The New B.C. Roadside Naturalist

THE NEW
B.C. ROADSIDE
Naturalist

A Guide to Nature along B.C. Highways

RICHARD CANNINGS
& SYDNEY CANNINGS

GREYSTONE BOOKS

Vancouver/Berkeley

Greystone Books Ltd.
www.greystonebooks.com

Cataloguing data available from Library and Archives Canada
ISBN 978-1-77100-054-3 (pbk.)
ISBN 978-1-77100-055-0 (epub)

Editing by Nancy Flight and Catherine Plear
Cover and interior design by Heather Pringle
Cover photograph by guenter guni/iStockphoto.com
Illustrations by Donald Gunn
Illustrations on pages 254, 278, 288, 293 and 299 by Lee Mennell
Illustration on page 137 by Robert Cannings
Maps on pages xii and 6 by Eric Leinberger
Map on page 3 by Maurice Colpron

Excerpt from "Northwest Passage" by Stan Rogers,
copyright 1981, used with permission from Fogarty's Cove.

Printed and bound in China by C&C Offset Printing Co., Ltd.
Distributed in the U.S. by Publishers Group West

We gratefully acknowledge the financial support of the Canada Council
for the Arts, the British Columbia Arts Council, the Province of British Columbia
through the Book Publishing Tax Credit and the Government of Canada
through the Canada Book Fund for our publishing activities.

Greystone Books is committed to reducing the consumption of old-growth forests
in the books it publishes. This book is one step toward that goal.

Contents

Preface

THIS BOOK has been in the back of our minds for years. We have been entertained and informed over many kilometres by books that describe the human history along the highways of British Columbia, but for some reason there has never been a book that covers the natural history along the main highways of the province.

The concept is simple enough, but executing it was a more daunting task than we thought it would be. There were fairly simple decisions to be made at first, such as "Which direction should we go?" We decided to use Vancouver as a starting point, so most highways are covered west to east and south to north. The few exceptions to that rule are Highway 20, which is covered starting in Williams Lake and ending in Bella Coola, as the vast majority of travellers encounter it; and Highway 17, which is covered east to west, starting from Vancouver.

A more difficult question was "Which highways should we write about?" We have included all the major roads that traverse the province, plus some shorter highways that are often travelled. In this new edition, we've added the major highways of northern British Columbia: the Stewart-Cassiar (Highway 37) and the Hart and Alaska Highways (Highway 97). Because anyone travelling the Alaska Highway to the Yukon border would certainly be continuing on for at least some distance, we have included the entire Yukon section of the Alaska Highway. A few smaller highways, some of them personal favourites, such as Highway 4 to Tofino and Ucluelet, Highway 101 along the Sunshine Coast, the Haines and Klondike Highways in the far northwest, and various short highways in the Kootenays, were left out. Nor did we cover the portion of Highway 16 on the Queen Charlotte Islands.

We have suggested one or more rest stops on each highway. These are spots located directly off the road where you can stretch your legs and enjoy nature at a more leisurely pace. Many of these sites have interpretive trails and displays that will enhance your enjoyment of the journey and your understanding of the land you are travelling through.

The official names of B.C. lakes and rivers often differ from those given on highway signs. In those cases we have given the official name followed by the alternate name in parentheses.

We also struggled with the style of the book—should it be a kilometre-by-kilometre series of bulleted notes or a more rambling narrative? We eventually went with the latter, since we wanted to produce an informative but easy-to-read tour. We hope that we have succeeded in this endeavour and that you enjoy your explorations of British Columbia as much as we enjoyed writing this book.

Acknowledgements

THIS BOOK is dedicated to the hundreds of naturalists in British Columbia, who pass on their immense knowledge of the natural world in fascinating stories told along the trail, in club newsletters, and through the Internet. Their curiosity about the world we live in and their keen observations are the backbone of books such as this one. In researching this book, we canvassed many of the naturalists and biologists across the province for their advice on topics of roadside interest and their detailed local knowledge.

We would like to especially thank June Ryder, who read much of the manuscript and made detailed corrections and additions. Margaret Holm, Trevor Goward, Barbara Moon and Tony Griffiths also reviewed parts of early drafts. Bruce Bennett, Chris Bull, Brian Chan, Trudy Chatwin, Maurice Colpron, John Deal, Frank Doyle, Tom Ethier, Bob Forbes, Trevor Goward, Cris Guppy, Mark Hobson, Rick Howie, Steve Israel, Tom Jung, Fred Knezevich, Rick Marshall, Don Murphy, Judy Myers, JoAnne Nelson, Tom Northcote, Jim and Rosamund Pojar, Don Reid, Anna Roberts, Murray Roed, Ordell Steen, Adam Taylor, Ron Tetreau, Michaela Waterhouse and John Woods also provided information and ideas. In our travels around British Columbia researching this book, we have been treated to the warm hospitality of many people, including Anne Hayes and Dave Wilson, Barry Booth, Steve and Hazel Cannings, Mary Collins, Cris Guppy, Anne de Jager, Doug and Myriam Leighton, Jim and Rosamund Pojar, Anna Roberts and Robin Weber. We thank you all.

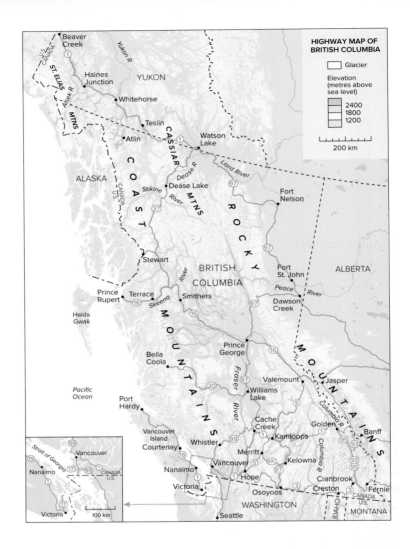

This book was also greatly improved by the photographs provided by Steve Cannings, Doug Leighton and others, and of course by the beautiful illustrations of Donald Gunn and Lee Mennell. Finally, we thank our editors, Nancy Flight and Catherine Plear, who made this book much easier to read.

Introduction

And through the night, behind the wheel,
the mileage clicking west
I think upon Mackenzie, David Thompson and the rest
Who cracked the mountain ramparts and did show a path for me
To race the roaring Fraser to the sea.
STAN ROGERS, *"Northwest Passage"*

WE LIVE in fast-paced times, with the luxury of high-speed highways to take us across a landscape with blinding speed, to say nothing of flying over it in airliners. We can easily drive across British Columbia in a day, a trip that took Thompson, Mackenzie and Fraser months to complete. But speed needn't be completely blinding. Although it is easy to motor through the province simply revelling in the magnificent mountains, enjoying the sun and cursing the rain, there are many fascinating features of the environment that can be appreciated at 100 kilometres per hour. These features are often part of the big picture of our world—changes in climate, changes in the crust of the earth, changes in whole ecosystems.

British Columbia is blessed with a diverse landscape, and the scene changes minute by minute. Landscapes can be read like books, the scenery changing like pages turning, and the British Columbian book is one of the best page-turners on Earth.

Facing page: Highways covered in this book.

➤ A Short Geological History

To put the big picture into focus, you need a general knowledge of the forces that built the western edge of Canada. Most of this part of the world is new land, not just lifted up from the ancient seafloor, but made up of pieces of the Earth's crust that travelled here from near and far through a process called plate tectonics. These pieces, called terranes, moved and met up with the western edge of the continent as part of the constant movement of the plates that make up the floor of the Pacific Ocean.

The major mountain ranges were formed by the collisions between ancient North America (Laurentia) and these terranes and from expansion and intrusion resulting from the tremendous heat of their subduction beneath the west coast. Even today the plates shift constantly, slowly, inexorably, building mountains while we sleep and only rumbling their intentions with earthquakes from time to time.

On the map of the geological terranes, you see these terranes divided into realms according to their origins. The peri-Laurentian terranes lie between the Omineca Mountains and the western Coast Mountains and underlie the Intermontane region in between. They once were the bedrock of chains of volcanic islands and small oceans that lay west of the old continent in a situation comparable with the other side of the Pacific Ocean Basin today—think of Japan or the Philippines. One of the ancient island arcs is named Quesnellia, after the town of Quesnel. It runs from Quesnel north to the Yukon border east of Teslin, and south past Princeton. The other old island arc, Stikinia, spans western British Columbia from Bella Coola to Atlin. The Slide Mountain Terrane is the seafloor of a minor ocean that grew between a rifted chunk of North America—the Yukon-Tanana Terrane—and its mother continent. It is spectacularly exposed in the Cassiar Mountains along the Stewart-Cassiar Highway of northern British Columbia, where it now rests atop the old western shores of North America.

Compared with the relatively local peri-Laurentian terranes, those of the Tethyan and Arctic realms have travelled astounding distances to arrive in their present Cordilleran berths. The Cache

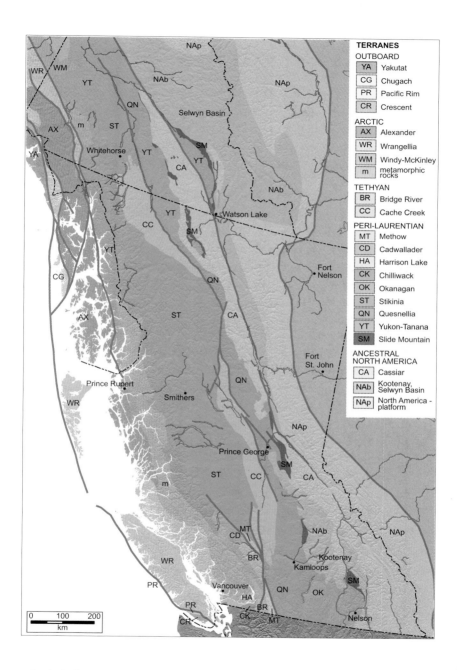

TERRANES

OUTBOARD

YA	Yakutat
CG	Chugach
PR	Pacific Rim
CR	Crescent

ARCTIC

AX	Alexander
WR	Wrangellia
WM	Windy-McKinley
m	metamorphic rocks

TETHYAN

BR	Bridge River
CC	Cache Creek

PERI-LAURENTIAN

MT	Methow
CD	Cadwallader
HA	Harrison Lake
CK	Chilliwack
OK	Okanagan
ST	Stikinia
QN	Quesnellia
YT	Yukon-Tanana
SM	Slide Mountain

ANCESTRAL NORTH AMERICA

CA	Cassiar
NAb	Kootenay, Selwyn Basin
NAp	North America - platform

Geological terranes.

Creek Terrane forms a discontinuous strip through the Interior from Cache Creek to the southern Yukon. Fossils in the limestones of the Cache Creek Terrane tie it to the Tethys Sea, an ancient ocean that lay south and west of China before India and Africa collided with Asia and Europe. The Cache Creek Terrane is made up of island reefs and ocean floor that was reeled toward the Laurentian margin by rapid subduction under Stikinia and Quesnellia.

Outside and west of the peri-Laurentian Terranes in British Columbia lie the Arctic Terranes (Wrangellia and the Alexander Terrane)—the bedrock of Vancouver Island, Haida Gwaii (the Queen Charlotte Islands) and the islands of the Inside Passage. These rocks once were part of the Arctic realm. Their older parts formed and remained somewhere near northern Scandinavia and eastern Siberia until mid-Paleozoic time, when they were propelled westward through the Arctic Ocean and into the Pacific. Unlike the ocean floor that ferried the Cache Creek oceanic islands toward Laurentia under traction from its subduction zones, the Arctic terranes were fragments of volcanic arc and continental origin that might have moved by a mechanism similar to that at play in the recent history of the Caribbean—an island arc that reformed into a bulging loop that surged over 1000 kilometres in 60 million years.

The mid-Jurassic, about 185 to 170 million years ago, was a time of crisis and profound change in British Columbia. During this time, all of these massive crustal blocks came together to collide and coalesce, creating the mountains we now know. Why did all this happen? Thousands of miles to the east, on the other side of Laurentia, the North Atlantic began to open—first a crack, then a seaway and then a nascent ocean. Its new ocean floor began to spread, and a new continent, North America, started to move ponderously westward. The once-independent terranes of the Cordillera simply got in the way.

The result was mountains: as the continent continued westward, sedimentary strata at its margin piled up like snow in front of a magnificent snowplow, riding up and over eastward to make the shingled stack that later would be sculpted into the Rockies. The physiography of British Columbia—its twin backbones of the Coast Mountains and the Ominecas and Rockies separated by the subdued Intermontane belt—is the result of the two slow-motion, simultaneous collisions. Where the Intermontane terranes piled up onto the old continental margin, the Omineca and Rocky Mountains rose. Where the Insular terranes collided with the outer edge of the Intermontane terranes, the Coast Mountains were born.

As North America drove under its western neighbours, large pieces of Quesnellia and the Slide Mountain Terrane peeled off the oceanic plate. Some slices up to 25 kilometres thick overrode the continental margin and became stacked like pancakes on top of it. The rocks of the terranes and the old continental shelf were squeezed, folded, and in some cases recrystallized to form the Columbia, Omineca and Cassiar Mountains. Compression continued and the layers of sedimentary rocks covering the continental core were pushed ever eastward. The layers first deformed into waves, but the resistant limestone layers eventually broke and became stacked up in gently sloping piles.

By 120 million years ago, the western ranges of the Rockies were stacking up, but the mountain-building wave continued to move eastward. The main ranges were rising about 100 million years ago, and by the time the pushing stopped about 60 million years ago, the eastern ranges and foothills had been created. When all was finished, the thrust sheets had been telescoped and shoved up to 250 kilometres eastward from their original position.

As the Insular terranes collided with the Intermontane terranes, a new subduction zone formed to the west. As the seafloor was subducted into the mantle, many igneous intrusions rose up in a succession of pulses from 170 to 50 million years ago, creating the Coast Mountains Batholith, one of the largest bodies of granite and granitoid rocks on the planet.

About 85 million years ago, the plate movement in the Pacific changed direction to the north. North America was still moving relatively westward, but this change meant that British Columbia's crust was not only squeezed but also sheared to the north. Something had

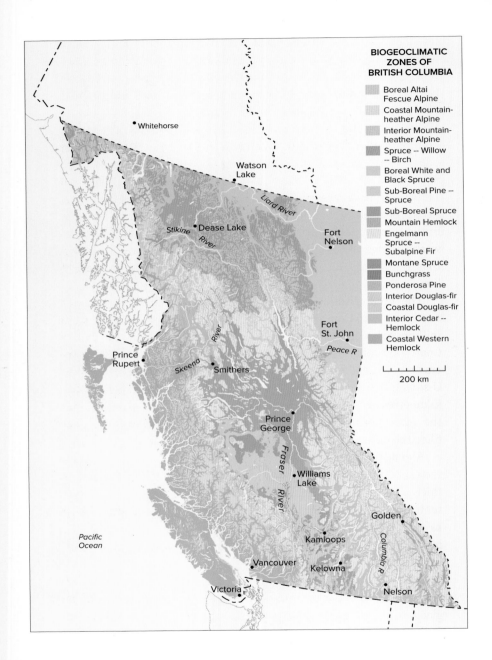

BIOGEOCLIMATIC ZONES OF BRITISH COLUMBIA

Boreal Altai Fescue Alpine

Coastal Mountain-heather Alpine

Interior Mountain-heather Alpine

Spruce -- Willow -- Birch

Boreal White and Black Spruce

Sub-Boreal Pine -- Spruce

Sub-Boreal Spruce

Mountain Hemlock

Engelmann Spruce -- Subalpine Fir

Montane Spruce

Bunchgrass

Ponderosa Pine

Interior Douglas-fir

Coastal Douglas-fir

Interior Cedar -- Hemlock

Coastal Western Hemlock

200 km

Whitehorse

Watson Lake

Liard River

Stikine River

Dease Lake

Fort Nelson

Fort St. John

Peace R

Prince Rupert

Skeena River

Smithers

River

Prince George

Williams Lake

Fraser River

Golden

Columbia R

Pacific Ocean

Kamloops

Vancouver

Kelowna

Victoria

Nelson

Biogeoclimatic zones.

to give, and the crust fractured. The westward blocks slid north along a series of faults, such as the Tintina (Northern Rocky Mountain Trench), Fraser, Cassiar, Teslin, Denali and Queen Charlotte Faults. These are all strike-slip faults, similar to today's San Andreas Fault in California.

Just as the dinosaurs were breathing their last breaths about 65 million years ago, the intense tectonic pressure eased, the crust relaxed and cracks appeared, forming valleys such as the Kitsumkalum and Okanagan Valleys and the Southern Rocky Mountain Trench. Volcanic activity was common over the next 50 million years, in part because the tectonic relaxation had thinned the Earth's crust in the Interior. Large quantities of basaltic lava poured out over the western edge of the Okanagan Valley about 50 million years ago, then all over the Cariboo-Chilcotin between 30 million and 2 million years ago.

The great rivers of British Columbia followed the northwest-southeast trending faults created over the millennia. About 1.6 million years ago, the climate cooled, the snow deepened in the Coast and Columbia Mountains, and these great rivers turned to rivers of ice. The Pleistocene glaciers carved out the valleys into broad U-shapes, with wide bottoms and steep sides. The ice, more than 2 kilometres deep in places, eliminated almost all signs of life, ground the lower mountains down and left a legacy of gravel and sand that filled the valleys to depths of hundreds of metres.

About twelve thousand years ago, the glaciers began a major retreat, disappearing at first in the highlands and plateaus. The thick tongues of ice left in the valleys blocked the flow of meltwater torrents, and the routes of even major rivers changed year by year as these ice plugs withered away. Gravel and sand pouring off the highlands built up against the valley glaciers, creating terraces still visible throughout the province.

While the continental glacier smoothed most of the province down to a more rounded version of its pre-Pleistocene form, alpine glaciers carved the upthrust mountain ridges into spectacular peaks. On your travels, look for the deep bowls, or cirques, left by alpine glaciers, and the sharp ridges, or arêtes, that divide the cirques. In many places, alpine glaciers remain only on the northeast faces of mountains, where they are protected from the warm afternoon sun.

Life forms returned quickly to this landscape, travelling not only from the south but from the north and east also. Arctic species migrated from the unglaciated interior of Alaska and the Yukon, filling northern British Columbia with tundra plants and myriad animals, from insects to grizzly bears. Conifer forests, having spread westward across the northern edge of the prairies as the thinner continental glacier disappeared, moved into northern British Columbia while the southern half of the province was still ice bound. Even today, the flora and fauna of northern British Columbia have a distinctly eastern character.

➤ High-Speed Natural History

The mountains and valleys of British Columbia were thus filled with a great tapestry of life—plateaus covered with pine forests, valleys of golden grass and coastlines with surging tides and wheeling gulls. Plant life forms patterns on the landscape. Rain forests cloak the western, windward slopes of mountain ranges; the leeward slopes are usually covered in drier, more open forests; and the southern valley bottoms often have no forests at all. Moving upslope from the coast, the rain forests change to snow forests and then to alpine meadows; similar, but subtly different, changes occur as you descend from the mountain peaks to Interior valleys. These patterns of terrestrial life have been formally categorized as biogeoclimatic zones in British Columbia.

The concept of biogeoclimatic zones is based on the fact that you can understand a great deal about the local ecology of an area simply by identifying the common trees and shrubs growing there. And you can identify these trees and shrubs from a car moving at highway speeds. If you are driving through the Coast Mountains and notice that the dark-green western hemlocks have been replaced by greyer mountain hemlocks, you can safely surmise that you have left the coastal rain forests behind and have entered a zone of high snowfall.

Thimbleberry. RICHARD CANNINGS

If you see stately orange-barked ponderosa pines instead of the fur-rowed trunks of Douglas-firs, you have entered a valley with long, hot summers. For help identifying trees, see the appendix.

High-speed natural history can involve animal sightings as well. A large flock of gulls gathered on the shores of a river is often a sign of a salmon run, whereas a high-flying, mixed flock of nighthawks and gulls usually means there has been a significant hatch of ants or termites in the area. Even the massed growths of tiny lichens can provide detailed information—orange lichen tends to grow only on rocks with a high supply of nitrogen in the form of animal droppings, and alder trunks are whitened with lichen only in areas of very high rainfall.

So sit back, enjoy the drive and listen to the stories of the scenery.

ONE

The Trans-Canada Highway

HIGHWAY 1

IGHWAY 1, the Trans-Canada Highway, is the quintessential land route across British Columbia, a magnificent traverse of the province that showcases many of its diverse landforms and natural stories. Although it technically begins (or ends, depending on your perspective) on Vancouver Island, our journey starts at Horseshoe Bay, the BC Ferries terminal in West Vancouver. From there Highway 1 cuts across the southwestern toe of the Coast Mountains, turns east up the Fraser Valley, skirting the northern end of the Cascade Mountains, goes through the Fraser Canyon and across the golden grasslands of the Thompson Valley, then makes its way into the green forests and stunning scenery of four mountain ranges—the Monashees, the Selkirks, the Purcells and the Rockies—before entering Alberta at the Great Divide.

➤ **Horseshoe Bay to Hope:** The Lower Fraser Valley
The first section of this highway takes you from the coast into the heart of the mountains, following the course of that greatest of all B.C. rivers, the Fraser. Unlike most highways into the mountains, this stretch has very little altitude gain; the high point is probably somewhere in West Vancouver or North Vancouver.

Facing page: Cheam Peak from Herrling Island. RICHARD CANNINGS

Butterfly bush, a colourful flowering shrub introduced from China, is common along the Upper Levels Highway through West Vancouver. As its name implies, it often attracts butterflies such as this monarch to the nectar in its flowers. STEVE CANNINGS

You begin in an area of relatively light rainfall—West Vancouver receives only about 130 centimetres of precipitation annually—but it increases sharply as you drive along Burrard Inlet to the Second Narrows, where annual precipitation is about 185 centimetres, only slightly less than the 190 centimetres recorded in Hope.

The shallow soils and southwest exposure of the section of highway through West Vancouver create a locally drier environment, and the forest is dominated by young Douglas-firs. Under the power lines above the highway, forest clearing has created an even drier climate, and that area is covered in arbutus, Canada's only broad-leaved evergreen, also known as madrone in the United States, and easily identified by its smooth, copper-coloured bark. Shrubs along the median are almost all non-native species, dominated in summer by the bright purple-blue flowers of butterfly bush *(Buddleia)*, a native of China; the yellow flowers and green stems of Scotch broom; and the ubiquitous thorny tangles of Himalayan blackberry. The dominant native trees change to western hemlock as the highway goes through North Vancouver and the precipitation increases.

The first major valley the highway crosses is the Capilano River, which separates Hollyburn Mountain from Grouse Mountain. The twin peaks of the Lions are visible up the Capilano Valley. The Seymour River separates Grouse Mountain (the vertical cut up its western slope is the gondola route) from Mt. Seymour (1453 metres; radio towers are visible on its southern flank). The Capilano and Seymour Rivers are relatively short coastal streams, but both have sizable runs of coho, pink, chinook and chum salmon as well as steelhead. They also supply 80 per cent of the drinking water for Greater Vancouver. Dams constructed upstream to create water supply reservoirs have the reduced flow levels below the dams; as a result, hatchery programs are necessary to produce adequate numbers of fish. Highway 1 crosses Burrard Inlet over the Ironworkers Memorial Second Narrows Crossing. Burrard Inlet ends 8 kilometres to the southeast at Port Moody, but a branch of the inlet, Indian Arm—a deep fiord carved by glaciers during the Pleistocene—continues around Mt. Seymour into the mountains for another 20 kilometres. The shores of Burrard Inlet are almost entirely industrialized, but a small section at Maplewood Flats—on the north side of the inlet just east of the bridge—has been kept in a reasonably natural state and is now a nature reserve. It is one of the few places where osprey and purple martins nest in the Lower Mainland.

The large grain elevators just west of the south end of the bridge are the main outlet for wheat and other grains exported from the Canadian Prairies to Asian markets. The grain attracts hundreds of pigeons, which bring in Peregrine Falcons looking for lunch.

As you emerge from the long Cassiar Tunnel, you are approaching the famous Willingdon crow gathering. If you are travelling around dusk, you should see thousands of crows converging on buildings near the Willingdon exit in Burnaby. About twelve thousand of these birds come from all over the Vancouver area and gather here before going en masse to their roost site in a Burnaby woodlot.

About 10 kilometres south of the bridge, Burnaby Lake is a natural oasis in the highly urbanized landscape. Surrounding the lake's marshy shores is a rich riparian woodland dominated by tall black cottonwoods and medium-height red alder. As the road descends to the flats along the river, check the big cottonwoods on the southwest side of the highway for the large stick nest of the local pair of red-tailed hawks; it's especially visible when the trees are bare. The road then swings southeast through a mass of big-box retail outlets and warehouses built on sand dredged from the river.

Mt. Baker, the volcano closest to Vancouver, is also one of the most active in the Cascades and could erupt at any time. Much of the potential damage from such an eruption would result from the melting of its glaciers, which cover about 52 square kilometres of the peak. STEVE CANNINGS

The highway crosses the Fraser on the Port Mann Bridge, and although it follows the Fraser Valley, it doesn't meet up with the mighty river again until east of Chilliwack. Through the municipalities of Surrey, Langley and Abbotsford, the highway travels through rolling uplands of glacial deposits and sedimentary rock. The forest is all second growth (mostly less than a hundred years old) and is fragmented by pastures, berry farms, subdivisions and industrial parks. Alouette Mountain, the Golden Ears and the more distant Mt. Judge Howay (2255 metres) dominate the northern skyline along this stretch.

One of the most conspicuous birds along this stretch is the red-tailed hawk, named after the brick-red tail of the adults (young birds have a plain brown tail). These big hawks use their acute vision to hunt for voles (meadow mice) in the long grass of the freeway median. They are commoner in winter, when twenty or more can be seen on a drive through the Fraser Valley, but some are present all year round.

The corpses of unlucky opossums are also an unfortunately common sight along the roadside. This marsupial was introduced to Washington State in 1925 and reached British Columbia in 1949. It has thrived in the Lower Mainland, since its omnivorous habits work well in a landscape filled with vegetable gardens and garbage cans.

If it is clear, as you crest a hill near Clearbrook after the 264th Street exit you may see the impressive glacier-covered cone of Mt. Baker (3285 metres), just over the border in Washington State. One of the most active of the Cascade volcanoes, Baker has had several small ash eruptions in the last two centuries, and there is almost continual venting of steam and hydrogen sulfide.

By the time you reach the flat floodplain of the Fraser River again at Abbotsford, the river itself is 10 kilometres away, on the north side of Sumas Mountain. Some geologists believe that the Fraser flowed through this part of the valley in the late Pleistocene but was diverted north into its present course by an ice dam.

This central section of the Fraser Valley is the warmest point in Canada as measured by mean annual temperature—10.7°C. Not surprisingly, it is home to a suite of species found nowhere else in Canada, including two tiny mammals, the Pacific water shrew and Trowbridge's shrew. The largest mole in the country, Townsend's mole, is restricted to a small part of the Abbotsford area from the Huntingdon border crossing to Sumas Mountain. The shrew mole, North America's smallest mole, is more widely distributed in the lower Fraser Valley. Small groups of shrew moles roam the forest floor, each of the essentially blind animals tapping the ground with its touch-sensitive nose to find insects and worms.

At Abbotsford the highway is only 5 kilometres from the U.S. border and turns due east again to parallel the Fraser. The mountains on the eastern skyline are the Cheam group, dominated by Cheam Peak (2107 metres) itself. The sloping strata of Sumas Mountain are easily visible on the north side just east of Abbotsford, followed by the main bulk of the mountain, cloaked in second-growth forests and a scattering of large, old-growth Douglas-firs. A few Garry oaks grow on Sumas Mountain as well, one of the few sites where this species is found in Canada away from southern Vancouver Island and the Gulf Islands.

Shortly after the highway crosses the Sumas River, you pass by a line of tall trees on the right on a low ridge. This ridge marks the shores of Sumas Lake, a large (4000-hectare) shallow lake that filled the valley until it was drained in 1926 to enhance agricultural opportunities in the valley. For the next few kilometres, you are driving along the perfectly flat lake bottom, 2 metres below sea level. The only high points on the valley bottom here are the dykes that still train the waters into the Fraser River.

The lake is not the only major feature of the valley now lost under the cornfields; there was a large grassy prairie in the Chilliwack area as well. The prairie and lake provided excellent habitat for ducks, geese and, of course, mosquitoes, as noted by Lt. Charles Wilson of the 49th Parallel Survey, 1858–1862: "The scenery is most lovely but as far as I have seen the place abounds in snakes, mosquitoes, sand flies, rain, thunder, with an occasional roasting day... The prairie runs down to the bank of the Chilukweyuk from which we are about 2 miles distant, the view from the camp is superb, the prairie in front with its beautiful waving grass and belts of poplar, willow, ash and maple in the foreground..."

The Oregon spotted frog is an endangered species known in Canada from only three sites near Aldergrove and Chilliwack. RUSS HAYCOCK

Sumas Lake was fed by the Sumas and Vedder (Chilliwack) Rivers and was drained by the construction of two large canals, the Sumas Drainage Canal and Vedder Canal. In the next few kilometres,

Turkey vulture

the highway crosses both. As you cross the Vedder Canal, the spectacular spire of Mt. Slesse (2375 metres) is usually visible to the south. West of Mt. Slesse is the glacier-covered Canadian Border Peak (2291 metres). At this point the Fraser River is just north of the logyard on the north side of the highway—this is where the Fraser used to empty into Sumas Lake every year. The small mountain to the east is Chilliwack Mountain (320 metres).

Once past Chilliwack the highway meets the northern edge of the Cascade Range at Bridal Veil Falls. Straight ahead is the impressive Cheam Peak (2107 metres). The Fraser Valley narrows abruptly here, and the river meets the highway again just past the village of Popkum. This is a great place to see bald eagles in winter, as they gather to feed on chum salmon spawning in the side channels of the river; watch for eagles perched in large cottonwoods along the river from here to Hope. In summer, turkey vultures are often seen at this end of the valley, perhaps attracted by the strong updrafts that are also used by local glider enthusiasts.

The large cottonwood stands along the river are now being harvested for pulp; the even-aged plantation across the river on Herrling Island consists of hybrid poplars developed to grow quickly. The square building on the south side of the highway opposite Herrling Island is a powerhouse that takes water from Wahleach (Jones) Lake from a tunnel through the north ridge of Cheam Peak; a colony of cliff swallows nests under its eaves each summer. For westward travellers, Cheam Peak is spectacular from the Herrling Island exit. A stop at the Hunter Creek Rest Area may be your last chance to see coastal forest birds, such as black-throated gray warblers. Hunter Creek itself tumbles out of a hanging valley.

Just past Hunter Creek, the highway rounds a series of high granitic cliffs, part of the mid-Cretaceous Spuzzum pluton, a massive block of magma that cooled beneath the Earth's surface about 100 million years ago. Windblown Douglas-fir and western redcedar along the road are clear evidence of the strong prevailing westerly winds here. Easterly outflow winds can be very strong here as well, especially when Arctic air flows out of the southern Interior during winter cold snaps.

➤ **Hope to Lytton:** The Fraser Canyon

At Hope the highway turns north to follow the Fraser, and Highways 3 and 5 plunge eastward into the mountains. Here the river flows at an average rate of 2720 cubic metres per second, making it the largest river in British Columbia (the Columbia is shared with Washington State). The flow peaks in June at around 10,000 cubic metres per second, dropping to under 1000 cubic metres per second in winter. The river and the highway follow the Fraser Fault System, which has shifted the land both vertically—land to the west has risen relative to the east—and horizontally—the west side moved northward about 90 kilometres relative to the east side about 45 million years ago. This fault separates the Coast Mountains on the west from the Thompson Plateau and Cascade Range on the east.

About 2 kilometres north of the junction with Highway 7, near the top of a long hill, there are large, angular blocks of rock on either side of the road, the debris of a rock avalanche that occurred here about eight thousand years ago. If you look high up to your left as you pass a small lake on your left, you can see the steeply inclined slabs where the avalanche broke away.

The trip up the Fraser from Hope to Lytton is a trip through a remarkable climatic and ecological gradient, from rain forest to near-desert, from towering hemlocks to sagebrush. The roadside vegetation changes with almost every bend in the road and river. The highway does not go over any high passes, though it occasionally climbs around rocky ridges to avoid impassable canyons below. Following the rise of the river, it climbs from about 40 metres above sea level at Hope to 250 metres at Lytton. This route was used for centuries by indigenous peoples, and in 1859 the Cariboo Road was built in its place to reach the goldfields in central British Columbia.

Chicory. RICHARD CANNINGS

The big cottonwoods about a kilometre north of American Creek grow in rich, moist streamside soils; the roadsides here are carpeted with thimbleberry—a low shrub with large, maplelike leaves—and bracken fern, species typical of moist woodlands throughout the province. A small lake on the east side of the road is ringed with red alder and big broadleaf maples, trees found only in coastal forests. But you are quickly leaving the Coastal Western Hemlock Zone, and just north of Texas Creek you will see the last of the hemlocks.

The town of Yale marks the upper limit of navigable waters on the Fraser and the beginning of the Fraser Canyon. From here north to Boston Bar, the Fraser River flows between steep valley walls of hard granitic or highly compressed metamorphic rocks.

Just over 2 kilometres north of Yale there is a small pull-off on the east side. From here you can look across the river to the Yale Garry Oak Ecological Reserve, the easternmost stand of Garry oak in Canada, about 160 kilometres away from their main distribution on Vancouver Island. Look for them on both sides of the railway tracks, fairly close to the river.

Although the Fraser is justly famous for its tremendous salmon runs, the lord of all fish in this river is the white sturgeon. These giant fish—one taken from the river in 1897 weighed 630 kilograms—have declined dramatically in number over the last century as a result of overfishing and a propensity to concentrate toxins.

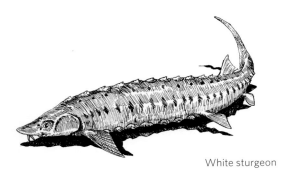

White sturgeon

The last of the western redcedar forests peter out a few kilometres north of Saddle Rock Tunnel, just before Sailor Bar Tunnel. Just south of Spuzzum, there is another old burn across the river that has grown back mainly to white birch, an indication that you are still in a fairly moist forest ecosystem. The dark canyon rocks are brightened with light green mosses, but as the climate shifts to a drier, hotter regime, these are replaced with more drought-tolerant lichens.

The highway crosses the river on the Alexandra Bridge, then passes Alexandra Lodge, one of the historic roadhouses along the Cariboo Road in the 1800s. Two tunnels later you are at Hells Gate, the narrowest point in the canyon, at least at river level. Hells Gate has always been a difficult point for salmon to traverse on their immense journey upstream from the Pacific to spawning grounds in the B.C. Interior, but a series of rockslides caused by railway construction in 1913 almost destroyed the entire upper Fraser River salmon population. Pink salmon runs of about 40 million fish per year were essentially wiped out, and sockeye runs, including those from the Adams River, were greatly reduced for many years.

Just north of Hells Gate, the river bends to the west around China Bar and Scuzzy Rapids, and the canyon opens up. This geological phenomenon has profound biological consequences—it marks the gateway to the dry Interior, an imaginary line between the moist, mossy coastal forests and the open pine forests and grasslands of the Interior valleys. The broadleaf maples in moist gullies are no longer the huge trees typical of coastal valleys, their rough bark softened with deep moss and sprays of licorice fern;

they are small, almost shrublike trees. Burned areas north of here are revegetated by trembling aspen and ponderosa pine, not red alder and white birch.

In this broader section of the Fraser Canyon, there was room for glacial gravel deposits to accumulate on the river floodplain and survive subsequent erosion. Boston Bar and its twin across the Fraser—North Bend—are built on wide river terraces. The gravel terraces and bars along this section of the river contain placer gold and were worked extensively by miners in the mid-1800s. As a result of placer mining, level terrace surfaces were changed to corduroy-like gravel ridges and their soils were washed into the river. These placer gravels are still largely unvegetated.

About 12 kilometres north of Boston Bar, at a pull-off on the west side of the highway, there is a big ponderosa pine, one of the southern vanguards of a species that is dominant in the dry valleys of southern British Columbia. Copses of white-trunked aspen appear amid second-growth forests of Douglas-fir. As you approach Lytton, the forest becomes almost pure ponderosa pine, with dense stands of young pines growing along the highway.

Lytton is a small community at an important geographical junction—the meeting of the muddy Fraser River and the clear Thompson River. The difference in the colour of the rivers results from the presence of large lakes on the Thompson system—notably Shuswap and Kamloops—that allows sediments to settle out of the water. Lytton is often the hottest spot in British Columbia in summer and holds the record for the highest temperature in the province—44.4°C. The steep valley walls act as an oven on calm summer days, holding in the hot air during the day and releasing heat through the short summer nights.

▶ **Lytton to Kamloops:**
The Dry Grasslands of the Thompson River
Highway 1 turns east at Lytton to follow the Thompson through a deep valley in many ways as impressive as the Fraser Canyon. Rock formations along the canyon walls are often spectacular—white

Ponderosa pines grow on a dry hillside above the Thompson River.
RICHARD CANNINGS

ribbons in black rock at Jade Springs just east of Lytton, and black ribbons in white rock only a few kilometres beyond that. These ribbons, called dykes by geologists, were formed about 60 million years ago as the Earth's crust relaxed in this area. This relaxation produced a myriad of cracks in the local granitic rocks, and the cracks were quickly filled by molten rock of varying composition.

At Skihist Provincial Park, you can camp or picnic in open ponderosa pine forests. Although these trees aren't towering giants, many of them are as much as 250 years old. Beyond Skihist, plants typical of the Interior valley grasslands begin to appear—rabbitbrush and big sagebrush.

About 10 kilometres from Skihist, you cross the mouth of the Nicoamen River, marked by deep (about 150 metres) deposits of sand and gravel. This material was deposited by the ancestral Thompson River during an interglacial period more than twenty thousand years ago. It was apparently protected from the scouring action of the last glaciation by the east-west orientation of the valley.

Ponderosa pine... seems to have a penchant for dramatic and lightning-prone settings. It is a tree that swims in memory and surfaces in dreams.

DON GAYTON, *Landscapes of the Interior*

In this environment of hot, dry summers, evaporation of soil moisture plays a key role in the distribution of plant communities. Across the river the south-facing slopes receive direct sun throughout the day, and the large ponderosa pines and Douglas-firs are widely scattered, indicating intense competition for moisture. The root systems of these trees, which must be very large to gather enough moisture, spread out underground to meet those of their neighbours growing many metres away. The north-facing slopes along the highway receive sunlight at a much lower angle; evaporation is much less of a factor and the trees can grow more closely together.

About 28 kilometres from Lytton, the highway crosses to the upper side of the railway track. For the next few hundred metres north of this point, you are crossing the Drynoch Slide, a remarkable earth flow that has been moving slowly out of the hills to the east for thousands of years. Notice the red clay soil exposed in road cuts. From 1951 to 1972, this flow averaged over 3 metres per year. At that time measures were taken that redirected water flow away from the slide, and since then the flow rates have been much slower.

Approaching Spences Bridge, you enter the area that was occupied by Glacial Lake Deadman during the end of the Pleistocene glaciation. This lake, dammed by ice flowing out of the Coast Mountains, extended well beyond Kamloops. The white, silty soils deposited into this lake can be seen in many places along the valley.

These fine-grained silt deposits are very susceptible to landslides and erosion. If you look across the Thompson River just south of Spences Bridge, you can see the hummocky remains of a large landslide that brought an entire hillside of silt deposits into the river on August 13, 1905. This slide produced a 5-metre-high wave that swept up and down the river, flooding a Nlaka'pamux village and killing fifteen people, including Chief Lillooet. The slide dammed the river for about five hours, creating a temporary lake.

At Spences Bridge the highway crosses the Thompson River just south of its confluence with the Nicola River, coming in from the east. Here the highway enters the bunchgrass steppes of the Interior. Steppes are ecosystems that are too dry to support trees but moist enough for perennial grasses. The mix of grasslands and rocky cliffs north of Spences Bridge is ideal habitat for bighorn sheep, and a herd of these animals is often seen along the highway in this area. This herd stems from an introduction of Rocky Mountain animals here in 1927.

Another typical species of this habitat is the Chukar, a beautiful partridge introduced from eastern Europe in the 1950s—watch for small flocks of dust-coloured, grouselike birds with red legs and bills and black necklaces. About 18 kilometres north of Spences Bridge, you can see the line between ponderosa pine forest and open grassland across the river to the southeast. This is the lower treeline, an ecological zone defined by summer drought, just as the upper treeline is defined by summer frost.

Most of the mature ponderosa pines in the Thompson Valley were killed in the summer and fall of 2006 by a tsunami of mountain pine beetles. These beetles were born in the lodgepole pines on the plateaus north of the valley and emerged as adults on a few days in early August 2006. The beetles flew out in all directions, with a portion of the massive flight going south into the Thompson Valley. The sheer number of beetles overwhelmed the ponderosa pines, and by the spring of 2007 more than 90 per cent of them were dead. A few trees are still standing as dead snags, but many have already toppled over, perhaps weakened by the fungal infections the beetles carry with them. Like wildfires, these catastrophic insect invasions change the ecosystems they operate in; the lower slopes of this valley, once covered in open pine forests, will revert to bunchgrass steppe for the next few decades or more until cool climatic conditions allow the trees to germinate once again.

The Red Hill Rest Area is named after the bright orange-red rocks that form the hill just east of the highway—these are iron-stained volcanic rocks. North of Red Hill, the highway passes through the lower treeline onto sagebrush flats that contrast with the grassy, shrubless hillsides above. The Thompson begins to swing to the east at this point, but the highway continues north across level benches. These benchlands are thought to be the level

Bunchgrass Steppes

As you drive from Lytton northeast to Cache Creek, you leave the forests behind and enter the bunchgrass steppe. A steppe is a cool, continental environment that is too dry for trees to thrive in. Grasses succeed in these harsh places because above ground they have small, simple, ephemeral structures and below they have huge, fibrous root systems, which seek out whatever moisture is available. Bunchgrasses also tolerate drought well because their leaves contain a great deal of dry support tissue—rather than wilting, they just become dormant. The leaf bunches act as big funnels, gathering the rain water from above and guiding it to their roots below.

The bunchgrasses of southern British Columbia are not affected by summer drought because they grow only in the late autumn and again as soon as the snow melts in late winter and spring. Growth is essentially over by mid-July, at which time the plants become dormant. This absence of green summer forage in the dry intermountain valleys may explain the absence of bison west of the Rockies. On the central Great Plains, the early summer is as moist as the spring, and the sod grasses the bison fed on grow well into the summer.

Bluebunch
wheatgrass

Junegrass

Needle-and-
thread grass

Rough fescue

Cache Creek Mélange

"... the Cache Creek Terrane can be thought to represent a long strip of glue that binds eastern and western British Columbia. The people of Cache Creek live on that glue."

C.J. Yorath, *Where Terranes Collide*

Cache Creek has given its name to a piece of crust that forms a slender stripe through the B.C. Interior (see map of geological terranes, p. 3). It appears as though it is the glue that binds Stikinia to the west and Quesnellia to the east—but these two terranes are "local" chunks of crust that rifted from ancient North America and formed island arcs just off-shore, whereas the Cache Creek Terrane had its origins in the far-off Tethys Sea, an ancient ocean that once lay south and west of China. How did it find itself between Stikinia and Quesnellia? Recent geological reconstruction has proposed a remarkable explanation. First, it was reeled across the ancient Pacific by rapid subduction under Stikinia and Quesnellia. Then, as it came into contact with the island arcs, they began to buckle in the middle, and the north piece, Stikinia, was pulled down to the west, eventually closing in behind Cache Creek, giving it a big geological hug. During the squeezing, some of these rocks were crushed into a wild mixture—a "mélange" in geological terms—samples of which are visible as blackish, messy rocks behind buildings west of the highway at the south end of Cache Creek.

Above: Cache Creek Mélange.
RICHARD CANNINGS

tops of deltas that were built into Glacial Lake Deadman by glacial meltwater that flowed down the Bonaparte Valley to Cache Creek and then directly south along the line of the present highway before turning east into the ancient lake.

About 10 kilometres south of Cache Creek, you pass Ashcroft Manor, another of the historic roadhouses along this route; the community of Ashcroft itself is 4 kilometres to the southeast on the Thompson River. Irrigation has allowed ranchers to grow huge acreages of alfalfa on these dry grassland benches, and it is used as winter forage for cattle. Just south of Cache Creek, you pass a large landfill mainly out of sight to the west; this is the destination of most of the garbage produced daily by the Greater Vancouver area. The site was chosen for its combination of geological formations that would contain the waste as well as the dry climate that reduces the rate of leaching through soil.

At the town of Cache Creek, Highway 1 meets Highway 97 and turns east to follow the Thompson Valley once again. Although Cache Creek looks like any junction town with its motels, gas stations and fast-food outlets, it is famous in geological circles and has given its name to an entire rock formation—the Cache Creek Group.

East of Cache Creek, the road first climbs up a small valley with a cottonwood-lined stream, then reaches the broad benchlands of the Semlin Valley. A stream to the south is lined with trembling aspen, then water birch. This is ideal habitat for long-eared owls—mouse-hunting nocturnal raptors that nest and roost in trees but prefer to forage over pastures and grasslands, looking for voles. The benchlands here are dominated by big sagebrush, though some of it has been mowed and replanted to crested wheatgrass, a non-native grass species that is often used to rehabilitate overgrazed sites (look for pure grass areas about 12 kilometres east of Cache Creek).

The highway is now travelling on a new terrane—Quesnellia. This land was likely an arc of volcanic islands similar to Japan or the Philippines, and much of its structure was therefore of volcanic origin. Most of the spectacular rock bluffs along the north side of the highway between Cache Creek and Kamloops Lake are made up of volcanic rocks of the Nicola Group, laid down about 235 to 200 million years ago on this group of islands before it collided with North America.

About 15 kilometres east of Cache Creek, the remains of an old flume are visible above the highway. Green shrubs—chokecherries, roses and mock orange—that have grown up under the flume's dripping water make the structure stand out even more against the dry grasslands and rock bluffs. This flume was built in 1908 to bring water from the Deadman River to the arid benchlands at Walhachin, where developers envisioned expanses of fruit trees. When World War I broke out, most of the British men who had settled the area returned to their homeland, and the settlement quickly disappeared, leaving only a broken flume as a reminder of its brief existence.

The structure of the benchlands that the highway has been travelling on is clearly visible as it drops into the Deadman River valley. The broad, uppermost bench here is the top of a large delta built partly onto ice and partly into Glacial Lake Thompson by the Deadman River about eleven thousand years ago. Glacial Lake Thompson was an earlier version of Glacial Lake Deadman with a higher water

Shrubs of the Steppes

Because they are both grey, big sagebrush and rabbit-brush are often confused by highway botanists—but they are easily distinguished. Big sagebrush has coarse, dark twigs and small leaves, whereas rabbit-brush has fine grey twigs and needlelike blue-grey leaves. In late summer and fall, they are even more dissimilar. Sagebrush has plumes of inconspicuous brownish-yellow flowers that bloom in late September and early October; rabbit-brush is crowned by brilliant golden flower heads in late summer. And they smell different—sagebrush exudes a strong, gorgeous scent, especially after a summer rainfall, whereas rabbit-brush, despite its specific name, *nauseosus*, has a mild, currylike perfume.

Common rabbit-brush

Big sagebrush

level—about 150 metres above the present level of Kamloops Lake. On the steep sides of the bench, you can see terracettes, looking for all the world like a network of cattle trails. In fact, they are wrinkles in the soil caused by slumping when the ground becomes supersaturated, as during snowmelt.

The Deadman River is the spawning grounds of the Thompson River steelhead. These sea-run rainbow trout move into the Deadman in April and May during spring freshet. This major run of steelhead has been known for many years, but it wasn't until 1977 that their spawning grounds in the Deadman were discovered.

The highway drops again to cross the Thompson River near its outlet at Savona, a small town at the west end of Kamloops Lake. A small group of trumpeter swans often winters at the river mouth here, where the water motion keeps a part of the lake ice-free. The highway climbs high above the south shore of Kamloops Lake, providing periodic views of the lake as it traverses volcanic and sedimentary rocks that are about 200 million years old. The volcanic rocks on the north side of the lake are mostly of the Kamloops group, laid down much later (about 50 million years ago) when westerly pressures on North America subsided and the crust was pulled apart, allowing magma to spew over the surface of much of the southern Interior of British Columbia. The highway then travels along a high bench of overgrazed grassland and saline soils. Large areas of grassland here have been converted to the production of ginseng, which is covered with black shade cloth to mimic the plant's natural forest-floor environment.

At Cherry Creek the highway follows the creek up a narrow valley filled with spruce and cottonwood, a sharp contrast to the arid grasslands on the open slopes. At the top of the valley, you are back in open ponderosa pine forests, though it is clear that these forests are filling in with young pines as a result of years of fire suppression. Cherry Creek follows the contact between the Nicola Group rocks and the Iron Mask Batholith, a mass of plutonic rock of similar age that has been extensively mined for copper. Old mine shafts are evident in the rock walls along the highway as it climbs the creek valley.

Spadefoot Toads

Dry grasslands are not the usual habitat associated with amphibians, but one very interesting species is common on these sagebrush flats—the Great Basin spadefoot toad. A unique toad, with cat-like eyes and small, shovel-like claws on its heels, the spadefoot spends most of the year underground, emerging in spring to breed in shallow ponds. Warm, wet spring nights are filled with the *wawk-wawk-wawk-wawk* calls of the males. The eggs hatch in two weeks, and the tadpoles develop into small toads in about five weeks. Rapid development is essential in an environment where ponds often dry up by August.

STEVE CANNINGS

Back on flat benchlands, sagebrush again becomes the dominant ground cover. The Afton copper mine stands next to two small ponds in the grasslands. These ponds are oases for wildlife in this dry environment and are important breeding habitat for Great Basin spadefoot toads.

Crested wheatgrass plantings are again visible where the sagebrush has been mowed and replaced by this non-native grass. At the junction with Highway 5, you pass the highly alkaline Ironmask Lake on the south side of the road. The salts in the lake are mostly sodium and magnesium sulfates.

After the junction with Highway 5, the highway drops through subdivisions and malls into the urban sprawl of Kamloops. Here the Thompson divides into its north and south tributaries; Highway 5 follows the North Thompson to Valemount and the upper Fraser River; Highway 1 continues its eastern journey along the South Thompson.

➤ Kamloops to Salmon Arm: The South Thompson River

The South Thompson flows through a broad valley between two sections of the Thompson Plateau, a rare example of an east-west valley in southern British Columbia. The valley is dominated by postglacial features such as white silt bluffs, prehistoric deltas and beaches, and gravel terraces.

The South Thompson flows through dry grasslands that have largely been converted to agriculture. Ponderosa pines, black cottonwoods and Russian olives grow along the shores. In summer, watch for Lewis's woodpeckers—black, crowlike birds with bright pink bellies—perched atop the large trees. Ospreys—large brown-and-white fish-eating hawks—are common in summer as well, and you can see their big stick nests atop power poles and pine snags along the river. In winter the main natural attraction is the flock of swans, both trumpeter and tundra, that feed on aquatic plants along the entire length of the South Thompson. Several hundred of the large white birds can sometimes be seen.

As you approach Chase, about 50 kilometres east of Kamloops, you can see the evidence of a forest fire on the hills to the south; this fire along the Harper Lake road occurred in 1967 and serves as an excellent example of how slowly forests regenerate in this dry climate. Chase marks the end (or beginning) of the South Thompson River at its outlet at the west end of Little Shuswap Lake. Watch for bighorn sheep on the hillsides along the south side of the lake. Like the Spences Bridge sheep, this band came from a group of Rocky Mountain bighorns that were relocated here in 1927. The herd suffered a serious dieback in 1987 and now consists of only about twenty-five animals. Often the most visible

Bands of salt-tolerant vegetation surround this alkali pond west of Kamloops. RICHARD CANNINGS

Swans

Three species of swans are found in British Columbia. The trumpeter swan is the largest bird in North America, breeding on lakes and marshes across the northern half of the province; the tundra swan breeds in the High Arctic but migrates through the Interior valleys in large numbers and winters in the Thompson-Okanagan area; and the mute swan is an introduced species on southern Vancouver Island, the Fraser Delta and in various city parks. All are typically large, white birds (though the immature birds are grey) but can be identified by their bills.

The mute swan has an orange bill with a black knob at the base, the tundra has a small black bill with a yellow patch in front of the eye, and the trumpeter has a large black bill with no yellow patch. The trumpeter also has a distinctive deep, sonorous honking call, whereas the tundra (formerly called the whistling swan) has a higher-pitched call; the mute swan, of course, has no loud calls at all.

Left to right: Trumpeter, mute and tundra swans. RICHARD CANNINGS

life on Little Shuswap Lake is the common merganser, a big, fish-eating duck with a narrow red bill. The males are largely white with blackish-green heads; the females are grey with rusty red heads and a shaggy crest.

Shuswap Lake lies on a relatively narrow boundary line between the grasslands and ponderosa pine forests of the dry Interior and the moist cedar-hemlock forests of the Interior wet belt. The grasslands of the South Thompson end more or less at Chase and are replaced by transitional ponderosa pine woodlands along Little Shuswap Lake. These pines are replaced by Interior Douglas-fir forests along the south shores of Shuswap Lake, and by the time you reach the eastern portions of the Shuswap beyond Sicamous, you are in the Interior cedar-hemlock forests.

Little Shuswap and Shuswap Lakes were separated by the Adams River delta as it filled the valley with sediments brought down from the north. The lakes are now joined by the 3-kilometre-long Little River. The Adams River is famous for its huge spawning run of sockeye salmon. Every fall, peaking in the last three weeks of October, hundreds of thousands or even millions of these fish make their way from the North Pacific Ocean through Johnstone Strait and the Strait of Georgia into the mouth of the Fraser River and, following Highway 1 all the way, travel over 400 kilometres of the Fraser and Thompson Rivers to Shuswap Lake and the Adams River. Every fourth year (in even years not divisible by four—for example 2002, 2006, 2010), the numbers are dramatically higher, and over two million adults return.

The highway follows the shore of Shuswap Lake for a short distance, then climbs to the town of Sorrento. From there you can see Copper Island in the lake. As the highway swings south through Notch Hill, the mark of a small forest fire, which occurred in 1973, can be seen on the hills to the southwest. The forests are now predominantly young Douglas-fir in this area, with white birch in moister areas and a mix of trembling aspen and lodgepole pine on drier soils.

Shuswap Lake is shaped like half an octopus, with four long arms. You leave the main arm at Sorrento and reach the southwest arm (called Salmon Arm after the Salmon River, which enters there) at the village of Tappen. The huge bluffs on the north side of this arm are composed of gneisses and schists of the Shuswap Metamorphic Complex. These rocks formed when the sedimentary strata of the old continental shelf of North America were buried at depths of more than 15 kilometres by the terrane of Quesnellia about 180 million years ago. Somewhere in the Salmon Arm area, you will drive off the Interior terrane of Quesnellia and onto the ancient edge of North America.

The Salmon River once hosted a tremendous concentration of spawning salmon, but various factors, including the Hells Gate slides of 1913–14 (p. 20) and habitat degradation due to clearing of riverside trees and shrubs, have caused a major decline in numbers over the last century. Only five hundred chinook and one hundred coho salmon now return annually to spawn, but it is hoped that habitat enhancement efforts will raise those numbers over the coming years.

The Salmon River has filled this end of Shuswap Lake with rich sediments, making it an important habitat for many plants and animals. Huge black cottonwoods thrive in the moist soils along the western shore south of Tappen, providing nest sites for bald eagles and other large birds. The canary reedgrass marshes along the lakeshore provide nesting habitat for western grebes, one of only three such colonies in the province (you can see these beautiful birds from May through September from the main wharf in Salmon Arm). The grebes feed on the abundant small fish that thrive in the bay.

As the lake levels drop in late summer, the mud flats at the river delta appear just in time for the thousands of shorebirds that stop at Salmon Arm on their way from breeding grounds in Alaska to wintering grounds in South America. These mud flats are the most important stopover site in the B.C. Interior for these shorebirds. They also harbour several rare plants, including moss-grass, a diminutive grass found nowhere else in Canada.

> **Shuswap Lake to the Great Divide:**
Three Mountain Ranges and One River

After passing the sawmill at Canoe, the highway climbs through diverse but increasingly wet forests of Douglas-fir, trembling aspen, white birch, western larch, western redcedar and white pine. Western larch is a seral species in these moist forests of the southern Interior—that is, it is the pioneer tree species that germinates when

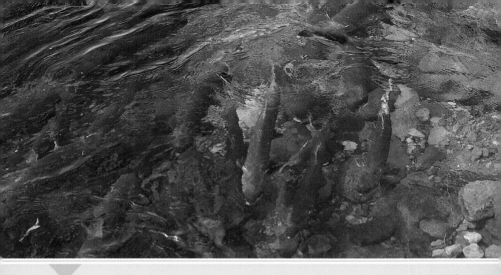

Shuswap Sockeye

Sockeye, originally transcribed as *suk-kai*, is the name given to this salmon by the Coast Salish people—the literal translation is "fish of fishes." With its rich, red flesh and its scarlet and green mating colours, this fish stands out among all others. Unlike other species of salmon, it has inserted a lake phase into its life cycle—fry usually spend one or two years feeding and growing in a lake below the spawning stream. They then move to the open ocean, where they spend two or three years, returning to their natal streams at age four or five. By that time they weigh about 3 kilograms.

In the lakes, young sockeye are plankton feeders in open waters. Because there is nowhere to hide in the waters they feed in, juvenile sockeyes usually spend the daylight hours deep in the dark, cold waters, coming up to feed in warmer, plankton-rich waters at dusk and dawn. Shuswap Lake is the rearing ground for fry from the runs on the Adams River and other tributaries and is therefore one of the best lakes for sockeyes. In good years, 93 million young sockeyes may be in the lake—a remarkable 3000 per hectare. Because lakes have a larger rearing area than streams, sockeyes are more abundant than stream-developing species, such as coho and chinook salmon. The lake-rearing habit of sockeye salmon has independently given rise to a number of populations that remain in the lake and never make the dangerous trip to the ocean and back. These fish are called kokanee.

Above: Sockeye salmon returning to spawn in the Adams River. STEVE CANNINGS

a site is cleared through logging or fire. Look carefully at the sites dominated by larch here—the very young trees growing under the larch are usually one of the climax wet forest species such as western redcedar. A few dead white pines are usually visible in the forest, their long branches red with dead needles. These are almost always victims of white pine blister rust. This fungus, accidentally introduced from Europe, infects mature trees and is first noticeable when bright orange blisters, full of rust spores, form on the trunk. These spores will infect the alternate hosts of the rust—gooseberries and currants.

The highway descends to the valley again at Sicamous, where it crosses Sicamous Narrows, the short stretch of water separating Shuswap Lake from Mara Lake. The Eagle River also flows into Shuswap Lake at Sicamous, and the highway follows this river eastward into the Monashee Mountains. Gravels laid down at Malakwa, about 18 kilometres east of Sicamous, show a complicated history

Western Grebes

Western grebes are elegant waterfowl with long, swanlike necks and bright yellow daggerlike bills. Most breed on rich prairie marshes, migrating westward each fall to winter on sheltered bays along the Pacific coast, especially in the Strait of Georgia and Puget Sound. Grebes are unrelated to other waterbirds and have lobed toes instead of webbed feet. They are excellent divers, submerging for minutes at a time to pursue small fish and large aquatic insects. Grebes build floating nests of marsh vegetation, anchoring them to reeds or other aquatic plants.

of flow patterns as this valley was deglaciated. At one point melt waters in the Eagle River valley flowed eastward to the Columbia at Revelstoke; later they flowed south into Mabel Lake and thence to the Okanagan before settling on their present route into the Shuswap.

A short distance east of Malakwa, the characteristic tree of British Columbia rain forests—the western hemlock—appears, and white pine becomes the common species of young tree growing along the roadside. Other roadside plants are also typical of openings in moist forests—goatsbeard, cow parsnip and bracken fern.

Just past the Enchanted Forest theme park, the highway crosses the Eagle River. This point is an excellent spot to see spawning sockeye salmon in late September and October. This run is a mix of the larger sea-run sockeye—which venture down the Thompson and Fraser to the open ocean after maturing for a year in Shuswap Lake—and the smaller kokanee, which remain in Shuswap Lake until they return to spawn when they are four years old.

The first large lake you reach on the Eagle River is Griffin Lake. On June 5, 1968, a major mud flow roared down the Camp Creek valley here, burying the highway and four motorists with 76,000 cubic metres of mud, trees and boulders. This type of slide is relatively common in steep-walled valleys such as this one, usually triggered in early summer as heavy rains saturate the snowpack below the treeline. The resulting flow of slush turns to a mud flow below the snow line, uprooting trees and rocks until the debris cleans the steep valley to bedrock. A similar slide swept into Clanwilliam (Summit) Lake on April 2, 1999. This lake is just east of Eagle Pass; the flow is clearly visible above the railway snowshed at the west end of the lake. The slide damaged the snowshed and filled the lake with trees and other debris, still obvious three years later.

After Eagle Pass, the highway makes a relatively quick descent to the Columbia River at Revelstoke. This is one of the short free-flowing stretches of the Columbia, between two of its many dams and reservoirs—the Revelstoke dam is only 5 kilometres to the north, and the Arrow Reservoir is less than a kilometre to the south.

As you climb out of the valley beyond Revelstoke, you have left the Monashees behind and entered the Selkirk Mountains. A view to the southwest reveals Mt. Begbie (2731 metres), a series of three glacier-capped peaks in the Monashees. To the northwest is the spire of Mt. Copeland (2560 metres), famous for its record snowfall. You soon enter Mt. Revelstoke National Park, best known for its summer wild-flower meadows and huge snow packs. To truly appreciate this park, you must drive up the Meadows in the Sky Parkway, a 26-kilometre road to the alpine, open to the top in the summer and fall only. The exact dates and distances it is opened depend on the snow pack.

A few large white pines tower above younger trees; their long, gan-gly branches, grey-green needles and banana-like cones make them easy to pick out. After about 10 kilometres, you enter an old hemlock forest, which soon gives way to a seral forest of aspen and birch.

The highway leaves Mt. Revelstoke National Park and continues to climb the Illecillewaet Valley toward Rogers Pass. Shortly after leaving the park, you cross a bridge over the Illecillewaet River and follow a rocky gorge. The black-and-white rocks here are grano-diorite gneisses—metamorphic rocks formed under the burden of Quesnellia, which buried the west coast of North America about 180 million years ago. About 9 kilometres out of the park there are areas of dead trees across the river; these are hemlocks killed by the hem-lock looper, the inchworm larvae of a small moth.

Soon another phenomenon that shapes local forests is evident—avalanche tracks through the forests on the steep valley slopes. These mountains have some of the highest annual snowfalls in the world—the Canadian record is 24.47 metres at Mt. Copeland, about 20 kilometres northwest of Revelstoke. The average annual snow-fall at Rogers Pass is 8.69 metres, and the maximum is about twice that amount. And remember that snowfall higher on the mountain slopes is much greater than that on the valley highway.

Deep snow and steep slopes add up to avalanches, as the series of snowsheds along the highway indicates. You will also see mounts for artillery guns that fire shells into the mountains to trigger ava-lanches when the danger levels are high. The highway is temporarily

REST STOP

Mt. Revelstoke National Park Nature Trails

ABOUT 25 KILOMETRES from Revelstoke, you come to the Skunk Cabbage Nature Trail, well worth a stop in spring and summer. This is one of the best places in these mountains to watch forest birds, and park biologists conduct annual studies on their breeding success here. Just a couple of kilometres or so up the highway is a forest of old hemlocks and cedars that you can explore on the Giant Cedars Trail, a boardwalk that winds up and down the hillside through an awe-inspiring stand of huge trees, some up to a thousand years old. Steller's jays call raucously from the picnic area, but some of the most interesting denizens of this forest are unseen by day. Five species of small bats use the huge, hollow cedars as roost sites.

The nature trails afford pleasant walks through a forest that is otherwise difficult to traverse on foot. Sir Sandford Fleming, one of the pioneer railway builders of the 1800s, described hiking through the Illecillewaet Valley thus:

> The walking is dreadful, we climb over and creep under fallen trees of great size and the men soon show that they feel the weight of their burdens... The dripping rain from the bush and branches saturates us from above. Tall ferns sometimes reaching to the shoulder and Devil's Clubs through which we had to crush our way make us feel as if dragged through a horsepond and our perspiration is that of a Turkish bath... The Devil's Clubs may be numbered by millions and they are perpetually wounding us with their spikes against which we strike... We wade through Alder swamps and tread down Skunk Cabbage and Prickly Aralias, and so we continue until half-past four, when the tired-out men are able to go no further...

Above: Devil's club. RICHARD CANNINGS

closed during these operations, of course. As well as snowsheds and howitzers, avalanche-control methods include the construction of various earth and rock barriers designed to stop or deflect avalanches before they reach the highway. Although Rogers Pass is relatively low at 1330 metres, this highway wasn't built until 1962 because it was so difficult to ensure safety from avalanches; until then motorists were forced to drive around the Big Bend Highway, which followed the Columbia River around its "big bend" 140 kilometres north of Revelstoke.

Because they shed their snow regularly through the winter, avalanche slopes are the first areas in the mountains to become snow-free in spring. And because they are treeless, they support a lush growth of grasses and herbs, perfect food for hungry bears that have just emerged from their hibernation dens. So watch for bears, both grizzly and black, on these slopes in spring and early summer.

After a series of three snowsheds, you enter Glacier National Park, created in 1886 to preserve the mountain forests through Rogers Pass for the enjoyment of the tourists who stopped there regularly on the train. You are also entering a different forest at this elevation; the hemlocks and cedars are replaced by Engelmann spruce and spirelike subalpine fir. This is the heart of the Selkirks, an area that William Van Horne, railway tycoon, described as "the climax of mountain scenery." It was here in 1888 that sport mountaineering was born in North America, not in the Rockies or the American West.

The highest mountain visible from the highway is Mt. Sir Donald (3277 metres); there is a good view of it from the Sir Donald picnic area as you approach Rogers Pass. From the Illecillewaet Campground area, you can see several of the glaciers that give the park its name, especially the large Illecillewaet Glacier 4 kilometres to the south. Like most glaciers around the world, the Illecillewaet has retreated significantly as a result of climate change. Photos taken by early tourists in 1897 show the toe of the glacier about 2 kilometres below where it is today. To the north, Mt. Rogers and Hermit Mountain (left and right, 3216 and 2094 metres,

Illecillewaet Glacier. DOUGLAS LEIGHTON

respectively) have small alpine glaciers. The Rogers Pass Discovery Centre has good exhibits of natural and railway history.

Once over the pass, the highway descends through another series of five snowsheds and within 10 kilometres is back in the hemlock forest again. Mountain goats are often visible on the steep slopes above Tractor Sheds Picnic Area, though it is probably best to try to spot them from the roadside rather than from a moving vehicle. The highway follows Connaught Creek to the large Beaver River valley, about 12 kilometres from Rogers Pass. This valley marks the boundary between the Selkirk Mountains on the west (made up here of early Cambrian rocks) and the Purcell Mountains to the east (consisting of Precambrian rocks). The Purcells are built, for the most part, from sedimentary and volcanic rocks, which are softer than the metamorphic gneisses and quartzite of the Selkirks and therefore appear much more rounded than the rugged Selkirks.

Shortly after leaving Glacier Park, you can see the next mountain range in the distance—the Rockies. Between the park boundary and Quartz Creek, the highway goes through several rock cuts that are rich in mica, and if the sun angle is right, you will get a blinding display of the mirrorlike qualities of that mineral. The highway begins

In spring and early summer, black bears gorge on the lush new plant growth along the roadsides and on avalanche slopes. One of their favourite spring delicacies is dandelion. RICHARD CANNINGS

a long turn back to the southeast as it enters the huge Rocky Mountain Trench and meets the Columbia River again. To the north you can glimpse the Kinbasket Reservoir, a huge lake behind the Mica Dam, 150 kilometres north on the Columbia. The forest also changes dramatically as you enter the trench. Now behind the high Selkirks and Purcells, you are in a rain shadow, and the forest becomes temporarily more diverse, as species preferring drier environments, such as lodgepole pine, mix with the moist forest species.

As you cross the Columbia River once again (this time it is flowing north to the Big Bend), you enter the Rocky Mountains. Predominant rock colours, which had been blackish in the Selkirks and Purcells, are now the greys of limestones and other carbonate rocks. South of Donald, the highway travels southwest down a long straightaway; in the distance is Moberly Peak, with a distinct white patch—a gypsum quarry—on its western shoulder.

The highway crosses the Blaeberry River on a small bridge; few motorists realize that but for fate, the highway could well be turning east here to cross the Rockies at Howse Pass. If elevation alone were the criteria for highway and train routes, Howse Pass would definitely be superior to other routes through this part of the mountains; at 1525 metres, it is more than 100 metres lower than Kicking Horse Pass. However, railway planners and politicians preferred the more southern Kicking Horse route since they felt it would discourage territorial incursions from the United States.

A few kilometres south of the Blaeberry River, you pass Moberly Marsh on the west side of the road; this is one of the many rich marshes situated along the Rocky Mountain Trench where backwaters and old oxbows of the Columbia River have created cattail and bulrush marshes and wet meadows that are teeming with animals not found in the coniferous forests that cover most of British Columbia. Most mountain valleys in British Columbia have never had many marshes, and few valleys have significant numbers remaining; it is fortunate that those in the Rocky Mountain Trench have largely survived unscathed.

The highway follows the trench south for about 25 kilometres, then turns east again at Golden and begins its climb up the Kicking Horse River into the heart of the Rocky Mountains. Because the mountains along the western wall of the Rockies were on the leading edge of the faulting that stacked up the Rockies, they are more folded and deformed than those in the central and eastern parts of the range. Even more important, their rocks are predominantly shales, which are more easily deformed and eroded than the brittle limestones and dolomites common farther east. The latter rocks were laid down off the coast of ancient North America. The shallow waters along the coast produced an abundant growth of coral-like reefs in Cambrian times, which form carbonate rocks such as limestones, while muds and silts that turn to mudstones and shales collected in deeper waters.

There is a distinct line between these two rock types in the Rocky Mountains. Dubbed the Kickinghorse Rim, it crosses Highway 1 and the Kicking Horse River at the town of Field. To the east you can see the classic pale grey, castellated peaks of the central Rockies; to the west, more rounded, dark grey mountains.

The Rocky Mountain Trench

British Columbia is full of geological wonders, but few are as large or as impressive as the Rocky Mountain Trench. Stretching from northwestern Montana to the Yukon, it is the longest linear valley in the world. Differences in structure and geography divide it into three segments: the Tintina Trench in the Yukon, the Northern Rocky Mountain Trench from Prince George north to the Yukon, and the Southern Rocky Mountain Trench. The two northern sections are huge "strike-slip" faults—that is, the land on the western side of the valley has moved northward in relation to the east side—in this case, more than 425 kilometres.

The formation of the Southern Rocky Mountain Trench is more difficult for geologists to explain, but it likely occurred after the relentless pressures that built the mountains over millennia suddenly stopped about 60 million years ago. The halt in these pressures allowed the Earth's crust to relax across southern British Columbia, and several large cracks opened up as the crust eased westward. The largest of these cracks was the Southern Rocky Mountain Trench, where the earth simply split along a line and the bottom of today's valley fell thousands of metres in relation to the land on either side.

Above: A view up the Rocky Mountain Trench at Golden. DOUGLAS LEIGHTON

As you leave Golden, watch for bighorn sheep along the high-way—they are often hard to miss! The south-facing slopes above the highway are relatively dry, with Douglas-fir and Rocky Mountain juniper predominating; there are even some grassy slopes. The lower Kicking Horse Valley is very narrow with a steep gradient and seems little altered by glacial erosion. Perhaps the Pleistocene ice in this section was more or less stagnant for some reason and didn't scour the valley out as it did higher up. The highway clings to the valley walls, often winding around cliffs, and it is best if the driver not steal any glances at this book during this stretch. At the second bridge, look at the vertical limestone beds on the north side of the river; this is an overturned thrust fault. If you see patches of dead, red-needled lodgepole pine in this area, they are almost surely victims of mountain pine beetle.

About 20 kilometres from Golden, though, the valley opens into a typical glaciated mountain valley. The forest is primarily young Douglas-fir and lodgepole pine, with some aspen and juniper scattered through it. Trailing mats of dark green kinnikinnick grow on the gravelly soils along with grey-leafed shrubs of soopolallie. Engelmann spruce appears just before you reach the boundary of Yoho National Park. About 3 kilometres past the park boundary, there is a blowdown area where a small area of forest was levelled by wind in November 1996; this is most easily viewed at the railway overpass as you travel westward.

As you pass Chancellor Peak Campground, the valley floor is almost level, and the sky-blue Kicking Horse River winds across braided gravel beds, carpeted with yellow mountain-avens in early summer. These flowers, so typical of gravelly soils in the mountains, have rather inconspicuous, bell-shaped yellow flowers, followed by silvery dandelion-like seed heads in August. Wind-dispersed seeds are typical of plants such as mountain-avens, which colonize new, bare-soil habitats. Bare soil or gravel often lacks nitrates, so another important characteristic of mountain-avens, and several other colonizing species, is the ability to create these nutrients from atmospheric nitrogen. Like clover and other legumes, mountain-avens do this with the help of bacteria in root nodules.

The mountain slopes here are forested with lodgepole pines, but most of the young trees growing under the pines are Engelmann spruce, foreshadowing a climax forest of spruce in two hundred years if no fire intervenes.

The rusty ridge to the west at Ottertail Campground is Mt. King (2892 metres); to the north is glacier-capped Mt. Carnarvon (3040 metres). Foxtail barley is common along the roadside at the bridge over the Kicking Horse, as are oxeye daisies and yellow hawkweed in summer. This is elk country (see page 190), so watch for these large deer in grassy areas along the river and highway.

The village of Field is situated in a spectacular part of the Kicking Horse Valley, surrounded on all sides by high mountains, including Mt. Field (2400 metres) to the north and Mt. Stephen (3199 metres) on the south. The soft sedimentary rocks on these steep

Mt. Stephen and Mt. Dennis

On the south side of the valley at the town of Field stand two high mountains—Mt. Stephen to the east, Mt. Dennis to the west. Mt. Stephen is typical of high peaks in the central Rockies, with high, light grey cliffs, whereas the rounded, dark grey shales of Mt. Dennis are characteristic of mountains along the western ranges. Geologists call this boundary a facies change, meaning that it has occurred because different rock types formed side by side rather than being brought together through later faulting.

The limestones of Mt. Stephen were laid down in shallow coral seas, whereas the shales of Mt. Dennis formed from muds and silts deposited at the same time but in deeper waters farther offshore. These rocks contain some of the most famous fossil beds in the world—the trilobite beds of Mt. Stephen and the Burgess Shales across the valley on Mt. Field.

slopes produce constant rock falls and large talus fans, which are the source of the abundant gravels that constantly fill the river valley and maintain the braided river course.

Yellow hawkweed. RICHARD CANNINGS

As the highway begins to climb the last big hill to the Great Divide, you can see mine openings in the lower slopes of Mt. Field on the north side of the valley. These were dug long after the park was formed to extract lead-zinc ores. A stop at the Spiral Tunnel viewpoint provides good views into the valley to the north, where you can see typical thrust fault mountains and glaciers. Wapta Lake lies at the top of the hill, and the Great Divide and the Alberta border await you 5 kilometres from there. To the south are some fine examples of hanging valleys and steep-walled cirques; alpine larch brighten the high slopes in early fall as their needles turn gold with the first hard frosts. The structure and shape of gravel deposits here suggest that at the end of the Pleistocene and after ice had retreated from most of the Bow Valley, the upper part of this valley (from Wapta Lake eastward) was covered in ice that extended to within 8 kilometres of Lake Louise.

> I followed up the Bow River to study the mountains more closely. Never before did I observe so close a resemblance to the waves of the ocean during a wintry storm. In viewing their wild appearance the imagination is apt to say that these mountains must once have been liquid, and when in that state, swelled to their greatest agitation, it was all suddenly congealed and made solid by power omnipotent.
>
> DAVID THOMPSON, *from his journals*

TWO

The Island Highway

HIGHWAYS 1 AND 19

THE ISLAND HIGHWAY begins at Mile zero of the Trans-Canada Highway, just north of the sea cliffs of Beacon Hill Park. From there it traverses the relatively dry, benign lowlands of eastern Vancouver Island north to Nanaimo, where the Trans-Canada crosses the Strait of Georgia to the mainland and Highway 19 continues north to Campbell River. There the lowlands end and the highway swings into the wetter, more rugged country of northern Vancouver Island. The highway ends at Port Hardy on the shores of Queen Charlotte Strait.

▶ **Victoria to Campbell River:** A Rain Shadow amid Rain Forests
The winds off the water are usually brisk and salty. The sculpted copses of trees and shrubs at the cliff tops are a testament to their power, and glaucous-winged gulls play on the updrafts. Across the Juan de Fuca Strait, the perfectly carved snow- and ice-capped peaks of the Olympic Mountains create a stunning southern skyline. On a very clear day, you can see Mt. Rainier (4392 metres), more than 200 kilometres to the southeast, rising above the eastern flank of the Olympics.

Facing page: The pale fertile stalks of the northern giant horsetail emerge in damp ditches and other wet places along the west coast. SYDNEY CANNINGS

A perfect Eden, in the midst of the dreary Wilderness...
JAMES DOUGLAS, 1842

The soil here is underlain by gravels and glacial till that piled up against a stagnant glacier that had grounded in the Juan de Fuca Strait about twelve thousand years ago. This mantle covers bedrock that previous glaciers had scoured as they moved slowly southward. Rocks embedded in the ice scraped against the bedrock below, leaving behind scratches and grooves that can easily be seen today. Along the shore below you, more and more rock is exposed each year by wave erosion, and surfaces are exposed that are so fresh they look as if the glaciers had melted only yesterday. Another superb place to see this reminder of the ice ages is on the bedrock beside the Centennial Fountain, immediately west of the Legislature on Belleville Street.

The strait itself is a huge saltwater river that switches directions twice a day, exchanging nutrients from the Pacific Ocean and the Fraser River and its smaller cohorts at each turn of the tide. Great ships move ponderously up the strait to Vancouver, and moving with them in summer are salmon of five species, returning from their great Pacific journeys, followed closely by their natural predators, the killer whales.

Your journey begins with a short drive through Beacon Hill Park, which, for a city park, maintains a surprising array of native animal and plant species. Grassy swards flow down the south-facing hillsides, and woodlands of Garry oaks merge with open stands of big Douglas-fir to the north. In April, the meadows are awash in blue camas and many other wildflowers, including a remnant clump of the globally rare deltoid balsamroot. As you drive north on Douglas Street, you pass a stand of large black cottonwood trees on the east side of the road; look up in the top of one of them to find the massive nest of a pair of bald eagles. Just north of the nest is a long-established breeding colony of great blue herons; look for the stick nests high in the Douglas-firs.

At the north end of Beacon Hill Park (Superior Street), Blanshard Street splits off from Douglas Street. For those going north up the

The grooves in these rocks along Victoria's shoreline were scratched by rocks frozen within moving glacial ice. COREL

east coast of Vancouver Island on Highways 1 and 19, Douglas Street guides you through Victoria; Blanshard Street is Highway 17, the route to Vancouver via the Swartz Bay–Tsawwassen ferries.

Highway 1 swings westward over the north end of Portage Inlet, then touches the north side of Langford Lake before entering the big trees of Goldstream Provincial Park. This small park protects the Goldstream River valley, where large Douglas-firs populate the hillsides and western redcedar and black cottonwoods grow along the river itself. The park's main annual attraction is the chum salmon run, when thousands of salmon return to the river from October through December to spawn. Following the salmon are hundreds of bald eagles and other fish-loving animals.

Davidson's penstemon. STEVE CANNINGS

The mouth of the Goldstream River lies at the south end of Saanich Inlet, a deep fiord carved by glaciers. Here the glaciers usually came in from the sea rather than going out, as they usually did. This glacier came from the Coast Mountains across the Strait of Georgia and pushed up Saanich Inlet south to Colwood.

Mt. Finlayson (416 metres), on the east side of Goldstream Park, marks the edge of two geological terranes. The main cliffs of Mt. Finlayson are metamorphosed igneous rocks of Wrangellia, a large land mass that collided with North America about 130 million years ago. The lower slopes of the mountain, separated from the upper cliffs by the Survey Mountain Fault, are made up of the softer, metamorphosed sedimentary rocks of the Pacific Rim Terrane, which was forced under Wrangellia about 65 million years ago. The Pacific Rim Terrane is relatively small, consisting of a narrow strip of land near Victoria and the shoreline of Pacific Rim National Park. About 5 kilometres north of the Goldstream Park entrance, the highway crosses over the Survey Mountain Fault onto Wrangellian rocks.

The highway climbs the steep fiord walls for a short distance and then leaves them for the gentler slopes of the Victoria Highlands; it eventually reaches the Malahat Summit, at 356 metres elevation. From here you can get a good view of Saanich Inlet, both across to Brentwood Bay and tiny Senanus Island and south over the treetops to the end of Finlayson Arm and the mouth of the Goldstream River.

The forests on the Malahat Summit are dominated by Douglas-fir and arbutus, the latter occurring as a pioneer species where the forests have been cleared by fire or machine. Rocky banks on the roadside are brightened by purple clusters of penstemon flowers in the spring. In summer, oceanspray shrubs bloom with drooping bouquets of creamy flowers. Once over the summit, the shadier northeast-facing slopes have more western redcedar and red alder. Scotch broom, an invasive alien species, is common along the roadside. The bright yellow flowers of broom make it an attractive plant to many people, but its prolific seed production—up to eighteen thousand seeds per plant per year—and vigorous growth has allowed it to take over huge areas of natural habitat on southern Vancouver Island.

As you approach Duncan, you can see the Koksilah River valley to the west and the ridges of western Saltspring Island to the east. At the south entrance to Duncan, you cross the Cowichan River, well known for its spawning runs of coho, chinook and chum salmon and steelhead. The steelhead arrive earliest in the year, appearing in January and peaking in February and March. The salmon spawn in the fall—the coho and chinook mainly in October and the abundant chum, sometimes more than a hundred thousand strong, in December.

Mt. Tzouhalem (498 metres) is the rounded ridge east of Duncan; its warm, southwest-facing slopes support a remnant of the rare Garry oak savanna. Housing projects are encroaching on this habitat from below, but a small ecological reserve protects endangered plants such as the deltoid balsamroot. Western Bluebirds formerly nested on Mt. Tzouhalem, but habitat loss has now eliminated this colourful species from Vancouver Island.

Once through the main business district of Duncan, you drive past a large marsh on the east side of the road. This is Somenos Lake, one of the largest and richest wetlands on Vancouver Island. It has been designated an Important Bird Area for the high populations of waterfowl that winter here, including one of the largest concentrations of trumpeter swans in the world. Up to a thousand of these huge white birds can be seen in winter in the marsh and on adjacent flooded fields. There is also a breeding population of mute swans, the classic park swans introduced from Europe. The orange bills of the mute swans quickly distinguish them from the native trumpeters (see page 32). Twenty-five pairs of great blue herons nest in trees on the west side of the road at Somenos.

Just north of Duncan, the highway turns northeast to skirt the eastern slopes of Big Sicker Mountain (714 metres). This mountain has given its name to the Sicker Group, the oldest body of rocks on Vancouver Island. The pale greenish rocks along the west side of the road were formed in volcanic explosions over 360 million years ago. Once past Big Sicker Mountain, you cross the Chemainus River and turn northwest toward Ladysmith.

Ladysmith Harbour is one of several estuaries on the southern B.C. coast that has nesting purple martins. These large swallows all but disappeared from the province in the mid-1900s, probably as a result of competition with European starlings for nest sites. Purple martins have since staged an encouraging comeback, thanks largely to nest boxes erected by naturalists on pilings in intertidal areas of eastern Vancouver Island and the Lower Mainland. About seventy-five pairs of martins now nest in the province every year.

The grasslands surrounding the Nanaimo airport at Cassidy are home to the only population of coastal vesper sparrows in British Columbia. These birds, like many plants and animals adapted to coastal grasslands, have declined precipitously in numbers as their fire-dependent habitats have been covered with housing developments, ingrowing forests or alien shrubs such as broom.

Deltoid balsamroot. GEORGE DOUGLAS

The Island Highway bypass around Nanaimo goes directly through Harewood Plains, another grassland remnant. The open slopes above the highway have shallow soils with many mossy seepage points; these beautiful meadows bloom pink and blue in April with masses of sea-blush and blue-eyed mary.

The pink flower heads of sea blush brighten spring meadows on southwestern Vancouver Island. RICHARD CANNINGS

Highway 1 turns west to a ferry terminal at Nanaimo, and the Island Highway becomes Highway 19. You return to the coast at Nanoose Harbour, a shallow, warm bay that is rich in shellfish and herring spawn. Much of its surface is now covered with mussel farms, marked by the blue floats, but it still attracts flocks of waterfowl and herds of sea-lions each spring when the herring spawn. Nanoose Hill, the ridge on the north side of the bay, has some excellent Garry oak meadows on lands owned by the Department of National Defence. The hill creates updrafts favoured by large soaring birds, such as bald eagles and turkey vultures.

The western horizon at Nanoose Bay is dominated by the dark cliffs of Mt. Arrowsmith (1817 metres), one of the more spectacular peaks on Vancouver Island. It is one of the best places to find Vancouver Island's unique subspecies of white-tailed ptarmigan, a small alpine grouse that turns completely white in winter. The rocks of Mt. Arrowsmith are entirely volcanic, laid down in underwater lava flows while this chunk of the Earth's crust was drifting through a tropical sea over 225 million years ago.

The highway climbs back onto the broad, rolling Nanaimo Lowlands, passing farmlands, pasture and second-growth forests dominated by Douglas-fir. At Parksville you get a glimpse of the Strait of Georgia again, this time at the mouth of the Englishman River. The large mud and gravel flats near Parksville are critical habitat for migrating Brant geese in spring. These geese time their journey from Baja California north to the High Arctic to take advantage of herring spawn, which are a rich source of fuel for their long flight.

North of the exits to Parksville and Tofino, you cross a series of streams, including French Creek, the Little Qualicum River and its larger cousin, the Big Qualicum River. These valleys often have scattered large, veteran trees that were spared the logging efforts on the flat land to either side of their valleys. There are some large Sitka spruce along French Creek and several impressive Douglas-firs at the Little Qualicum. The Big Qualicum has several important salmon runs; as in other Vancouver Island rivers, the Qualicum salmon stocks are dominated by a large chum run that averages about 100,000 fish. Its coho population is about 10,000, only half of the former numbers; chinook numbers vary widely but are usually around 1000 or 2000.

Beyond the Big Qualicum River, a high fence on the west side of the highway keeps Roosevelt elk from wandering onto the road. You get another view of the salt chuck just past Rosewall Creek and again around the exit to Buckley Bay and Union Bay. Denman Island lies just offshore at both these sites, with Baynes Sound running between it and the mainland of Vancouver Island. Baynes Sound, shallow and warm, is the oyster capital of British Columbia and is another Important Bird Area, so designated for its huge concentrations of waterfowl during spring. Hundreds of Pacific loons, mew gulls and other waterbirds gather for the herring spawn, while large flocks of black turnstones forage on exposed mussel and oyster beds.

The grassy shoulders of the highway have been planted to lupines, while the bright pink spears of fireweed blossoms dominate the cleared areas on either side. North of the Tsolum River, western hemlocks begin to appear, indicating a moister climate, but Douglas-fir remains common.

At the exit to Courtenay and Comox, you can glimpse the Comox peninsula and one or two of the farms that fill the Comox Valley. The Comox Valley has the highest concentrations of wintering trumpeter swans in the world. Once considered near extinction, these huge birds—the heaviest wild bird in North America—have greatly increased in numbers over the last thirty years. About two thousand now spend the winter in the Comox Valley, mostly from November through March. The swans are considered by many farmers to be a pest species, consuming large quantities of pasture grass planted for dairy cattle, but the impact of the swans on local agriculture has been minimized by a cooperative project between the farmers, the

Toad Fences

A young western toad ventures out of Keddie Slough. RICHARD CANNINGS

If you look at the elk fencing between Millar Creek and the Hamm Road exit, you will see a layer of fine mesh at its base. This is a toad fence, probably the only one of its kind in British Columbia.

On the east side of the highway, hundreds of western toads gather to breed every summer in Keddie Slough. Each female toad lays a large clutch of eggs—often more than twelve thousand—in long strings. The eggs hatch quickly into small, black tadpoles, which metamorphose into tiny toads six to eight weeks later. In August and early September, these toadlets move out of the marsh en masse to disperse throughout the forested habitats west of the highway that are the species' natural feeding grounds. To prevent catastrophic highway mortality of toads, these low fences were built to direct the toads through a number of culverts on their westward journey.

Canadian Wildlife Service and Ducks Unlimited Canada. The swans also favour culled potatoes and carrots left in fields but apparently turn up their beaks at Brussels sprouts and broccoli.

The Comox Valley is also famous for its fossils. Extensive deposits of Cretaceous shales here commonly contain ammonites and other molluscs, but there have been other, more remarkable finds. In 1988, a fossilized skeleton of an elasmosaur was discovered along the Puntledge River. Elasmosaurs were long-necked swimming reptiles that hunted fish about 80 million years ago. And yes, there has been one dinosaur found in the Comox-Courtenay area. The tooth of a small carnivorous theropod dinosaur—the group to which *Tyrannosaurus* belongs—was found in marine shales along the Trent River. The animal had likely died along another long-vanished river and was washed out to sea, where it sank into the mud that later formed the shales.

As you reach the uplands north of Courtenay, you can see the distant Mt. Albert Edward (2093 metres) and, slightly north and much closer, Mt. Washington (1589 metres) on the western horizon. Mt. Albert Edward is a rough layercake of lava flows formed at the same time as Mt. Arrowsmith.

About 9 kilometres south of Campbell River, the Oyster River has a major pink salmon spawning run from August to October, with smaller numbers of chinook following in September and October, chum in October and November, and coho from October to December. Campbell River dubs itself the Salmon Capital of the World (a title hotly disputed by Port Alberni), based on its important sports fishery. The salmon of Campbell River enter the Strait of Georgia from the north, forced through the narrow, turbulent waters of Discovery Passage. This small strait is the last of the many narrows that the tidal flood must pass through before reaching the open waters of the strait. Tidal currents of 5 to 7 knots are normal here during spring tides.

Campbell River itself has significant salmon runs, with thousands of pink and chum spawning in its waters annually. Formerly large runs of coho and chinook have in recent years been reduced from thousands to hundreds of fish.

Large Douglas-firs stand watch along Nimpkish Lake. RICHARD CANNINGS

Campbell River was also the home of the late Roderick Haig-Brown, one of British Columbia's foremost conservationists and nature writers. His house, now an official British Columbia historic site open for tours, is on the south side of the river only a few hundred metres west of the highway. Haig-Brown's concerns around local events in Campbell River, especially the building of the John Hart dam on that river in 1948, led to a lifetime of writing and activism. The dam was one of several body blows to local salmon populations.

Campbell River to Port Hardy: The North Island Rain Forests

The trip from Campbell River north to the end of the Island Highway at Port Hardy contrasts markedly to the southern section of the route. The northern section passes through the true rain forests of Vancouver Island, though most of the forests along the highway have been clear-cut in the last two or three decades, leaving only ragged remnants of old forests along the ridge tops. Between Sayward and Port McNeill, the only human habitations are the logging camps of the Nimpkish Valley. Most of the route is well inland, and there are only two sites where you can gaze out over the wild coast of the north island.

The first of these is about 11 kilometres north of Campbell River, where you can look north to Seymour Narrows, a 3-kilometre stretch of very turbulent water between Vancouver Island on the west and Maud Island and Quadra Island on the east. Tidal currents can reach 16 knots through Seymour Narrows at flood tide. Ship navigation through these waters was hampered for many years not only by the tidal currents but also by a dangerous underwater shoal named Ripple Rock that caused 119 shipwrecks, starting in 1875. In 1958 engineers drilled a tunnel under the rock from Maud Island, packed 1250 tonnes of explosives under the twin peaks of the rock, then set off one of the largest non-nuclear explosions in history to erase the rock from the narrows.

North of Campbell River, the highway moves inland, away from the sea and into a new forest. You have left the dry Coastal Douglas-fir Zone and have entered the wetter Coastal Western Hemlock Zone. Although much of the forest here is second-growth Douglas-fir, if you

REST STOP
Dalrymple Creek

THE DALRYMPLE CREEK Nature Trail offers self-guided interpretive walks along a 500-metre trail on land owned by the Weyerhaeuser forest company. Huge, fire-scarred four-hundred-year-old Douglas-firs grow here in a younger forest of western hemlock and western redcedar. Watch for the workings of red-breasted sapsuckers along the trail, especially near the start. These small woodpeckers drill neat rows of tiny holes in hemlock bark, returning to lap up the sap with their special brushlike tongues. In summer, they add ants and other insects attracted to the sweet sap to their diet.

Facing page: Douglas-firs. RICHARD CANNINGS

look at the small trees growing on the forest floor, you can see they are the droopy-tipped western hemlock that is so characteristic of the B.C. coastal rain forests.

Beyond Roberts Lake you follow Roberts Creek down to its junction with Amor de Cosmos Creek, then over a small pass into the Salmon River drainage at the unfortunately named Big Tree Creek Rest Area. Big Tree Creek flows through a thick growth of small red alder, western hemlock and western redcedar, but no large trees can be seen. The thick, shrubby understorey is salal on the uplands and salmonberry and swordfern along the creek. A much better rest stop is offered about 9 kilometres farther on at Dalrymple Creek.

From Dalrymple Creek, you descend to the Salmon River and its hay farms, the last evidence of agriculture you will see on the journey north, and cross the river at its junction with the White River, which comes in from the southwest. There are no fewer than six rivers in British Columbia with the name Salmon River; this one has spawning runs of all five Pacific salmon species, dominated by runs of up to 200,000 pink salmon.

Beyond the Sayward junction, you climb along Elk Creek into the mountains of northern Vancouver Island. At the Keta Lake Rest Area, the western hemlocks are joined by some amabilis fir. You are on the boundary between rain forest and snow forest—amabilis fir, with its dark green needles and smooth grey bark, is one of the diagnostic species of the coastal subalpine forests, known as the Mountain Hemlock Zone. Keta Lake is nestled in a large area of logged-over slopes. Its shores are lined with hardhack, a pink-flowering spirea typical of cold swamps, and its waters dappled with yellow pond-lilies. A surprising anomaly, probably the work of tree planters with a sense of humour, is a stand of young ponderosa pines—trees typical of the hot, dry Interior valleys—along the north side of the road opposite the rest area. These trees are surviving here but do not appear to be thriving.

After crossing the Adam River, the highway turns northwest, heading deeper into the interior of the island. There is a patch of old-growth western hemlock at Rooney Lake, but most of the

Like many other bog plants, black crowberry is a member of the heath family.
RICHARD CANNINGS

forests along this highway have been completely cut in the last fifty years. The Eve River, logged to the water line a few decades ago, flows in from the west in a dense swath of young hemlock, the river course only detectable by the red alders along its bank. As you move inland closer to the high mountains of the central island, the forests become drier once again; at the Tsitika River, western white pine, typical of moist—but not soggy—forests, becomes a common pioneer species. By the time you reach the Schoen Lake junction, the forests are distinctly drier; along the Nimpkish River there are old-growth Douglas-firs on steep, south-facing slopes. Gravel islands in the river are forested by black cottonwood, red alder, willows and Douglas-fir.

North of the Zeballos junction, the highway passes a wetland complex of beaver ponds, streams, fens and bogs. The wetland vegetation includes sweet gale, hardhack, cattail, sedges, Labrador tea and salal. Small, round-topped lodgepole pines grow in the boggy areas. The upland forest here is also rich in species, including Douglas-fir, western redcedar, Sitka spruce, western hemlock, western white pine and lodgepole pine.

The Nimpkish River has significant runs of sockeye and chum salmon. The sockeye run, sometimes numbering as many as 200,000 fish, occurs in the summer, and the chum run, peaking at about 100,000 fish, occurs in late fall. These runs often attract considerable numbers of bald eagles, especially during the late fall, when the birds are not restricted to breeding territories. About twenty pairs of eagles nest in the valley, using huge veteran Douglas-fir trees to hold their bulky stick nests, some as large as Volkswagen beetles. Eagles in territories closer to the coast are more successful at raising young than those along the lake, since the adults have access to gulls and other seabirds that are the preferred prey during summer. There is an Eagle Nest Rest Area, but no trees large enough to support an eagle nest are now visible from the stop.

Nimpkish Lake lies far below the highway and is visible only through the trees at a few sites. North of Storey Creek there are areas of older forest along the highway, dominated by large, craggy Douglas-firs. Although these trees are impressive, they are only about 175 years old—less than half as old as and much smaller than Douglas-firs on Nimpkish Island, a small island in the Nimpkish River far from the highway. The Nimpkish Island trees are among the tallest trees in Canada.

Just north of the Port McNeill junction, there is a sphagnum bog on the northeast side of the highway. Mats of crowberry and clumps of Labrador tea cover the bog, and salal bushes grow on the drier hummocks. Crowberry is related to blueberries and huckleberries but has black berries and foliage resembling short fir needles. The berries are edible but far from choice. An ingrowth of young lodgepole pines on this bog suggests that its water level has dropped recently, perhaps because of highway construction.

From the Broughton Strait viewpoint, you can look over the northern end of Malcolm Island to the Coast Mountains on the mainland. Malcolm Island is one of the islands that mark the southern edge of Queen Charlotte Strait, where it narrows into Johnstone Strait. Every summer the millions of salmon that will spawn in the rivers emptying into the Strait of Georgia must pass through these narrows, and following the salmon are killer whales and other fish-eating animals. Shearwaters, gulls, auklets and other seabirds gather here as well. Numas Island, the small island you can see north of Malcolm Island, has a small seabird colony, including 750 pairs of rhinoceros auklets. These seabirds are nocturnal puffins that lay their eggs in long burrows dug into the mossy soils of forested islands.

About 17 kilometres north of Port McNeill is the Misty Lake Rest Area. This small lake is an Ecological Reserve, set aside to protect one of only three populations in the world of the giant black stickleback. The other two populations are on the Queen Charlotte Islands.

Many of the redcedars here and elsewhere in wet areas along the British Columbia coast have dead spike tops or candelabra-like growth forms with several gleaming silver trunks almost devoid of growth. Scientists are unsure of what causes this distinctive growth form, but it seems to be caused by repeated die-off of the leading tip of the tree followed by regrowth from the side branches. Part of the answer may lie in the fact that many of these trees are very old and very hardy—there are few insect species here that will kill these trees, and forest fires are exceedingly rare because of the wet climate.

Just south of Port Hardy, the highway crosses the Quatse River; this small stream flows 10 kilometres from Quatse Lake north to the Pacific at Hardy Bay. It is noted for its spawning runs of steelhead and coho salmon. The Island Highway ends at Port Hardy, at a cobble beach facing the waters of Queen Charlotte Strait and the distant Coast Mountains.

THREE

The Crowsnest Highway

HIGHWAY 3

IGHWAY 3, the Crowsnest Highway, is one of the three main east-west routes across British Columbia. Constrained by Canada's southern border, it is forced out of several low valleys to ascend and descend nine mountain passes as it wends its way across the province. It is perhaps the most naturally diverse of these routes, climbing over the Cascades through Manning Park and traversing the desertlike grasslands of the Okanagan Valley, the wet forests of the West Kootenays and the open grandeur of the Rocky Mountain Trench before reaching Alberta at Crowsnest Pass. One of the characteristics of this highway is the almost constant dramatic change in climate and vegetation encountered along its length, from wet to dry, hot to cold, rain forest to desert in stretches of only a few kilometres.

▶ Hope to Princeton: The Cascades

The highway begins its long journey just outside Hope in the narrow valley of Nicolum Creek, a small stream tumbling over granitic boulders in the heart of the wet coastal forest. Western redcedars

Facing page: A spray of fresh thimbleberry leaves spreads across the trunk of a red alder. RICHARD CANNINGS

The Sumallo River is a good spot to look for harlerquin ducks, beautiful sea ducks that forsake the coastal surf in summer to nest along white-water streams in the Interior. The colourful males are only present while the females are laying eggs in late April and May; the drab brown females and young can be seen as late as October. RICHARD CANNINGS

dominate the coniferous forests along the creek, whereas Douglas-firs grow on the rocky southwest-facing slopes above. The deciduous trees along the creek, especially where it was disturbed during highway construction, are red alders. Their trunks are whitened by lichens, a sure sign of high rainfall—normally alder trunks are grey or even greenish.

About 5 kilometres from the Highway 5 junction, you begin a steep climb to avoid a stretch of narrow canyon along the creek. Looking down into the creek, you will soon notice that the valley bottom is filled with more red alders, a result of a large mudflow from the Hope Slide above. The highway cuts into impressively deep, layered deposits of sand, gravel and boulders. These are terraces deposited against a tongue of the Fraser Valley glacier at the end of the Pleistocene, about twelve thousand years ago.

One of the major points of interest on the highway is reached about 10 kilometres from its beginning. The Hope Slide buried the

REST STOP

Sumallo Grove

ONLY 13 KILOMETRES from its source near the Hope Slide, the Sumallo River empties into the westward-flowing Skagit at Sumallo Grove. This stand of huge cedars, hemlocks and Douglas-firs makes a nice spot to break your journey and stroll under the magnificent trees, watch the rivers flow or have a picnic lunch. Remnant stands of old-growth trees like this are essential habitat for spotted owls, one of the rarest birds in Canada.

Above: Sumallo River. SYDNEY CANNINGS

headwaters of Nicolum Creek and the Sumallo River early on the morning of January 9, 1965. The landslide contained about 130 million tonnes of rock, mud and other debris and buried the former highway, which was on the east side of the valley, to a maximum depth of 80 metres. Four people were killed in the slide, the largest landslide in Canadian history. The slide took a major portion of the north valley wall down into the valley floor, picking up mud and water from the marshy lakes there and throwing it up onto the south valley wall. A large mudflow roared down Nicolum Creek,

Hair Lichens

Two types of lichens commonly drape themselves on coniferous trees in this region—the cream-coloured witch's hair lichen and the dark brown horsehair lichen. Both are important winter food for caribou, and both are indicators of old forests. Horsehair lichens break apart easily and spread from tree to tree on the strong mountain winds; hundreds of metres from the nearest source of lichens, snow fields often look like the floor of a barber shop. Horsehair lichens cannot tolerate being wet for long, though, and only grow well on open branches typical of older trees; there the wind can dry them quickly after misty rain or snow. Witch's hair lichens are much stronger and don't break so easily and therefore spread into new forests much more slowly than horsehair lichens.

Witch's hair lichen on rhododendron branches. RICHARD CANNINGS

flattening the cedars along its banks (which have been replaced by the red alder mentioned above). Along the south edge of the slide, forests have regrown to young black cottonwood, Douglas-fir and western hemlock, but the main slide scar on the northern slope remains mostly barren.

The small lakes just south of the Hope Slide are the source of the Sumallo River, one of the tributaries of the Skagit River. Ducks use these lakes during spring and fall migration—watch for goldeneye, bufflehead and mergansers diving for small fish and insect larvae.

The Sumallo winds along a narrow valley floor set between towering rock walls. You may see mountain goats on the southwest side of the river. The shaded mountainsides and dark cedars contrast beautifully with the often colourful shrubbery along the river. The scarlet stems of red osier dogwood brighten even the greyest of winter days in dense thickets along the meandering stream, while the rocky slopes on the opposite side of the highway glow with the fiery foliage of vine maple in the fall. In spring, look for the bright pink flowers of the red-flowering currant on the slopes. The small, dark-green shrubs on the open slopes are false box; their evergreen foliage makes them a favourite with florists.

A large statue of a marmot marks the west gate of Manning Provincial Park, one of the best-known and most popular parks in British Columbia. The park straddles the crest of the Cascade Range and offers many exciting trails for hikers and beautiful scenery for travellers.

Just past Sumallo Grove, the highway turns sharply east to follow the small but turbulent Skagit River, which in this area is completely different from the sedate Sumallo. As you pull out of this sharp corner, you are entering Rhododendron Flats, one of only a handful of sites in British Columbia where Pacific rhododendrons grow. In mid-June the shrubs are covered in huge pink flowers set against the dark green foliage of hemlocks. A trailhead on the south side of a long straight stretch allows motorists to appreciate these plants on foot.

At Rhododendron Flats you can also see a subtle shift to a drier forest type more typical of Interior mountains. The presence of western hemlocks under the Douglas-firs, the older trees draped with pale swaths of witch's hair lichen, shows that you are still in a moist, coastal forest. But the lodgepole pines appearing among the Douglas-firs on the south-facing slopes are characteristic of drier sites. You are on the edge of a new forest type.

The highway rounds another sharp bend as it crosses Snass Creek at the top of Rhododendron Flats, then quickly winds on to the Skagit Bluffs. Drivers should pay attention to the road on this stretch. A few kilometres on you cross Skaist River, another major tributary of the Skagit. The road begins to climb again, with a few western white pines adding spice to the mix of more common trees. At the first crossing of the Skagit, you'll notice that it's now a very small stream, even smaller than the short Sumallo. Another indication of changing forests is the appearance of a few spirelike subalpine firs along this part of the Skagit.

After a few more tight corners (this highway has more than its share), the forest opens up into a burned-over area. This fire raced through in 1945 just after the Hope-Princeton highway was opened. Almost sixty years later, the forest at the lower end of the burn is beginning to fill in with young Douglas-firs, especially on the south-west-facing slopes. A few large veteran Douglas-firs tower above the new growth on the other side of the creek. Higher up, regeneration has been slower, and the forest is dominated by lodgepole pines, in part because of drier, rockier conditions, and in part because of a second fire in 1971. The steep slopes here produce avalanches periodically throughout the winter; an earthen berm has been created at the base of one gully on the southwest side of the road to deflect snow slides away from the highway.

The burn effectively marks the boundary between the lower coastal forests and the higher subalpine forests, the first of several significant forest changes along the highway from here to Princeton. Above the burn the forest is mature Engelmann spruce, part of the Engelmann Spruce–Subalpine Fir Zone.

Within 3 kilometres you reach Allison Pass, the major divide in the northern Cascades, at an elevation of 1342 metres. East of the

Left: The red-naped sapsucker meets its close relative, the red-breasted sapsucker *(right)* at Allison Pass. STEVE CANNINGS *(left);* RICHARD CANNINGS *(right)*

pass, drainage flows to the Columbia River system via the Similkameen and Okanagan Rivers. The pass often marks a significant change in weather, the coastal clouds parting to reveal a blue Interior sky in the rain shadow of the mountains.

Until recently, lodgepole pine was the dominant tree in the forests east of the pass, but mountain pine beetles have killed most of the pines in this area. Mountain pine beetle outbreaks have been one of the most important forces directing the logging industry on the plateaus of British Columbia over the last four decades. Serious epidemics usually begin during warm, dry periods when trees are stressed and summer temperatures ideal for larval growth, and winter temperatures are too warm to kill off the beetles. The outbreaks end a decade or more later when a cycle of higher precipitation and colder winters begins. Large pine beetle infestations serve to speed up the succession processes in most forests. Young firs and spruces, released from the shade of the pines, grow quickly into a climax forest. You can see this in the forests along the Similkameen River, where the grey snags of newly killed pines are being crowded out by a vigorous growth of younger conifers, primarily Engelmann spruce.

REST STOP
Manning Park Beaver Pond

THE MANNING PARK Beaver Pond is a traditional summertime rest stop on this highway. A trail winds along the north shore of the wetland, allowing children to look for spotted frogs and adults to simply enjoy the birdsong and aroma of the forest. Although lodgepole pine forests are not known for their diversity of birds, sedge- and willow-lined ponds such as this one attract a wide variety of songbirds, including swallows, warblers, flycatchers and sparrows. They come for the sunlight, the water and, of course, the bugs.

Above: STEVE CANNINGS

Several coastal species meet their Interior counterparts at Allison Pass. One example is the red-breasted sapsucker, a permanent resident of the wet coastal coniferous forests, and the red-naped sapsucker, a summer resident of deciduous woodlands in the Interior. For a few kilometres, these species meet and occasionally interbreed. Another local boundary is that between the Douglas' squirrel, a small, orange-bellied coastal species adapted to eating hemlock and cedar cones, and its big, white-bellied cousin the red squirrel, adapted for larger cones such as those of lodgepole pine and Douglas-fir.

The highway is now following the Similkameen River and will stay close to it for the next 200 kilometres or so. At Manning Park Lodge, the highway swings to the east—you are now only 6 kilometres from the U.S. border. As the highway curls in behind the

Cascades, the climate becomes even drier and spruce are found only along the river and on shady north-facing slopes.

East of Hampton Campsite, a few ponderosa pines can be seen on these slopes as well (some have also been killed by beetles), their long needles, large size and reddish trunks making them easy to identify. Ponderosas are trees of dry forests, so they are a clear indication of the lower annual rainfall on the east side of the mountains. Evidence of drier conditions now comes from all sides—copses of aspens appear among the pines, and clumps of penstemon, with bright purple flowers in summer, cover the rocks instead of moss.

The Similkameen River winds back and forth across the valley, affording intermittent views that might yield a dipper, a harlequin duck or even a mink. About 6 kilometres east of Manning Park (the eastern boundary is marked by a large wood sculpture of a black bear), the river plunges through a narrow gorge. This is Similkameen Falls, cut by the river through a barrier of tuff—rock composed of volcanic ash and other fragments. Three kilometres farther on, the Similkameen River enters a much larger and broader canyon, and the highway climbs to the west to avoid it.

The high point of this canyon detour is Sunday Summit. At 1282 metres, Sunday Summit is about the same elevation as Allison Pass, but the forests here are completely different. Widespread fires in the early 1900s produced vast monocultures of lodgepole pine, with scattered Douglas-fir and ponderosa pines on south-facing slopes; spruce and subalpine fir are essentially absent. These pine stands are perfect breeding grounds for mountain pine beetles, and there are almost always patches of red trees in this area, despite the best efforts by foresters to control this tiny insect. Three-metre-high stubs in the clear-cuts north of Sunday Summit are left to provide nest sites for woodpeckers and the other birds and mammals that use woodpecker holes.

The highway stays relatively high for the next 15 kilometres, travelling through more lodgepole pine and Douglas-fir forests. Across the valley to the east, you can see the large open-pit copper mine on Copper Mountain. The highway begins to pass tailing piles from this mine, then descends steeply to Whipsaw Creek, passing the mine ore concentrator on the way. The view from the hill hints at a major ecosystem change, as large areas of natural grassland spread north from Princeton.

As you cross Whipsaw Creek on a sharply curved bridge, you enter a very different landscape. The bedrock changes from 200-million-year-old lava flows to sandstones only 50 million years old. Coal seams are common in these sandstones, and many fossils have been found, including those of horsetails, ferns, dawn redwood, pines, alders, birch and sycamores.

The big change visible to most travellers is the forest, where dense stands of Douglas-fir and lodgepole pine are replaced by a parklike grove of large ponderosa pines. Dramatic changes such as this are common when you cross bridges in British Columbia, since you go between cool north-facing slopes and dry south-facing slopes, but the Whipsaw Creek boundary is impressive.

The change continues as you travel north along a flat terrace toward Princeton. Sagebrush appears on the low hillsides, and mountain bluebirds, the colour of clear summer skies, perch on fenceposts next to the nest boxes put there for them. As you near Princeton, you can look down to the northwest to the winding Tulameen River and to the southeast to the Similkameen. Landslides are gradually eating back into the gravel terrace, narrowing it and threatening the road.

The Tulameen River gets its name from *tulmin,* the indigenous Thompson word for the red ochre used as a bright paint for pictographs and face painting. The red cliffs a few kilometres up the Tulameen were an important source for this iron oxide pigment, and one of the early names for Princeton was Vermilion Forks.

As you reach the valley bottom and downtown Princeton, glance quickly to the north—behind Billy's Restaurant is a beautiful outcrop of steeply dipping sandstone layers overlain by glacial outwash gravels. After crossing the Similkameen River, you soon see large, sandy banks above you to the south. These are tailings from the old Copper Mountain mine's Allenby concentrator, which last operated in 1957. Concern has been raised about the high metal content of these tailings, which are easily picked up as dust in the wind; in an attempt to stabilize the surface, sewage effluent has been used to make the soil more amenable to grasses.

▶ **Princeton to Osoyoos:** The Lower Similkameen Valley
The highway now closely follows the Similkameen River, hugging its southwest shore through a steep-walled valley. About 5 kilometres east of downtown Princeton (opposite the junction with Taylor Way), look north to the big rock bluff across the river—you can often see mountain goats on the cliffs. At dusk watch for mule deer in the large hayfields along the highway. Groves of black cottonwood line the river—this is a wonderful route for autumn colour in mid-October, when the cottonwoods are bright gold. The forests above the highway are generally dense Douglas-fir, but the ponderosa pines and Douglas-firs on the opposite hillsides grow well apart, clinging to rocky soils baked by afternoon sunshine. The rocky slopes appear blackish because of the crustose lichens on the rocks; patches of new slide activity appear whitish.

About 30 kilometres from Princeton, the highway crosses the Similkameen River again, leaving the Douglas-fir forests behind and entering the dry ponderosa pine forest. The grasses under these pines are mostly bluebunch wheatgrass, the classic bunchgrass of the B.C. Interior. Another 6 kilometres and you are at Hedley, viewing a magnificent rockscape towering above the old mining town. The mountain on the east side of town is Nickel Plate Mountain, site of a gold mine that produced 3 million ounces of gold between 1896 and 1958. The gold was concentrated where molten acidic rock was neutralized by limestone—a geological antacid—precipitating the valuable metal out of solution. Stemwinder Mountain, to the west of Hedley (20-mile) Creek, consists of sedimentary and volcanic rocks that are thrown into an amazing series of folds.

As you leave Hedley, the highway passes newly worked tailings from the gold mine; these soils contain high levels of arsenic and, unless treated, will support little vegetation. About 3 kilometres on, the rocks on the east side of the valley are beautiful, massive granodiorite, part of the Okanagan Batholith, which is about 180 million years old.

About 15 kilometres from Hedley, the Ashnola River carves a deep scar into the mountains south of the highway, entering the Similkameen across a cottonwood-covered delta. Watch the north road bank near the Ashnola delta for a broad white band running through the cut. This is a striking deposit of volcanic ash from the cataclysmic eruption of Mt. Mazama in Oregon about seven thousand years ago, when the summit cone of the volcano collapsed, creating Crater Lake.

A pull-off on the south side of the highway 1.5 kilometres east of here provides a good opportunity to get out and scan the slopes for mountain goats and bighorn sheep. Another attraction is a tiny butterfly, the Mormon metalmark. This beautiful orange-and-black butterfly is found in Canada only in a few spots in the Similkameen

Mountain Goats

Mountain goats, though distantly related to farm goats, are more properly called goat-antelopes; their closest well-known relative is the chamois of the Alps. Both males and females have sharp black horns and whitish fur. They are remarkable climbers, aided by soft, textured pads under their hooves that provide grip on the rocky terrain they favour. Mountain goats eat a wide variety of plant material, from grasses and flowers to shrubs and conifer twigs.

Photo: RICHARD CANNINGS

Adult Mormon metalmarks feed on the nectar of rabbit-brush and snow buckwheat; the caterpillars eat nothing but snow buckwheat leaves. CRISPIN GUPPY

Valley; the caterpillars feed exclusively on wild snow buckwheat plants in dry gravelly habitats.

You encounter the first of the Okanagan-Similkameen orchards, along with a myriad of fruit stands, on the western edge of Keremeos. The fruit trees of Keremeos tend to bend eastward under the influence of strong prevailing westerly winds blowing through the narrow valley each time a Pacific storm centre moves inland.

As the valley widens at Keremeos, note that the flat valley floor consists of three distinct landforms: the active flood-plain of the Similkameen River, an extensive low river terrace on which the town of Keremeos is situated and a higher terrace consisting of glacial outwash gravels. The highway climbs steeply onto the higher terrace immediately after passing through the downtown area.

At the eastern edge of Keremeos, Highway 3a branches off north to Penticton; Highway 3 continues to follow the Similkameen toward Osoyoos. Like the adjacent south Okanagan, the lower Similkameen Valley has a hot, dry climate with relatively mild winters. The valleys also share habitats that are unique in the province and in the nation and that are especially diverse in bird life. There is a plethora of birds

Bobolinks—female and male

to watch out for—many species that are commoner here than any-where else in Canada.

The valley broadens somewhat to a lush bottomland of hay fields, willow thickets and scattered large ponderosa pines. The hay fields provide nesting habitat for long-billed curlews—large sandpipers with long, down-curved bills. Bobolinks also nest in these fields. The males are small black birds that are mostly white and cream above, whereas the females are cryptically coloured in drab browns. Most animals are coloured pale below and dark above, but male bobo-links show the opposite pattern, designed to make them stand out against the sky as they sing. Striking colour patterns such as this are common in grassland birds that use song flights for display in an environment that lacks trees and other high perches.

As the Similkameen nears the U.S. border, the highway swings to the east to stay in Canada. At the top of the hill, the junction of the Nighthawk road offers a shortcut to the Chopaka border crossing and a magnificent swath of sagebrush grassland. Open your window to let in the glorious aroma of sage—especially if it has been raining recently. This is the best place in Canada to look for sage thrash-ers, and it was the last place in British Columbia where white-tailed jackrabbits were seen—in 1981. Much of these grasslands are now protected as a new provincial park, preserving one of Canada's rarest ecosystems.

A long climb through ranch land brings you to Richter Pass, a low pass between the Similkameen and Okanagan Valleys. Most highway passes in British Columbia come reasonably close to the upper treeline; Richter Pass is so low that you never reach the lower treeline, which is between the dry grasslands and the ponderosa pine and Douglas-fir forests. A road leaving the north side of the highway at the pass leads to the peak of Mt. Kobau (1870 metres), a high ridge that once was to be the site of a large reflecting telescope until changing government priorities relocated the project to Chile. Mt. Kobau is also one of the few places in Canada where dry grasslands ascend a mountain slope all the way to the upper treeline without a solid forest in between.

Once over the pass, the highway goes by a couple of small ponds. The second one on the south side of the road is Spotted Lake, an outstanding example of a saline lake, with spectacular white salt rings. These epsom salts are mostly magnesium and sodium sulfates, with small amounts of sodium carbonate and calcium sulfate. The rings

Sagebrush Birds

Two species of birds are rarely found farther than hopping distance from big sagebrush: the brewer's sparrow and the sage thrasher. The sparrow is also locally common in southern Alberta and Saskatchewan, but the thrasher is regularly found only in the sagebrush grasslands west of Osoyoos. Both species are drab—the colour of sage—but highly talented songsters. Brewer's sparrows have long, loud canary-like songs, whereas the subtle warbling of the sage thrasher seems to fit perfectly with the dawn sky and the smell of sage.

Like all alkaline lakes, Spotted Lake has no outlet. In the spring it fills with snow melt, then evaporates under the hot summer sun. STEVE CANNINGS

are thought to be formed through crystallization processes shaped by the alternate flooding and drying of the lake.

Shortly beyond Spotted Lake, the highway descends into the Okanagan Valley on a long traverse. Below you at the viewpoint is the Osoyoos Desert Centre, an interpretive site featuring the unique desertlike grasslands of the south Okanagan and lower Similkameen Valleys. There is a wonderful view of Osoyoos Lake and the vast orchards and vineyards that irrigation has created. To the southeast are the high grasslands of northern Okanogan County, Washington (note that *Okanagan* is spelled differently south of the border); the highway winds up Anarchist Mountain just north of these grasslands, again forced over a pass to avoid the United States.

The sandy, dry benchlands of the south Okanagan Valley are referred to as "Canada's Pocket Desert." Although the area is desertlike—populated with cacti, scorpions and rattlesnakes—it is technically not a desert. Because it supports perennial grasses, ecologists refer to this region as a mid-latitude steppe. Narrow valleys closer to the Coast Mountains, such as the Similkameen and lower Nicola, which have only 200 millimetres of precipitation a year, are drier than the Okanagan but are much colder in winter. Desert or not, the south end of the Okanagan and Similkameen Valleys is a special place—about a third of British Columbia's rare or endangered plants and animals make their home there.

At the bottom of the hill, Highway 3 meets Highway 97, only 4 kilometres north of the U.S. border. For more information on the Okanagan Valley in general, turn to the chapter on Highway 97. After a few blocks of urbanized Osoyoos (pronounced uh-soo'-yus), you cross the narrows of Osoyoos Lake. The lake is advertised by the local Chamber of Commerce as the "warmest lake in Canada"; it is certainly a shallow, productive lake, but it is unfortunately at the bottom end of the Okanagan drainage and therefore receives all the nutrients and chemicals introduced throughout the valley to the north. Although still relatively healthy, it is the most sensitive of the large lakes in the Okanagan Valley to added pollutants. It is an extremely important lake to local fish stocks, being the nursery lake for the Okanagan sockeye salmon, which spawn in the Okanagan River north of Oliver.

➤ **Osoyoos to Christina Lake:** Boundary Country

You almost immediately begin to climb out of the valley, passing a few orchards and vineyards before the highway takes the first of many 180-degree turns to ascend the slopes of Anarchist Mountain. The dark green, gangly shrubs are antelope-brush, which grows on sandy soils; the pale grey sagebrush is common on the steeper slopes. The rocky roadside is a great place to see yellow-bellied marmots and mountain cottontails, both of which are favourite meals for the golden eagle. Smaller animals are of interest here, too—this is the only site in Canada where the dusky hairstreak is found. This small, dark butterfly feeds on lupines in the dry grasslands of Anarchist Mountain.

The views to the west are stunning from this ascent of the mountain, and a stop at the viewpoint halfway up is highly recommended, if only to keep you from driving off the road while trying to take in the scenery. Haynes Point stretches like a long finger across Osoyoos

Lake, just south of the isthmus you crossed the lake on. Osoyoos gets its name from the Okanagan word *soo-yoos,* which refers to this narrow point; legend has it that the initial "O" was added in the 1850s by a magistrate of Irish descent. Mt. Chopaka (2402 metres) and Snowy Mountain (2592 metres) dominate the western horizon, with Mt. Kobau in the middle distance to the northwest. Imagine this landscape as it would have been about fifteen thousand years ago, at the climax of the last great glaciation, when the ice sheet was 2 kilometres thick. Only one summit—Snowy Mountain—would have been visible in the south Okanagan.

You can see how the character of the Okanagan Valley changes dramatically south of the border, where the hills become smaller and dark forests are replaced by pale grasslands. At this point the political border coincidentally falls on a biological boundary as well—the southern edge of the Okanagan Highlands—and with it the southern boundary for several species of plants and animals adapted to cold northern forests.

Just above the viewpoint, the highway turns up Haynes Creek and leaves the scenery behind. The grass and sagebrush are replaced by water birch, black cottonwood and Douglas maple. Once out of the creek valley, the forest becomes pure ponderosa pine. Most of this forest has been heavily logged; a few big snags give an indication of how large the original trees were. As you gain altitude, more and more western larches are mixed in with the pines, a sign that the climate is becoming moister with higher elevation. Larches are a deciduous conifer; their soft green needles turn a brilliant gold in October, then fall to carpet the forest floor before the snow flies.

About 10 kilometres past the lookout, the forest is largely replaced by pastures and high grasslands. The U.S. border lies a few hundred metres south, along the edge of the cultivated fields. These are very different grasslands from those in the valley bottom. There is little or no sagebrush here, and the bunchgrasses are primarily fescues instead of the wheatgrass, needle-and-thread and three-awn found below. The birds are different as well; soaring Swainson's hawks and singing horned larks give the hills a prairie

The effects of irrigation of the Okanagan Valley are very clear in this view of Osoyoos Lake. The dry benches of bunchgrass and antelope-brush, one of the rarest ecosystems in Canada, have been almost entirely converted to orchards and vineyards. RICHARD CANNINGS

flavour. Similar grasslands occur at lower elevations in the north Okanagan and in the Nicola Valley.

Anarchist Summit is reached at 1233 metres elevation, and the road quickly begins to descend past aspen copses to the village of Bridesville. You have left the narrow Okanagan watershed and entered the Kettle River drainage, another of the main tributaries of the Columbia River. The grasslands beyond Bridesville have been severely degraded by diffuse knapweed, a weedy species that is native to southeastern Europe. The open grasslands on the north (south-facing) side of the valley contrast sharply with the dense larch and Douglas-fir forests on the north-facing slope. Several kame terraces—flat-topped benches of outwash sand and gravel laid down against stagnant ice at the end of the last glaciation—are visible to the south along the Baker Creek valley.

The highway crosses the 91-metre-deep Rock Creek canyon. Johnstone Creek, 5 kilometres farther down the road, is less spectacular, but a stand of sizable ponderosa pines and western larch

Diffuse knapweed is a devastating weed in the dry grasslands.

RICHARD CANNINGS

is protected in a small provincial park there. Soon you are descending steeply to the Kettle River at the village of Rock Creek.

The Kettle Valley provides a welcome stretch of level ground, a rare commodity on this highway. The rocks of the sloping parallel ridges north of the river were laid down as lava flows about 50 million years ago at the time the Okanagan Valley was being formed. After these rocks were formed, this section of the Kettle Valley, from Rock Creek to Midway was faulted downward almost 2000 metres. About 9 kilometres east of Rock Creek, you cross to the north side of the Kettle Valley, where broad, grassy slopes descend to the highway. Like many of the dry grasslands in the Kettle Valley, these are infested with diffuse knapweed.

The Kettle River continues south from Midway into northern Washington, so the highway turns northeast up Boundary Creek. The narrow creek valley provides shade and moisture for a very different plant community—larch, Douglas-fir, spruce and cottonwoods line the creek, in direct contrast to the dry grasslands on the other side of the road.

You will soon notice that most of the forested slopes in the Boundary Creek valley are covered by trembling aspens, a species that appears after a fire or other disturbance. These are the result of the smelter at Greenwood, which belched sulfur dioxide for years, killing all the trees within 5 kilometres. The smelter was fed copper, gold and silver ore by the Motherlode Mine starting in 1901, and although it closed in 1918, the forest has yet to fully recover.

Just north of Greenwood, the highway leaves the Boundary Creek valley to climb to Eholt Summit. Although the summit is only 1028 metres in elevation, the forest changes quite dramatically from the grasslands of Midway as you swing around the north side of the mountain; at Wilgress Lake Rest Area, the forest is western larch, white birch and Engelmann spruce, and within 2 kilometres western redcedar appears.

About 14 kilometres from the summit, the highway emerges from the larch forests into south-facing, grassy slopes once again. Around the corner is Grand Forks, set at the confluence of the Granby and Kettle Rivers. The town is built on a series of four successively lower terraces—watch for the "steps" as the highway descends from one to the next. The highest terrace may have been formed by glacial out-wash at the end of the last glaciation, but the lower three are river terraces, formed during postglacial times as the river has gradually lowered its bed.

You cross the Granby River at the east edge of town, then travel along the north side of the Kettle Valley. The Granby flows down a major geological fault that marks the western boundary of a large block of rocks identical to those on the east side of the Okanagan Valley. From here to the Kettle River fault at Cascade, the northern side of the valley is studded with cliffs of metamorphic rocks, such as schist, marble and gneiss.

The combination of bunch-grass slopes and rocky bluffs north of the highway is ideal habitat for bighorn sheep, so watch for small herds of these animals, especially during winter. The dry grasslands between here and Christina Lake are the last you will see until you

Spotted knapweed, a close cousin of diffuse knapweed, prefers somewhat moister climates and is a common road-side plant along the highway from here to Alberta. RICHARD CANNINGS

reach Cranbrook, at the edge of the Rocky Mountain Trench. This is the westernmost point in the ranges of many small animals, including the Great Basin spadefoot toad and the tiger salamander. The bluffs are dotted with smooth sumac, which turns brilliant scarlet in September, and mock-orange with its fragrant, white blossoms in June. The small grey shrubs are rabbit-brush, which bloom yellow in late summer.

At Cascade the Kettle River flows south into Washington and eventually to the Columbia River; the highway turns north to Christina Lake. Cascade is named after the large waterfall where the Kettle River pours over the Kettle River Fault. This waterfall is a very effective barrier to fish travelling upstream, so the fish populations in almost the entire Canadian section of the Kettle River are completely isolated. Cascade was known by the Okanagan-Colville indigenous peoples as *k'lhsaxem,* meaning "end of fish going up." This isolation has resulted in some distinctive populations of fish, including the speckled dace, which may have evolved into a new species. Even those populations below the falls were historically isolated from fish in the rest of the Columbia system by Kettle Falls, where the Kettle River enters the Columbia. Cascade was the site

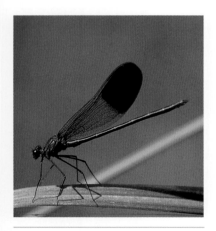

River jewelwing. DENNIS PAULSON

of an early hydroelectric project— when it was built in 1899, it had the most powerful alternating current turbines in the world.

The Christina Lake valley follows the Kettle River Fault, the eastern edge of the metamorphic rocks mentioned above. As the highway turns north, it cuts through highly deformed rock at the edge of the fault; a pale band of granitic rock in the rock cut is a dyke—formed where molten rock filled a crack in the main rock mass after the fault occurred.

Christina Lake is about 14 kilometres long and is advertised by the local tourism boosters as "the warmest tree-lined lake in Canada" (antelope-brush-lined Osoyoos Lake claims the title of "warmest lake"). It is certainly a lake at an ecological transition point in British Columbia, its southern end lined with dry-loving ponderosa pines and its northern end with a rain forest of western hemlock and western redcedar. You are now entering the "Interior wet belt," the moist forests of the West Kootenays.

The lake drains into the Kettle River via Christina Creek, which the highway crosses just south of the lake. Christina Creek is a beautiful stream in a surprisingly natural state despite its low elevation. It is a warm creek (since it drains such a warm lake) and has a wonderful diversity of life, especially of aquatic insects.

The jewel in the crown of Christina Creek is the river jewelwing, a stunning emerald-green damselfly with smoky-black wingtips. This is one of only a handful of creeks in British Columbia where this beautiful insect is found.

▶ **Christina Lake to Creston:** The West Kootenays
Above the creek to the east, the Kettle Valley Railroad grade, now a part of the Trans-Canada Trail system, clings to the side of granitic bluffs. Just north of the village of Christina Lake, you get a good view to the north end of the lake, now protected as part of Gladstone Provincial Park. A few kilometres beyond, the highway climbs away from the lake and swings northeast up a slope scattered with oceanspray shrubs, which have cream-coloured flowers in summer. The road levels out on a flat terrace cloaked in young Douglas-fir, then gets into much moister woodlands at the McRae Creek Rest Area, consisting of western white pine, Engelmann spruce, western redcedar and white birch. This terrace is a "raised" delta, consisting of sand and gravel deposited in Christina Lake by McRae Creek when the lake level was higher than at the end of the last glaciation. Drier ponderosa pine forests are evident once again on south-facing slopes as the highway turns east up the creek, with white birch and trembling aspen dominating burned-over areas on the north-facing slopes.

The highway begins to ascend steeply up the McRae Creek valley, crossing the creek on the 84-metre-high Paulson Bridge. Above the bridge, the highway follows Walker Creek to the summit. Mature western larch grow on the west side of the road; western hemlock, in the creek bottom; and Douglas-fir, on the drier rocky slopes to the east. About 4 kilometres from the bridge, you enter the true subalpine forest of Engelmann spruce, subalpine fir and lodgepole pine. Record snow depths in 1998 caused widespread damage to the forest at the headwaters of Walker Creek; a large clear-cut on the north side of the road was the result of salvage logging in 1999.

The road soon levels out to provide a view of the plateau-like character of the south end of the Monashee Mountains. You cross Bonanza Pass at 1535 metres elevation but stay high on the rolling plateau for another 20 kilometres. For a short distance, you are in the Big Sheep Creek watershed, then you cross over a pass into the Blueberry watershed, which the highway follows all the way to Castlegar. Shortly after Blueberry Pass and just before the Highway 3b junction to Rossland, you will see Nancy Greene Lake on the south side of the road.

The pyramidal peak visible about 12 kilometres to the south of Nancy Greene Lake is Old Glory Mountain (2376 metres). The forestry lookout personnel on the summit of Old Glory kept weather records for over twenty years, and these provide some of the best climate data for an alpine site in British Columbia. Two of the more interesting pieces of information are that the mountain has an average of 25 days per year of blowing snow and 226 days per year with fog. The latter point is often touted as a world record. Contrary to what you might expect, it is not especially cold on top of the mountain in winter. In fact, the lowest temperature ever recorded on Old Glory is a bit higher than the lowest temperature recorded at Grand Forks. The big difference in climate above treeline in southern British Columbia is the frost-free period—only three weeks on Old Glory, compared with about twenty weeks or more in the valleys.

About 5 kilometres beyond Nancy Greene Lake, Blueberry Creek and the highway begin a steep descent to the Columbia River. At first the forest is lodgepole pine, and the soft, maplelike leaves of thimbleberry are prominent in the roadside shrubbery. Farther down the mountain, the first hints of the tremendous diversity of tree species in the Kootenays become apparent. On the south-facing slope above the highway, a patch of western hemlock and western redcedar, typical of very wet forests, is followed by a mix of ponderosa pine and western white pine. The latter two species are typical of dry and wet sites, respectively, but are often found together in Kootenay forests.

At Castlegar you cross the mighty Columbia River just below its meeting point with the Kootenay River. The Columbia comes in from the northwest part of the valley, draining the Arrow Lakes, now a reservoir behind Keenleyside Dam. The Kootenay flows out of the northeast, having gone over five dams between Castlegar and Nelson alone. The water flow is thus highly regulated here and averages

The Trail Smelter Case

The smelting industry at Trail began in 1896 but expanded dramatically between 1925 and 1927, when two large smokestacks were built and production doubled to make the smelter the largest lead-zinc smelter in the world. A problem was the high level of sulfur emissions—over 8000 tonnes per month. Release of sulfur into the air creates sulfur dioxide, and high concentrations of that chemical can severely damage plants over a wide area. The Columbia Valley quickly lost almost all of its forests between Castlegar and the U.S. border, and in 1928 the U.S. government complained to Canada that emissions from the Trail smelter had damaged forests and agricultural crops in Washington State. As a result of the legal proceedings following these allegations, Canada paid over $400,000 in damages to the United States, and Cominco, the owners of the smelter, built a large fertilizer plant that removed the sulfur from the emissions by the late 1930s.

The decisions made by the International Joint Commission and its special tribunal remain one of the most important legal precedents cited in international laws regarding cross-border pollution. Sixty years later, the Trail Smelter case formed the basis of one of the principles cited in the Rio declaration of 1992.

about 2000 cubic metres per second, about two-thirds the average flow in the Fraser River at Hope. Although the Columbia is a major river, a good part of its watershed lies south of the border and its Canadian watershed is less than half that of the Fraser (88,000 square kilometres versus 210,000 square kilometres).

The highway travels along a flat river terrace (because it is the only large flat piece of land in the valley, the terrace is also the site of the Castlegar airport), then climbs out of the valley to the east. The striking thing about the Columbia Valley south of Castlegar is the almost total lack of large trees, a result of the millions of tons of sulfur dioxide spewed into the valley by the Trail lead-zinc smelter from 1900 to 1940. The hillsides are cloaked in blue elderberry, young lodgepole pine, white birch, mountain alder, black cottonwood and Douglas-fir, slowly healing the vast scar created by rampant air pollution.

About 7 kilometres from Castlegar, the highway turns east away from the valley, and the healthier, though still young, forests of western larch and Douglas-fir quickly appear. Some huge larch stick out of the smaller trees, giving an idea of what the forest once looked like. At Bombi Summit (1214 metres) you are in subalpine forests of Engelmann spruce and subalpine fir. On the other side of the summit, the diverse Interior Cedar–Hemlock forest appears—western hemlock, Douglas-fir, western redcedar, western white pine and trembling aspen. Cream-coloured witch's hair lichen blows in the wind, absorbing moisture from the abundant mist.

The highway descends to the Beaver Creek valley, then turns east and quickly crosses over a minor divide marked by cattail and lily pad marshes on both sides of the road. Beaver Creek flows south from here into the Columbia west of Trail; Erie Creek meets the Salmo River on its way south to the Pend Oreille, which empties into the Columbia a few metres north of the U.S. border. The Erie Lake Rest Area is in a grove of ponderosa pines, western larch, Douglas-fir and western redcedar. Beyond the lake the highway crosses broad valley bottom flats into the outskirts of Salmo, where Highway 6 branches off north to Nelson and Erie Creek meets the Salmo River.

Caribou

Caribou are unique among Canadian deer in that both males and females have antlers. They also have unusually round, broad hooves, which allow them to walk on the surface of deep, crusty snow; other members of the deer family are forced into valley bottoms, where the snow is not so deep. In summer, caribou forage in high mountain meadows, feeding on grasses, sedges and ground lichens. They move into mountain forests in winter, standing on the deep snow to reach arboreal lichens. These lichens are only abundant in older forests, so caribou have been affected by logging much more than most wildlife species.

DOUGLAS LEIGHTON

The Salmo Valley is relatively broad, the clear green river flowing through stands of large black cottonwoods. Over a hundred years ago the scene was not quite so placid, as placer gold brought in prospectors from all over in the early 1860s. A few mines developed, especially during the boom years of 1896–97, and a tailings pond remains along the road about 10 kilometres south of Salmo. A few kilometres south of the tailings, the highway swings east out of the Salmo Valley and follows South Salmo Creek, beginning its long, steep ascent of Kootenay Pass into the heart of the Selkirk Mountains. After about 12 kilometres, you turn northeast into the Stagleap valley. Patches of young lodgepole pine and trembling aspen grow on old forest fire sites, and alpine meadows beckon in the distance.

If you are lucky, you might see mountain caribou along the upper sections of this highway. This small threatened herd is the only one along a highway in southern British Columbia. The

Beargrass. RICHARD CANNINGS

animals are attracted to the salt put on the highway in winter and spring. They can also be seen travelling through the area in summer, when there are bighorn sheep along the highway as well.

As you approach Kootenay Pass, you enter the subalpine forests of Engelmann spruce and subalpine fir, with some western hemlock mixed in. The hemlock indicates high precipitation, but the road is known not for high rainfall but for deep snow. Winter closures are common as Pacific storms produce blizzard conditions and extreme avalanche danger. Avalanche slopes are obvious as light green swaths cut vertically through the dark forests.

Ripple Mountain, the peak south of the highway just west of the summit, shows a deep cirque on its north face, carved out by an alpine glacier that has since melted away. At 1774 metres, Kootenay Pass is the highest pass on a major highway in British Columbia. A beautiful alpine lake lies at its summit, and creamy spikes of beargrass flowers bloom amid the subalpine fir and Engelmann spruce in midsummer; there are few other places in the province where you can easily find this beautiful plant.

East of the summit, avalanche slopes dominate the mountainsides, overgrown with alder that can withstand the impact of powerful snow slides. Small spruce and fir grow up amid the alder but will be snapped off when their trunks become too brittle to bend under the force of an avalanche.

For the next 30 kilometres, the highway descends steeply down the Summit Creek valley through typical moist West Kootenay forests. A clear-cut south of the creek, about 15 kilometres from the pass, has scattered larch trees, left as a seed source for reforestation. A few kilometres on, the Blazed Creek Rest Area is in western redcedar/western hemlock forest, but as you approach the valley bottom, ponderosa pines appear in open, dry forests on the north side of the highway.

As the highway levels out just above the Kootenay River flood-plain, Summit Creek flows through an impressive stand of black cottonwoods before emptying into the meandering channels of the bigger river. The Kootenay is flowing north here, coming out of

REST STOP

Creston Valley Wildlife Management Area
Interpretation Centre

TURN SOUTH ON the West Creston road for a short drive to the Creston Valley Wildlife Management Area Interpretation Centre. The centre has informative displays on the natural history of the valley and guided canoe trips through the wetlands. You can also walk the board-walk through the marsh and along the dykes to see turtles, terns, grebes and herons and other water-loving species.

Above: Painted turtles. DOUGLAS LEIGHTON

Idaho and emptying into Kootenay Lake 12 kilometres north of Creston. Between Creston and the lake, the "floodplain," which includes extensive marshes and back channels, is actually a huge delta of silt and sand that the Kootenay River has built into Kootenay Lake. The highway crosses the floodplain, leaving the Selkirk Mountains behind and facing the Purcell Mountains.

The Kootenay River floodplain was reclaimed by dyking in 1935, when over 9000 hectares of marshland were turned into fields of grain, alfalfa and clover. Although floods in 1938 turned the farmland into marshes once again, the dykes were immediately rebuilt. However, almost 7000 hectares of marshland remain, managed by the Creston Valley Wildlife Management Area, making this valley one of the most important migration and breeding sites for water birds in the B.C. Interior.

Huge numbers of tundra swans move through the Creston Valley on migration. Although numbers are down from historic levels (mostly because the birds are using a different migration route), hundreds of swans still stop over in early spring and late fall. Thousands of ducks and coots also pass through each year.

The Creston Valley is also of national significance for its breeding birds. It has the only Forster's tern colony and one of only three western grebe colonies (p. 36) in British Columbia, a large colony of black terns and significant numbers of nesting American bitterns, eared grebes and red-necked grebes. Perhaps one of the most conspicuous nesting species here is the osprey. Although populations plummeted over most of North America in the second half of the 1900s because of pesticide poisoning, Creston always had a healthy osprey population. Today the large stick nests can be seen on trees and poles throughout the valley.

At Creston the highway meets up with Highway 21, which travels south to Idaho, and Highway 3a, which goes north along the east shore of Kootenay Lake, and thence by ferry to Balfour and Nelson. The apple orchards of Erickson, on the east side of Creston, testify to the warm summers and relatively mild winters experienced in this valley.

Disappearing Frogs

Ecologists have noticed a rapid drop in the numbers of many frogs around the world over the past few decades. One species that has disappeared over much of its range is the northern leopard frog. Once common throughout the Kootenays and south Okanagan, it is now known from only one site in British Columbia—the Creston marshes. Biologists are monitoring this local population to try to understand why the frogs have disappeared from other sites and perhaps how we can help the population to increase once again.

Leopard frog. MARC-ANDRÉ BEAUCHER

▶ **Creston to Cranbrook:** The Purcells

After leaving Creston, you follow the Goat River northeast into the Purcell Mountains. South of the Goat River, the Ramparts form a spectacular 1000-metre-high wall of Precambrian rocks about 1.5 billion years old. In typical Kootenay fashion, the forests are diverse, with moisture-loving western redcedar, western larch, grand fir, western white pine and black cottonwood mixed with dry-country species such as lodgepole and ponderosa pines. In dry summers the redcedars become stressed and cut off water supply to inner branchlets. This condition is called flagging, since the sacrificed patches of foliage turn bright red.

The Goat River valley turns due north about 10 kilometres northeast of Creston, and the highway follows Kitchener (Meadow) Creek east to a low pass at Goatfell. Much of the Kitchener valley is forested with a mix of Douglas-fir and young lodgepole pine, the latter dominating in gravelly areas. Open hillsides to the north indicate an old forest fire and warm, dry summers that prevent rapid regrowth of trees. A large wet meadow fills the headwaters of Kitchener Creek, and willows trace the creek to the south.

As you descend to the Moyie River, the forest becomes moister once again, with white spruce and western white pine giving way to redcedar and cottonwood. An alder swamp just before the Moyie River bridge is filled in with hardhack, a moisture-loving spirea with columnar pink flower heads.

In a turnaround typical of highway ecology in southern British Columbia, the forests immediately change as the road swings north-east behind the Moyie Range of the Purcells. Big ponderosa pines are prominent on the south-facing slopes, indicative of the rain shadow effect the mountains have created. The forests on the north-facing slopes are dominated by western larch and lodgepole pine; forest-harvesting patterns in this area often leave selectively cut forests in which some larch are left as seed trees. After passing through the tiny community of Yahk, the highway continues to follow the Moyie northeast to Moyie Lake.

The rocks along the Moyie River were deposited in deep water in a basin that sprawled across the interior of North America's mother continent, Rodinia. As you drive northeastward toward Moyie Lake, you are travelling forward in geological time, past newer and newer rocks. As the newer sediments were laid down, they filled the basin. The newest rocks, those along the northern part of Moyie Lake, come from very shallow water; some even show ripple marks from wave action.

Moyie Lake has been cut in two by the alluvial fans of Lamb Creek, which flows into the west side of the lake, and Barkshanty Creek, which flows in from the east. Flowing into the north end of the lake is Peavine Creek, which follows the Moyie Fault. Rocks south of that fault have dropped 4000 metres in relation to those on the north side, so you immediately encounter older rocks after you cross Peavine Creek—rocks similar in age and structure to those you passed 40 kilometres to the southwest in Yahk. The Moyie Fault crosses Moyie Lake and continues to the southwest up the valley of Lamb Creek.

As you approach Cranbrook, the forests of western larch, lodgepole pine and Douglas-fir give way to ponderosa pine. These are the dry forests of the East Kootenay, the rain shadow of the Purcell Mountains. Wetlands in these dry forests are especially attractive to wildlife, and one of these is Elizabeth Lake on the western outskirts of Cranbrook. Black terns and yellow-headed blackbirds are some of the characteristic summer residents here.

▶ **Cranbrook to Crowsnest Pass:** The Southern Rockies
From Cranbrook the highway goes northeast to meet the greatest of all geological structures in British Columbia—the Rocky Mountain Trench (p. 44). Just past the Kimberley Junction, you turn southeast and descend to the western edge of the trench. A distinctive shrub appears on the coarser soils here—antelope-brush. Although it is the same species that occurs in the south Okanagan, antelope-brush in the East Kootenays has a much smaller stature. It is still a favoured browse for deer and elk.

These gently rolling, grass-covered hills are Rampart Prairie—an area of rather saline soils and an endangered plant community, salt grass. Another indicator of the alkaline soils is the abundance of gumweed along the roadside. This small, sunflower-like plant has sticky stems and a distinct rosemary-like aroma when handled. Small ponds dot the kettled terrain. About 20 kilometres from Cranbrook, the highway nears the Kootenay River, with a good vista of the Steeples and the Bull River valley to the east.

At Wardner the highway crosses the Kootenay River once again. Here the Kootenay is flowing south out of its headwaters in Kootenay National Park toward Montana. Wardner marks the northern shores of Lake Koocanusa (Kootenay + Canada + USA), a large reservoir extending 145 kilometres northward from a dam at Libby, Montana. In recent years the reservoir has not been filled to capacity, and the northern end is usually a meadow of waving grass.

Part of the reason for the lower water level is the recent discovery that white sturgeon in the Kootenay River below the Libby Dam had not reproduced successfully since the dam was built in 1975.

This spawning failure was due to the low water flow below the dam in spring, just the opposite of the normal pre-dam flow, in which water flow was greatest in spring and early summer. Since Kootenay River white sturgeon are considered endangered in the United States, the springtime flows from the dam were increased, lowering the reservoir levels. High summer flows are also critical in the Columbia River for the few salmon runs remaining on that river in the United States. Rather than lower the level of Lake Koocanusa further to alleviate those concerns, the Bonneville Power Authority has made an agreement with BC Hydro for summer releases of water from the Keenleyside Dam above Castlegar to increase flow for Columbia salmon.

On the east side of the Rocky Mountain Trench, the highway angles southeast through rolling, hilly country with a mixed forest of trembling aspen, western larch, Douglas-fir and ponderosa pine. Much of the local topography was shaped by the last glacier that flowed southward here. Numerous low, streamlined hills (drumlins), paralleling the ice flow direction, were formed when the ice flowed over previously deposited rock fragments, sand, silt and clay. In the vicinity of Jaffray and Galloway, the road cuts straight through at least one drumlin.

About 50 kilometres south of Wardner, the highway turns east to Elko, climbing onto gravel terraces deposited against the east wall of the Kootenay Valley glacier. For a time at the end of the last glaciation, the Elk River was dammed by the great ice mass in the trench, creating Glacial Lake Elk, which extended upstream from the vicinity of Elko to beyond Sparwood. The outlet from this lake flowed south from Elko to cross the 49th parallel at Roosville before flowing west into the Kootenay. Watch for the silty, largely stone-free deposits of Glacial Lake Elk exposed here and there in road cuts and riverbanks (where they will be capped by stream gravels) along the valley to beyond Sparwood.

At Elko, Highway 93 follows this ancient route of the Elk River south to Montana, and Highway 3 follows the Elk upstream into the Rocky Mountains. The south-facing slopes along the highway are excellent winter range for wildlife, with little snow cover and abundant browse in the form of antelope-brush and saskatoon bushes. This is a good area for wildlife viewing in winter and spring, especially from January through May, when bighorn sheep, elk, white-tailed deer and mule deer can be seen on the slopes. In the 1920s there were about four thousand bighorns in this area, but disease outbreaks and other factors have cut those numbers in half.

As the highway goes through a tunnel and travels along the eastern slopes of the Lizard Range, the vegetation quickly begins to reflect a moister climate, the ponderosa pines disappearing and western redcedar appearing on the riverbanks. The forests along this part of the Elk River are typical of the diverse Interior Cedar–Hemlock Zone—sometimes more than ten species of trees can be found within 100 metres.

The Lizard Range, the site of most of the ski developments in the area, towers in the west as you approach Fernie. These impressive mountains are entirely upside down, consisting of over one hundred million years of sedimentation flipped over by the relentless forces that pushed up the Rocky Mountains. In contrast to the normal geological situation, in which the rocks on mountaintops are younger than those at their bases (since the mountaintop rocks were laid down as sediments on top of the lower rocks), the peaks of the Lizard Range consist of rocks about 360 million years old, whereas the forests on the lower slopes grow on bedrock less than 250 million years old.

The processes that could flip a mountain range upside down are difficult to imagine, but Mt. Hosmer (2506 metres), on the west side of the valley just north of Fernie, provides an example of what the midpoint of such an event might look like. The rock strata forming this mountain have been pushed into an essentially vertical position, and it is easy to imagine that continued pressure would have flipped this mountain over as well.

While upside-down mountains are impressive, the big geological story of the Elk Valley is coal, which has driven the economy of this area for more than a century. A 160-kilometre-long stretch of

Natal Ridge contains part of the huge coal deposits of southeastern British Columbia; some of the coal deposits are more than 600 metres thick, and it is estimated that the total amount of coal in the area exceeds 50 billion tonnes.
RICHARD CANNINGS

mountains between Fernie and the Alberta border contains huge coal deposits that were laid down about 150 to 110 million years ago. The coal was formed in great primeval forests of cycads (primitive trees with palmlike leaves) and conifers growing in a warm, wet climate. Flowering plants had yet to blossom, but the dinosaurs were at the height of their rule. In fact, dinosaur footprints have been found in these coal seams. The highway travels through some of these coal deposits after passing Sparwood and turning southeast up the valley of Michel Creek. Large coal heaps are visible on the top of Natal Ridge, east of the highway.

At the junction of the Coal Mountain road, the highway leaves Michel Creek and follows Summit Creek eastward. The forests on this south-facing side of the valley are relatively dry, dominated by young lodgepole pine and trembling aspen, with juniper in the understorey. You are approaching the Great Divide; the microwave towers on the high ridge ahead are in Alberta. The border is just beyond Summit Lake, and on the east side of the border is the Crowsnest River, whose waters flow into the Oldman River and the South Saskatchewan River and eventually mix with the cold waters of Hudson Bay.

The Coquihalla and Southern Yellowhead Highways

HIGHWAY 5

U NLIKE THE other highways connecting the B.C. coast with Alberta, Highway 5 travels north-south instead of east-west. Taking advantage of the province's northwesterly slant, it begins in Hope, slices across the northern tip of the Cascade Range, arcs over the Thompson Plateau, then follows the North Thompson River in its course between the Columbia and Monashee Mountains before meeting Highway 16 along the Fraser River and finally turning east to cut through the Rockies at Yellowhead Pass.

➤ **Hope to Kamloops:** From Snow Forests to Golden Grasslands
The first section of Highway 5 is the Coquihalla Highway. It begins climbing southeastward out of the valley floor at Hope on the western slopes of the Coquihalla Valley and initially follows the old route of the Kettle Valley Railway, which was abandoned for decades because it was constantly buried in avalanches through the long mountain winter. From Hope, the highway soon crosses over Two-Mile Creek, notable for its trapezoidal concrete chute designed to facilitate the flow of debris torrents under the bridge. This structure

Facing page: A youthful Fraser River near its headwaters in Mt. Robson Provincial Park. SYDNEY CANNINGS

was built after a heavy rainstorm on January 4, 1984, that triggered a major rock fall on the east wall of Hope Mountain about 1000 metres above the highway. About 40,000 cubic metres of rock, some of it boulders 4 metres in diameter, thundered down the Two-Mile Creek channel, severely damaging the bridge. Slides such as this are common in B.C. mountains, particularly during heavy rains, and much work has been done to minimize the danger to highway structures and motorists during these events.

After Two-Mile Creek you turn northeast to follow the Coquihalla. The highway stays firmly ensconced in the valley at first, through typical coastal forests of western hemlock and western redcedar. About 20 kilometres from Hope, it begins to climb out of the valley on its northwest side, up Boston Bar Creek. The climb is steep, and the forests begin to change. Red alder, the classic pioneer tree species on coastal roadsides, disappears quickly after Shylock (the railway sections along the Coquihalla were all named after Shakespearean characters, including Juliet, Othello and Iago).

The valley of Boston Bar Creek is a typical glacial valley—U-shaped with steep sidewalls. The steep slopes and high snowfall add up to frequent avalanches—there are 71 avalanche paths in this valley alone, and an average of 103 avalanches occur along the creek each year. The highway is constructed in the middle of the valley wherever possible to decrease the number of avalanches reaching it, and various earth barriers and deflecting berms have been built to redirect serious slides. At one spot the highway had to be built across a very active avalanche track with an average of 8 avalanches per year, so the Great Bear #5 snowshed was built to allow these slides to flow harmlessly over the highway. Occasionally, when the avalanche danger is severe, the highway is closed and explosive charges are either fired by artillery cannons or dropped from rope ways on the slopes onto critical sites to trigger slides.

The coastal rain forests change to snow forests at higher elevations, and the western hemlock is replaced by the greyer mountain hemlock; the western redcedar, by yellow cedar. Amabilis fir becomes common as well, its smooth grey bark contrasting with its dark green needles. All these trees depend on high snowfall, since they cannot live in areas where the ground freezes. On the windward side of the coastal mountains, snow comes so deep and so fast that the ground never freezes, and the trees can maintain a flow of sap throughout the winter.

Yak Peak. DOUGLAS LEIGHTON

The frequent avalanches maintain permanent treeless tracks on the mountainsides. In areas of granitic rocks, the avalanches often sweep the soil and vegetation off the mountain, and the valley walls are clean bedrock. Near the summit of Yak Peak, on the north side of the highway, you can see a good example of this process.

As in most high mountain passes in British Columbia, the climate and vegetation change abruptly from one side of the pass to the other. Beyond the Coquihalla toll booths, the forest takes on an Interior subalpine character, with subalpine fir, Engelmann spruce and lodgepole pine predominating. Copses of trembling aspen are common, especially where forest fires have removed the coniferous trees. In the fall, look at these copses for patches of aspens that have turned the same colour at the same time. These are clones, the result of the aspen's tendency to reproduce through suckers, especially after a fire has burned the trunk above the ground.

Once over the pass, the highway follows the Coldwater River north to Merritt. Rearing channels have been built along the river to provide habitat for young coho and chinook salmon so that they can escape the torrent of the main river channel during high water in spring and early summer. Normally the young salmon use natural side channels, but some of these have been destroyed by highway construction.

The forests gradually open as you lose altitude, changing to montane woodlands of Douglas-fir and eventually ponderosa pine as you near Merritt. When you come down the final hill into Merritt, the forests disappear altogether and you enter the bunchgrass ranch lands of the Nicola Valley.

The highway bypasses Merritt to the west, going across the willow-covered floodplain of the Nicola River. Watch for the large stick nests of ospreys atop poles in this area. Red-tailed hawks are often seen as well, soaring above the grass, watching for mice. Large alfalfa fields, producing hay for winter feed in the large local cattle operations, cover the lowlands to the east. The dry hillsides above are sparsely treed with ponderosa pines and scattered saskatoon shrubs. After only about 10 kilometres in the Nicola Valley, you begin to climb once again, this time up the Clapperton Creek valley onto the Thompson Plateau.

On the east side of the valley south of Nicola Lake, you can see a low terrace formed by a basaltic lava flow. Its steep sides are cloaked in large Douglas-firs, able to grow in the valley bottom there because they can intercept groundwater flowing over the top of the basalt. These rocks are rather young in geological terms, laid down only 500,000 years ago.

The pattern of forest change continues, going from ponderosa pine to Douglas-fir and then to the subalpine forests of Engelmann spruce and subalpine fir. Most of the ponderosa and lodgepole pines between Merritt and Kamloops have been killed by a recent outbreak of mountain pine beetle. The beetle ravaged lodgepole pine forests on the plateau north of Kamloops; then in a matter of days in early August 2006, a huge flight of beetles invaded the ponderosa pines of the Thompson Valley. That invasion killed almost all the ponderosa pines around Kamloops within a single year. The outbreak spread south into the ponderosa pines of the Nicola Valley in following years and caused significant mortality there. Twenty kilometres from Merritt, the highway begins to level off and the rounded features of the plateau become apparent. The upper section of Clapperton Creek is slow moving, lined with willows and dammed by beavers. It rises in a series of three lakes, all named after English counties—Kent, Sussex and Surrey. The high point of this section of highway is the Surrey Lake Summit, at 1444 metres elevation. About 5 kilometres farther on, you descend to the well-named Meadow Creek, meandering west to meet Guichon Creek and eventually the Nicola River.

The highway climbs to the Lac Le Jeune area, then begins the long descent to Kamloops. Partway down the hill, on the west side of the road, you pass Timber Lake, a small, forested lake that usually contains a pair of nesting Common Loons during the summer. The road flattens out and skirts around Sugarloaf Hill, through open ponderosa pine forests, bunchgrass and squaw currant. On the western horizon, you can see the broad ridge of Greenstone Mountain, scarred by a large forest fire that overran the mountain in 1998. The highway comes out into sagebrush grasslands, then circles west toward the junction with Highway 1. The small alkaline lake at that junction is Ironmask Lake. This lake is one of the saltiest in the B.C. Interior, its chemistry dominated by sodium and magnesium sulfates. Once merged with the Trans-Canada, the highway quickly enters the outskirts of Kamloops, passing fast-food outlets and franchised motels.

At the bottom of the hill, it leaves Highway 1 to cross the South Thompson River and begin its long journey north to the Rockies.

▶ **Kamloops to Valemount:** The North Thompson Valley
Kamloops was founded at the junction of the North and South Thompson Rivers. Heading north on Highway 5, you immediately cross the South Thompson, a large but relatively short river that begins 55 kilometres to the east at Little Shuswap Lake and ends at Kamloops, where the two rivers merge to form the Thompson. The North Thompson is a much longer and wilder river, and Highway 5 follows it for much of its length. While crossing the South Thompson, you can see that its waters are usually clear and green, since most of the silt that was carried out of the mountains by its tributaries was dropped into Shuswap Lake. The North Thompson is much more turbid, since it has no lakes along its channel.

The North Thomspon River at Fishtrap Rapids slices through deep layers of sand and gravel laid down at the end of the Pleistocene Epoch at the mouth of Fishtrap Creek. The rapids and creek are named after salmon traps formerly set here every year by Secwepemc (Shuswap) people. RICHARD CANNINGS

Once over the bridge, you can see T'kumlups Marsh on the west. This rich cattail marsh on the Kamloops Indian Reserve and the city next door get their names from the Secwepemc (Shuswap) word for "meeting place." In summer you can often see yellow-headed black-birds and other marsh life here.

The highway skirts the lower slopes of Mt. Paul, a mosaic of steep talus slopes, rocky outcrops and bunchgrass. The high page-wire fence along the east side of the highway is designed to prevent big-horn sheep from wandering onto the road. There is a healthy herd of these animals from Paul Mountain east along the north shore of the South Thompson River to Chase. They can be seen along this stretch of the highway at various times of year.

About 5 kilometres from the Highway 1 turnoff, the Paul Lake road branches off to the east; a line of black cottonwoods marks the path of Paul Creek. To the west, the grassy Batchelor Hills roll up to the ponderosa pines and Douglas-firs of the Lac du Bois area. The valley bottom here is dominated by sagebrush grasslands. In early August

2003, the summer when hundreds of forest fires burned over much of western North America, a fire burned 5700 hectares of the slopes of Strawberry Hill, the mountain on the east side of the highway north of Paul Creek. Just before the community of Rayleigh, you can see an osprey nest on a double power pole on the east side of the highway, and there is another nest visible on the east side of the highway opposite the big sawmill at Heffley Creek about 7 kilometres north of there.

North of Rayleigh you leave the very hot grasslands, and sagebrush is no longer to be seen. The grey shrubs are now all rabbit-brush, easily identified in August and September, when they are topped with yellow flower clusters. In May the slopes are brightened by the big yellow flowers of the arrowleaf balsamroot, known locally as the "spring

Ice Bugs in the Desert

Mt. Paul (825 metres) looms high to the east of Kamloops, its huge scree slopes descending from rocky cliffs to the sagebrush-covered slopes below. These talus fields were the site of one of the most surprising biological finds in the annals of Canadian entomology. One chilly day in November 1936, local biologist Jack Gregson was climbing up these scree slopes and noticed a strange, wingless insect on a rock he had accidentally overturned. What he had found was a grylloblattid or, as it was then known as, an ice bug. These primitive insects—some call them living fossils—are related to crickets and cockroaches and at that time were known only from a few specimens collected near glaciers in the Canadian Rockies. Few biologists would have predicted that they would be found under the sun-baked rocks of Kamloops. Gregson's find encouraged others to look elsewhere for these creatures, now called rock crawlers, and there are now twenty-four known species in western North America and eastern Asia.

Rock crawler

Bank swallows

sunflower." Rock bluffs on the east side of the road have created steep talus slopes over the years. The big trees on these slopes are Douglas-firs, which don't normally grow on hot valley-bottom slopes, but these rocky spots provide enough water by concentrating ground run-off.

The riverbank along this stretch, where newly created gravel bars are clothed with short willow shrubs, provides a wonderful example of succession. Above the willows on older gravel are young cottonwood trees, which give way to large, old cottonwood trees on the oldest gravel bars. The large cottonwoods are among the most important trees for a wide variety of wildlife, primarily because they tend to develop hollows as they age, making them favourites with woodpeckers and other birds and animals that live in tree cavities. One species to watch out for here is the Lewis's woodpecker (p. 212).

One of the most serious problems facing the grassland eco-systems of British Columbia is the invasion of alien plant species. These species can aggressively outcompete native grasses, especially if the grasses have been stressed by overgrazing. One of the recent invaders is sulfur cinquefoil, a low plant with small yellow flowers and dark green leaves. Sulfur cinquefoil can spread across many hectares of grassland very quickly and can be seen along this highway at several sites.

Near McClure the common shrubs are chokecherry and haw-thorn, both covered with whitish blooms in May and blackish berries in late summer—favourites with birds and bears alike. Indeed, shrubs and grass become the dominant vegetation over the next 20 kilometres or so because of one of the most devastating forest fires in British Columbia history. On July 30, 2003, a carelessly dropped cigarette started a fire near McClure. Fanned by strong south winds, the blaze raced north, crossing the North Thompson River from east to west, then back again from west to east. The village of Louis Creek was destroyed, including a large sawmill. When the fire was brought under control a month later, it had consumed seventeen homes and over 26,000 hectares of forest.

North of Barrière the highway crosses to the west bank of the North Thompson and continues northward through rolling farm country, mostly hay fields and pas-tures. As you gradually climb with the gentle gradient of the river, the climate becomes cooler and moister. This slow change is reflected in the tree species. North of Darfield pon-derosa pines become rare and local, and white spruce and western red-cedar begin to show up along the river; a little farther along, lodge-pole pine appears. Trembling aspen and white birch are the common deciduous trees along this stretch, offering ample practice in identi-fying these superficially similar, white-trunked trees.

Oxbows of the North Thompson River provide valuable wildlife habitat in this essentially lakeless valley.
RICHARD CANNINGS

On the north edge of Little Fort a high, sandy terrace on the west side of the highway provides enough drainage and southern exposure to support a flourishing stand of ponderosa pines, the northernmost outpost of this species in the North Thompson valley. These sand banks, deposited by Lemieux Creek at the close of the Pleistocene, are also ideal for nesting bank swallows. The small brown swallows have dug a cluster of nesting burrows into the north end of the banks.

About 10 kilometres north of Little Fort, the highway crosses an oxbow of the North Thompson to travel across a flat, meadow-covered island. This is the Roundtop Wildlife Area, managed by the B.C. government and Ducks Unlimited. Riparian habitats such as these are especially valuable in mountainous British Columbia, not only for large mammals such as bear and deer, but also for a wide variety of songbirds and, of course, waterfowl. Wood ducks and goldeneyes nest in the huge cottonwoods here and raise their young on the rich, quiet backwaters of the river.

A few of these shallow backwaters provide habitat for one of Canada's rarest and most unusual ferns. The Mexican mosquito fern forms dense colonies of tiny plants that float on the water surface. In Canada, this fern is found in only six sites in the North Thompson and Shuswap Valleys and can be easily recognized in late summer when the plants form reddish carpets on the water.

As you approach Clearwater, a basalt bluff to the west signals the volcanic origin of this landscape. The highway crosses the Clearwater River just south of the town—the Clearwater is the major tributary of the North Thompson, flowing out of the very moist Cariboo Mountains. Trophy Mountain (2577 metres) is visible to the north, its upper slopes famous for vast flower meadows in summer and deep snows in winter. These deep snows are characteristic of the Cariboo Mountains, which spawned many of the huge glaciers that covered the Interior during the Pleistocene, carving the valleys traversed by most of the highways in this book.

Driving northeast of Clearwater, you enter a small rain shadow of Trophy Mountain, and the south-facing hillsides have a dry, open forest of Douglas-fir at Vavenby. North of Vavenby, the climate becomes successively cooler and wetter, and agriculture, in the form of hay fields, persists for only about 17 kilometres north of here. The valley becomes narrower and the river more turbulent at the mouth of the Mad River; you'll see some impressive standing waves over large rocks in midstream. Western white pines along the road to the north hint at a moister climate, as does a marsh filled with hardhack, flowering pink in summer, about 20 kilometres north of the Mad River. Just beyond this marsh is a large horsetail-filled wetland. Red paintbrush, white oxeye daisy and yellow hawkweed flowers are common along the roadside, as are the maplelike leaves of thimbleberry.

At Avola the highway crosses over to the east side of the river, and the forest begins to change quickly. Spruce becomes common in the river bottom, with cottonwoods growing in isolated areas. Western hemlock, that ultimate indicator of wet forests in British Columbia, shows up as well. The roadsides are cloaked in water-loving goatsbeard and cow parsnip. About 5 kilometres north of Avola, you pass a beautiful beaver pond on the west side of the road. The beavers have likely been living at this pond for some time; lines of thick cattail growth mark the lines of the original dams.

Just beyond this pond, you reach the southern edge of the Elevator Fire, which burned 1600 hectares of second-growth forest (a forest born of fires that swept through here during the 1920s) in August 1998. The fire was set by a three-hour lightning storm that also started a hundred other fires in the Monashees between Clearwater and McBride.

At Finn Creek the road leaves the river and begins to climb to Messiter Summit, at 765 metres elevation. This climb is to avoid Little Hells Gate, where the North Thompson roars through a canyon only 4.5 metres wide. Above the canyon the highway rejoins the river, now a true mountain stream—blue and fast. Western white pine is now common through the valley, though many of the mature trees are recently dead, likely killed by the ubiquitous white pine blister rust. Paintbrush is still a common roadside flower, joined by orange tiger lilies and the small white spikes of rein orchids.

As you approach Blue River, you drive by a section of forest logged in 1977 and 1978, now a thick growth of young lodgepole pine, white birch and trembling aspen. This forest is growing on a relatively dry, south-facing terrace slope built by the Blue River at the close of the Ice Age. A black spruce bog in the valley bottom is the first example of this truly boreal habitat on the route north.

About 5 kilometres north of Blue River, you cross Cook Creek, and for the next 20 kilometres you will notice a lot of dead western redcedar and western hemlock on the hillsides. These trees were killed by an outbreak of hemlock loopers in the 1990s. Loopers are small moths; the caterpillars are also known as inchworms, since they form successive loops as they walk along a twig, as if they were measuring inches off a ruler. It is the caterpillars that have been defoliating the trees in this valley.

Eight kilometres north of Miledge Creek, Pyramid Creek cascades out of a hanging valley across the river. A hanging valley is formed when a large valley glacier carves out the main valley more deeply than the smaller side valley. When the glacier eventually melts, it leaves the side valley hanging, and the result is often a significant waterfall. North of this waterfall is a fine stand of old-growth western hemlock, on the east side of the river.

Over the next few kilometres, the highway crosses the North Thompson three times. After the third bridge, the river swings to the west and the highway follows the Albreda River north. Between Clemina Creek and Mt. Albreda from the south, make sure you look over your shoulder at the magnificent Albreda Glacier. One of the province's more spectacular views, it is unfortunately marred by several large, rectangular clear-cuts just below it.

Once you are over Mt. Albreda—the divide between the Fraser and Columbia watersheds—lodgepole pine becomes common again, along with a creeping understorey of kinnikinnick on sandy, gravelly soils. The pines are joined by larger Douglas-firs on upland slopes,

Hemlock looper. BOB DUNCAN

REST STOP

Cranberry Marsh

JUST SOUTH OF Valemount, the highway crosses a broad area of cattails and bulrushes. This is Cranberry Marsh, now protected as the Starrat Wildlife Sanctuary. A pull-off on the south side of the Holiday Inn makes a great break in a long journey; there is an easy walk through woodland to a viewing tower, as well as forty-five-minute and two-hour loop trails around the marsh.

Cranberry Marsh is the remnant of a much larger, flat-bottomed glacial lake that filled the valley here at the end of the Ice Age. It is the only large marsh within hundreds of kilometres, and its strategic position at the north end of the Thompson and Columbia Rivers migration corridors makes it an important stopover for many kinds of waterfowl. The sanctuary was donated by Mrs. Robert Starrat in 1969 in memory of her husband and is now co-managed by Ducks Unlimited, the B.C. government and the district of Valemount.

Above: The northern tip of the Monashee Mountains provides a backdrop for the rich waters of Cranberry Marsh near Valemount.
SYDNEY CANNINGS

Ancient Dunes

About 10 kilometres north of Valemount, the soil becomes pure sand and the highway cuts through several old dunes. This is Jackman Flats, a new provincial park created to protect a unique habitat. At the end of the Pleistocene, the Rocky Mountain Trench south of Valemount (in the Cranberry Marsh area) was filled with a string of lakes. Rivers deposited large amounts of sand into these lakes, but about nine thousand years ago the climate became warm and dry and the lakes disappeared. Strong prevailing winds from the southwest blew the sand northwards to this spot, forming dunes with gentle slopes on the southwest and steeper slopes on the northeast sides. About five thousand years ago the climate became cooler and wetter, allowing plant life to flourish and to stabilize the dunes. They are now vegetated with an open forest of lodgepole pine, carpeted with fascinating lichen gardens and kinnikinnick.

Above: RICHARD CANNINGS

whereas the banks of Camp Creek are lined with white spruce and alder. Camp Creek flows into the Canoe River, which flows into the Columbia River at Big Bend, though most of the Canoe is now a reservoir lake behind the Mica Dam. Shortly after crossing the Canoe River, you enter the broad valley of the Rocky Mountain Trench, where British Columbia literally opened up along a crack hundreds of kilometres long and thousands of metres deep (p. 44). Here the highway stands at the junction of three mighty mountain ranges— the Rockies to the east, the Cariboo Mountains to the west and the Monashees to the south.

> **Valemount to Yellowhead Pass:** The Rocky Mountains
North of Valemount the highway travels along the western edge of

the broad trench, through lodgepole pine forests on sandy, gravelly soil. The Mt. Terry Fox Rest Area provides a good view of the mountain that was named after the courageous young Canadian who attempted to run across the country to raise awareness of cancer and money for research.

A few kilometres north is the village of Tête Jaune Cache (French for "yellowhead"; pronounced tee'-jzhawn by the locals), a historic meeting place where the Fraser River comes out of the Rocky Mountains and turns north to follow the trench to Prince George. Tête Jaune was the nickname of a local fur trader, who also gave his name to the pass through the Rockies and the highway that now passes through it. The highway now turns eastward to follow the Fraser into the Rockies.

Four kilometres from the junction the river goes over Rearguard Falls. The falls are not spectacularly high, but they offer enough resistance to migrating chinook salmon that they afford a magnificent opportunity to watch these huge fish leaping up the cascades. These fish—some weighing over 15 kilograms—enter the mouth of the Fraser in June and travel over 1000 kilometres upriver to fight these falls in August. They spawn in gravel beds a few kilometres upstream at the mouth of Swiftcurrent Creek, unable to go beyond Overlander Falls.

The mountains along the western edge of the Rocky Mountains are impressive enough, their high ridges patched with snow well into summer, but they do not prepare the first-time traveller to this area for what lies ahead. A few kilometres east of Rearguard Falls, the highway rounds a bend and there, filling the eastern landscape, is the highest and most magnificent peak in the Canadian Rockies— Mt. Robson. At 3954 metres elevation, Mt. Robson rises more than 3 kilometres straight up from the valley floor. It is one of the most spectacular rock walls in the world.

The Robson River, sky blue from glacial melt waters from its mountain namesake, flows in from the north just west of the Mt. Robson Visitors Centre. Beyond the centre the highway begins a steep ascent for about 15 kilometres. It passes Overlander Falls (a

A few chinook salmon conquer Rearguard Falls to spawn at the mouth of Swift-current Creek, the longest trip made by any salmon on the Fraser River.
SYDNEY CANNINGS

short hike to the south), then climbs the northern slopes of the valley, which are forested with Douglas-firs. As the valley and the highway level out, the forest becomes predominantly Engelmann spruce.

Moose Lake, the only lake the Fraser River flows through on its long journey to the sea, fills the valley for about 10 kilometres. Its south shores rise almost vertically to Emerald Ridge and the Comb, the former named for the massive avalanche tracks down its slopes, bright green with fresh alder foliage in early summer. Emerald Ridge, like Mt. Robson itself, has the classic Rocky Mountain structure of cliff-talus-cliff-talus. The high cliffs of the Rockies are generally hard carbonate rocks such as limestone, and the sloping talus slopes are softer rocks, such as shales. Between Emerald Ridge and The Comb, Thunder Falls plummets out of a hanging valley, formed where a small alpine glacier flowed into a large valley glacier.

At the east end of Moose Lake, the Fraser River has formed a large, diverse marsh of sedge and buckbean, willow and alder. This is one spot where the southern willow and northern alder flycatchers, closely related species that are usually separated by geography and habitat (see Highway 97, p. 201) can be heard calling side by side. The highway crosses Grant Brook, passes a black spruce bog, then crosses to the south side of the Fraser. Just beyond this crossing you will get a good view of Mt. Fitzwilliam, a pyramidal peak to the east. This mountain is made up of two dramatically different types of rock—the pale dolomite rocks that form its lower half were laid down in the Precambrian Era, and its dark upper sandstones date from the Cambrian Period. The boundary between the two halves thus clearly marks the beginning of complex life forms on earth.

About 5 kilometres farther on, the highway crosses the Fraser River for the last time as it comes out of the mountains in the southern part of the park. Yellowhead Lake lies along the north side of the highway; Yellowhead Mountain rises above it at 2458 metres elevation. Beyond the lake the valley is filled with sedge marshes, black spruce bogs and beaver ponds. The highway passes a few low, rocky bluffs, then crosses the Great Divide at Portal Lake. This is Yellowhead Pass (1131 metres); east of here, the waters of the Miette River eventually flow via the Athabasca and Mackenzie Rivers into the icy Beaufort Sea.

FIVE

The Yellowhead Highway

HIGHWAY 16

HIGHWAY 16 traverses central British Columbia from the Pacific Ocean to the Continental Divide at Yellowhead Pass. Beginning in the cool marine air of Prince Rupert, it follows the magnificent valley of the Skeena River, then climbs along the Bulkley River to the edge of the Fraser Plateau at Smithers. After crossing the broad plateau, it reaches the Fraser River at Prince George and follows that river to its headwaters—through the unnaturally straight Rocky Mountain Trench to Tête Jaune Cache, then turning east with Highway 5 to penetrate the Rockies themselves.

➤ **Prince Rupert to Smithers:** The Waters of the Skeena

Prince Rupert is a city whose existence and essence is centred on water. Situated on Kaien Island, it is surrounded by the sea, and its two main industries—the fishery and shipping—rely on the sea. The one striking natural feature of the Prince Rupert shoreline is its very high tidal range. Unlike the average tidal range at Vancouver, which is about 4 metres, the tides at Prince Rupert vary by almost 7 metres daily. At low tide the exposed rocks and pilings are golden-brown with wrack *(Fucus),* giving the air that characteristic salt tang.

Facing page: The Bulkley River churns through a narrow rock chasm at Moricetown Rapids. RICHARD CANNINGS

REST STOP
Prince Rupert Trailhead

IF YOU NEED to stretch your legs after a long drive in from the east or are trying to get your land legs back after a ferry trip, you might want to stop at the city trailhead on Highway 16 on the east edge of town. Trails from this point lead up Mt. Oldfield (575 metres elevation) to Grassy Bay and to the Butze Rapids viewpoint. Butze Rapids is one of the most spectacular tidal rapids in British Columbia and one of three narrows around Kaien Island where tidal waters race through four times each day—twice in each direction.

The dominant feature of the local climate is rain. Prince Rupert is Canada's cloudiest city, with only 1212 hours of sunshine a year, and one of its wettest, with 255 centimetres of precipitation a year. Precipitation levels drop markedly as you go east along Highway 16— to 129 centimetres at Terrace and only 51 centimetres at Smithers. Western redcedar and western hemlock are the common trees in the forest, and they are festooned with cream-coloured old man's beard lichen, an indicator of a very wet climate.

Prince Rupert sits on a bedrock of metamorphic rocks, primarily schists, that were crushed, folded and refolded several times during the collision between the Alexander Terrane and Stikinia, which formed the coast of British Columbia at that time. The journey eastward along Highway 16 is over these rocks until you reach the Skeena River, where the massive granitoid core of the Coast Mountains lies.

As you continue along the highway east of Prince Rupert, you soon pass Oliver Lake on the west side of the road, a small park with a lake and a boardwalk through a picturesque bog. Bogs are common along the north coast of British Columbia, where the heavy rainfall and cool air result in saturated soils and the subsequent growth of mosses, especially peat mosses *(Sphagnum)*. Because peat mosses hold on to the abundant rainwater even better than the thin soils, they take over poorly drained areas and a bog is born. Watch for the white tufts of cottongrass waving in the bogs. Stunted, bonsai-like lodgepole pines also grow in these bogs, living up to their scientific name—*Pinus contorta*. Over most of its range in the Interior, this pine reflects its English name, as it grows ramrod straight in dense stands.

Just past Oliver Lake is the turnoff to Ridley Island, the major industrial port in northern British Columbia, where grain from the Canadian Prairies and coal from northeastern British Columbia are loaded onto freighters bound for Japan, Korea and other Asian destinations. The highway then leaves Kaien Island across Galloway Rapids, where tidal waters race between Morse Basin to the east and Wainwright Basin to the west. Wainwright Basin is drained westward by Zanardi Rapids.

The highway goes through a prominent rock cut just east of Galloway Rapids, most of which is schist similar to that seen in Prince Rupert, though there are several layers of dark grey marble at the eastern end of the cut. As the high-

Cloudberry. RICHARD CANNINGS

way ascends to Rainbow Summit, it passes by several lakes (Taylor, Prudhomme and Diana). Diana Creek remains ice-free in winter and is a good spot to see American Dippers at that time. There are several nice bogs visible on the west side of the highway before Rainbow Summit as well. At Rainbow Summit (160 metres), you are in the northern head of the Ecstall Pluton, a 130-kilometre-long mass of granite that cooled beneath the surface about 98 million years ago. The eastern edge of the pluton is about 13 kilometres east of

Eulachons

Beginning in mid-March, millions of small, silvery fish leave the protected marine inlets of British Columbia and enter coastal rivers. The eulachon swim upstream—up the Skeena, the Nass, the Kitlope, the Klinaklini, the Fraser and a host of other streams—just far enough to find good spawning gravel for their eggs.

The First Nations peoples welcomed the return of the eulachon because they came at the end of the cold, wet winter and they came bearing rich gifts—bodies laden with energy- and vitamin-rich oil. In an industry full of tradition and ceremony, which is still very much alive, the Native people netted the fish in tremendous quantities and extracted the oil.

Eulachon were a major trading commodity among First Nations, for both oil and fish were carried through the Coast Mountains on well-trodden *kleena*, or "grease" trails. Both the Klinaklini River and the settlement of Kleena Kleene on the Chilcotin Plateau derive their names from this trading network. Like *kleena*, the word eulachon is from the Chinook trading language and was pronounced "oorigan" by some Cree guides used by early European explorers. They talked of the "Oorigan River" as an easy route to the Pacific, referring to the Fraser River, but American explorers thought that this river was farther south, and Lewis and Clark were specifically ordered to find it as part of their explorations from 1804 to 1806. This led to the name "Oregon" being mistakenly applied to the area around the Columbia River. Alexander Mackenzie reached the Pacific twelve years before Lewis and Clark, travelling west along the grease trails from the Fraser River.

Eulachon populations have declined by about 90 per cent over the last century, and much of that decline has occurred in recent decades. The Committee on the Status of Endangered Wildlife in Canada has assessed the populations breeding in the Nass and Skeena Rivers as Special Concern, and those from the Fraser River and central coast areas as Endangered.

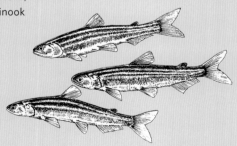

Rainbow Summit. The Ecstall Pluton is a small part of the Coastal Plutonic Complex, one of the largest contiguous areas of granite exposure on the planet.

The highway descends from Rainbow Summit through more lichen-draped cedars, the roadside lined with red alder, and enters the magnificent Skeena Valley. The mighty Skeena is about 3 kilometres wide at this point, about 13 kilometres from its mouth. To the south you can see the wide mouth of the Ecstall River valley. Frizzell Hot Springs, on the opposite side of the Skeena, illustrates how active tectonically this region of geological boundaries is; it is one of several hotsprings in the area.

Because of the high tidal range typical of Hecate Strait, the Skeena is strongly tidal as far east as Kwinitsa Creek and moderately so up to the Kasiks River. Estuarine sedge marshes along its shores provide excellent feeding grounds for migrating waterfowl in the spring. The marine influence is perhaps best illustrated by the presence of harbour seals and northern sea-lions in the river. The sea-lions are especially common in March, when the eulachon run is on. Bald eagles gather along the Skeena to feast on eulachon as well— sometimes more than a thousand of these huge birds can be seen along the river in early spring.

As with all the major rivers of British Columbia, the biggest story on the Skeena is that of salmon. Thousands of pink, chum, coho and chinook salmon and two million sockeye migrate up the Skeena each summer and fall to spawn in its tributaries. Steelhead, the oceangoing populations of rainbow trout, also make this a legendary fishing river. If you are travelling the highway in July, you may see one or two gillnetting fish boats along the shore just upstream from where the highway meets the river. These are test boats, contracted by the Department of Fisheries and Oceans. When they have caught a certain number of salmon, the commercial fishery near the mouth of the river is opened; the actual length of the season depends on the estimated size of the run that year. The Skeena is one of the world's great sockeye salmon streams—about two million sockeyes migrate up the river annually, most spawning in the Babine system.

The Skeena River is still strongly tidal at Kwinitsa, 50 kilometres from the open ocean. RICHARD CANNINGS

The forests along the Skeena are noticeably different from those on Kaien Island and the Tsimpsean Peninsula. Away from the influence of summertime marine clouds, the climate is somewhat drier and more continental—warmer in summer and cooler in winter than on the coast. The dominant conifer along the highway is the Sitka spruce, its long branches outstretched like straight arms from the trunk.

The scenery, especially on a clear day, is spectacular. The highway and railway cling to the north bank of the river, the steep granite walls of the mountains rising almost straight out of the river itself. The mountains that plunge into the Skeena at the McLean Point Rest Area are part of the Quottoon Pluton, a huge, single block of granite extending from Juneau, Alaska, to the Douglas Channel, 60 kilometres to the south of the Skeena. It is separated from the Ecstall Pluton by the Work Channel lineament, one of the many straight, northwesterly trending fault lines along the B.C. coast.

The steep granite walls along the Skeena are constantly shedding sheets of rock to the valley below—the technical term for these massive, rounded mountains is "exfoliating domes." The high snowfall in these mountains also results in frequent avalanches along the route.

The round, concrete turrets along the highway serve as mounts for howitzers that blast the slopes above to trigger avalanches under controlled conditions while the highway is closed.

The shedding of both rock and snow makes it almost impossible for forests to become established on these mountains; much of the steeper slopes remain as smooth granite, while alder forests cling to marginally less steep slopes. Several small but spectacular waterfalls can be seen, especially the one on Slickenslide Creek just west of the Kasiks River. The granitic rocks in this area are part of the Kasiks Pluton; just west of the Exchamsiks River, the prominent rock bluffs are metamorphic gneisses and other related rocks. The bluffs literally hang over the road at one point, allowing the traveller to appreciate the natural rock gardens of yellow stonecrop and other spring and summer flowers.

Much of the Skeena River between Kwinitsa and Terrace is filled with large and small islands forested with magnificent cottonwoods. One of these islands, just west of the Exchamsiks River, has been designated an Ecological Reserve to preserve this habitat. Black bears are commonly seen along the river, and occasionally a grizzly bear can be seen foraging along the riverbank or feeding on fresh greenery on the roadside in spring. This part of the Skeena Valley warms up quickly in spring and provides green forage for bears and deer earlier than sites closer to the coast or at higher elevations to the east. If you are extremely lucky, you may see a Kermode bear, the white form of the black bear found from the Terrace area south through Kitimat to Princess Royal Island. Mountain goats are plentiful; their population density here is the highest in the world. They are not easy to see, however, since they spend the summers high on the mountain cliffs and descend to lower elevation forests on the mountainsides in winter.

Metamorphic rocks of the coastal zone continue for the next few kilometres, but about 1 kilometre west of the Shames River the character of the bedrock changes. These rocks represent the boundary between the Coastal Plutonic Complex to the west and the Stikine Terrane to the east, a boundary where the western terrane was thrust over the Interior terrane about 100 million to 70 million years ago. East of the Shames River, greenish, nondescript, moderately metamorphosed volcanic rocks are common in road cuts.

You cross the Zymagotitz (Zymacord) River just before Terrace; in summer its milky colour indicates its glacial origins on the ice-caps of Mt. William Brown (2015 metres), about 25 kilometres to the northwest. As you enter Terrace you cross the Kitsumkalum (Kalum) River. Its beautiful blue colour also hints at its glacial origins, but most of its glacial silt is deposited in Kitsumkalum Lake 20 kilometres to the north.

The dominant feature of the Terrace area is the broad Kitsumkalum Valley to the north and the similar Kitimat Valley to the south. These valleys are the same geographical entity, a trench formed about 50 million years ago when subduction ceased off the coast, easing the pressure on the crust to the east and allowing it to crack in a straight line, the bedrock dropping 1500 to 2000 metres into the crack. The Kitsumkalum-Kitimat trench is still volcanically active—250 years ago the Aiyansh lava flow 60 kilometres north of Terrace partially filled the Tseax valley and destroyed two Nisga'a villages. About 30 kilometres to the south, Lakelse Hot Springs produces water at a piping 85°C.

The mouth of the Kitsumkalum River is usually lined with sports fishermen during the summer, as are the shores of Ferry Island, just upstream. These fishermen are trying for chinook salmon; the fly-fishers off the gravel bar just east of the Skeena bridge are seeking sockeye salmon. After passing through Terrace—named after the gravel terraces built against the valley glaciers at the close of the Pleistocene—you again find yourself along the Skeena, and the highway turns north to continue following the river.

Just past the Copper River, straight, Interior-type lodgepole pines appear, hinting that the climate is getting drier and colder as you go upriver. However, Western hemlock is still the dominant tree of climax forests here, and cream-coloured witch's hair lichen still festoons trees in places; both are signs of high rainfall. Red alder, the

Part of the Rocher Déboulé Range above Kitseguecla. RICHARD CANNINGS

pioneer tree species of coastal forests, lines the disturbed areas along the highway until you cross Legate Creek, after which it is replaced by lodgepole pine. Legate Creek thus marks the boundary between the Coastal Western Hemlock Zone and the Interior Cedar–Hemlock Zone. The latter forest type is a mix of coastal and Interior forest species, growing in combinations you see in no other forest zone. For instance, it is common along this stretch of highway to see stands of lodgepole pines with young hemlocks growing in the understorey. Normally lodgepole pines shelter young spruce and fir.

Beyond Oliver Creek, the spectacular Seven Sisters Peaks (2755 metres) dominate the scenery east of the highway. This is an area of forest transition, since the Seven Sisters are high enough to create their own rain shadow. Behind the peaks the young forests are dominated by trembling aspen. Near the Seven Sisters, Sitka spruce, a coastal species, meets up with white spruce, the Interior species, and from here to Moricetown most of the spruces are hybrids of those two species.

At Whiskey Creek there is a sign describing forest succession in the area. Young cottonwoods, the primary pioneer species in this

The sedge marshes along Toboggan Creek are fed by the Toboggan Glacier on Hudson Bay Mountain. RICHARD CANNINGS

habitat, dominate the area around the sign. If you want to take a break and improve your tree-identification skills, the rest area just west of Boulder Creek has signs illustrating the common local species.

The massive ridge of Rocher Déboulé (2377 metres) fills the eastern skyline as you approach the village of Kitseguecla. A small road is visible beneath Red Rose Peak at the centre of the mountain; it was built to serve the Red Rose Mine, an operation that mined tungsten until 1954. The northernmost peak is Hagwilget, which overlooks the community of Hazelton at the junction of the Skeena and Bulkley Rivers. Hazelton is named after the abundant growth of hazel bushes on the river terraces here.

About 15 kilometres east of Kitseguecla, you pass Seeley Lake, interesting for a number of reasons. One is the black spruce bog around its edges, the knobbly trees mostly dead from recent inundation by the rising lake level. These particular trees are further blackened by a luxuriant growth of hair lichen using the dead branches as an ideal base for gathering light from the sun and moisture and nutrients from the air.

But the most interesting story is how the lake was formed. About 3500 years ago, a massive debris slide roared down the Chicago Creek valley just east of here. The slide buried the Gitksan village of Temlaxham and created a natural dam that formed the lake. The event is recorded in graphic detail in the oral history of the Gitksan, which attributes the destruction to the actions of a giant grizzly bear. That ancient story, and the modern geological science that corroborated it, was critical in establishing the importance of oral traditions in the landmark *Delgamuukw* case, in which the Supreme Court of Canada considered the aboriginal rights of the Gitksan and Wet'suwet'en people.

At Hazelton the highway begins a broad turn to the south around the Rocher Déboulé Range, following the Bulkley upstream. Rocher Déboulé is part of the Bulkley Ranges, an eastern flank of the Coast Mountains that the highway skirts as far as Houston. The forest becomes even drier behind these mountains as you enter the Sub-boreal Spruce Zone at Moricetown. Western hemlock is no longer evident, replaced by white spruce as the dominant climax tree.

At Moricetown the Bulkley pours through a narrow gap in the rocks. These rapids have been a traditional fishing spot for the local indigenous people for centuries. Salmon—chinook, pink, sockeye, coho and steelhead—are dip-netted as they struggle through the turbulent water from August through early October. The larger chinook salmon are present in July as well, when they are usually taken by gaff in the higher water. About twenty thousand steelhead—representing almost 40 per cent of the entire Skeena run—migrate up the Bulkley River.

About 10 kilometres south of Moricetown, the highway crosses Toboggan Creek. There is a good view to the west up the Kitseguecla Valley to the mountain aptly named the Nipples. The Bulkley takes a bend to the east here, so the highway follows the straighter route up Toboggan Creek to Smithers.

The Toboggan Creek Fish Hatchery, just north of Toboggan Lake, raises coho and chinook salmon. The hatchery work includes enhancement of the Upper Bulkley River coho, one of the most threatened salmon stocks in British Columbia.

Hudson Bay Mountain towers over Toboggan Lake, its northeastern ridges carved by glaciers. The first is the Toboggan Glacier, and the next, above Lake Kathlyn, is Hudson Bay Glacier. Both have obviously retreated in recent years, leaving bare moraines below.

➤ Smithers to Prince George: The Fraser Plateau

Beyond Smithers, the highway skirts the eastern edge of the Coast Mountains as far as Houston, then turns east across the Fraser Plateau. From Houston to Fraser Lake, you cross the Nechako Plateau, a landscape dominated by Endako volcanic rocks, laid down about 50 million years ago, long before the Miocene volcanics covered the Chilcotin and Cariboo Plateaus to the south. This is a hilly landscape, with small mountains, scattered buttes and colourful outcroppings. East of Fraser Lake, you enter the Fraser Basin, a rather flat landscape with almost no rocky outcrops. Most of the features of the Fraser Basin are eskers, drumlins and glacial lake silt deposits created at the end of the Pleistocene.

At Smithers you meet the Bulkley once again, crossing over to its east bank. Continuing south, the highway travels across flats forested by lodgepole pine. The hills to the east are dotted with aspen copses and grassy balds. You descend to the river again at Telkwa, where the Bulkley is joined by the Telkwa River; from this point the Bulkley is significantly smaller.

From here to Endako, the highway passes through important winter range for ungulates. Moose and mule deer are abundant, and you can sometimes see a small herd of elk on Hungry Hill, about 30 kilometres east of Telkwa. Caribou were formerly more common, but Smithers was constructed on their prime wintering range, and now only about fifty roam the Telkwa Range southwest of the highway. The grassy openings in the forest on the south-facing slopes north of the highway are especially valuable to deer in winter and have interesting summer residents as well. Mountain bluebirds can be seen at the Bulkley View Rest Area about 5 kilometres east of Telkwa, and just beyond that is the Hubert Hill grassland, which has a unique plant community that includes Rocky Mountain junipers. At several points along this section between Telkwa and Houston you can see Barrett Hat (947 metres), a distinctive volcanic plug west of the highway and north of Houston.

At Houston the highway turns 90 degrees to the northeast and leaves the Coast Mountains behind. Nadina Mountain (2125 metres), immediately south of Houston, provides a beautiful farewell to this range (or a welcome, if you are travelling westward). You rejoin the Bulkley River, now smaller and meandering through stands of large cottonwoods. Houston celebrates its famous steelhead run with a display of the biggest fly rod in the world. In winter this section of river valley is filled with moose, so be especially careful if you are driving at that time.

At Six-Mile Summit, 10 kilometres east of Topley, you can see China Nose to the south. This isolated cliff, an outcrop of 50-million-year-old volcanic basalt, has a small population of mountain goats. At Taman Creek you cross the divide between the Bulkley and the Nechako watersheds. Taman Creek flows into Bulkley Lake, whereas the water in Rose Lake, 2 kilometres to the east, flows into the Nechako River to meet the Fraser at Prince George.

The Nechako Plateau is exceptional moose country; a big wet pasture about 12 kilometres east of Rose Lake is especially good habitat. The big white flower heads of cow parsnip are common in the moist ditches along the road. At Decker Lake you begin to traverse "Lake Country," an area noted for its large lakes, such as Ootsa, François, Burns and Stuart. The highway manages to miss most of these lakes, however. Burns Lake is a narrow lake set in an old watercourse that flowed even below the ice of the last glaciation. Its southwestern shores (opposite the highway) are an esker, made of gravel deposited beneath the ice by this meltwater stream. After going through downtown Burns Lake, you climb over a gravel ridge, then descend once again to the valley bottom. A marshy pond on the south side of the highway is lined with sedges and marsh cinquefoil, an excellent place to see dragonflies and nesting solitary sandpipers.

After going through more sedge meadows, the highway climbs over Hicks Hill, then descends to the Endako River and even more moose habitat. You cross the Endako River in lodgepole pine forest; drier slopes on the north side of the highway are open and grassy. The pioneer tree on these slopes is trembling aspen, and several spots have carpets of young aspens, sprouting from roots after a fire. These aspen copses are usually clones, all growing from a single rootstock.

At the west end of Fraser Lake, the highway jogs to the south to cross the Stellako River, a short stream that drains François Lake, only 10 kilometres to the southwest, into Fraser Lake. For a time during the Pleistocene, the Nechako was blocked by ice and the entire Nechako watershed drained through the Stellako, creating a deep canyon in bedrock.

Today the marshy river mouth of the Stellako shares a delta with the Endako River and is an important wintering site for trumpeter swans. Many of the rivers in central British Columbia have wintering populations of this rare waterfowl, the largest bird in Canada. The swans require shallow water with abundant water plants so that they can tip up and feed on the nutritious plant roots. In winter, when most of the lakes in this region are frozen, slow-moving rivers have water plants as well as open water. In summer the swans are replaced by cliff swallows, which flock to the bridge over the Stellako to build their mud nests underneath. Before bridges and buildings dotted the landscape, these birds built their semispherical mud nests under the ledges of rock cliffs, as their name suggests.

Cow parsnip. SYDNEY CANNINGS

The reddish ridge north of the Stellako is a colourful outcrop of volcanic rock, again part of the Endako group, as are most of the rocky hills around Fraser Lake. The lake has several islands, one of which is home to a colony of ring-billed and herring gulls. As you pass the village of Fraser Lake, you can see Mouse Hill on the east side of town. At the east end of Fraser Lake, you skirt the northern side of Fraser Mountain, one of the last good-sized hills you will see for the next 140 kilometres as the highway heads out over the flatter parts of the Fraser Plateau. You then cross the Nechako River as it flows north to brush by the east end of Fraser

Variable darner dragonfly emerging on marsh cinquefoil leaf.

Lake, to which it is connected by the Nautley River. A mere 1.5 kilometres long, the Nautley is even shorter than the Stellako. Like the Stellako, the Nautley is another important trumpeter swan wintering site.

East of Fort Fraser, you enter the relatively flat landscape of the Fraser Basin. Most of the land here was inundated by a large glacial lake at the end of the Pleistocene, and the silty lake deposits further smoothed an already smooth land surface. Some relief is provided by occasional small rounded hills on the north side of the road, especially about 10 kilometres east of Fort Fraser and at the Fort St. James junction. These are drumlins, gravel deposits formed beneath melting glaciers.

Just past the junction of Highways 16 and 27, Highway 16 meets Stony Creek as it winds through lush pastures on the south side of the road. These pastures are an important migratory stopover for Canada Geese travelling to Arctic breeding grounds. The fields

Orange hawkweed. RICHARD CANNINGS

around Vanderhoof have recently been colonized by pioneering long-billed curlews. These large sandpipers normally breed in the dry grasslands of western North America but have been moving north to take advantage of new habitat opportunities provided by fields cleared for cereal crops in the forests of central British Columbia. As you enter Vanderhoof through the Nechako Lumber sawmill, watch for the big stick nest of a pair of ospreys on a pole in the log yard. You might also see a raven's nest on the large powerline towers east of Vanderhoof.

About 34 kilometers east of Vanderhoof, you cross Cluculz Creek. This stream is relatively warm, since it drains Cluculz Lake, and has some interesting inhabitants. One of the most interesting is the boreal snaketail, a beautiful apple-green, brown and yellow dragon-fly that is found in British Columbia in warm creeks in the central and northern parts of the province. Most clubtails develop as larvae in creeks and rivers rather than in marshes or ponds, where many familiar dragonflies develop.

Other signs of a relatively warm climate around Cluculz Lake are the big Douglas-firs that grow on south-facing slopes here. These trees, along with some on the banks of the Nechako River around

Puddling Swallows

Cliff swallows are often seen flocking at roadside puddles in late spring to gather mud to build their nests. As the birds pick up the mud in their bills, they flutter their wings high over their backs.

It was long assumed that they fluttered their wings so they wouldn't get them muddy or wet, but a sharp-eyed B.C. biologist, Rob Butler, began to think there was more to the story. He noticed that the closely related barn swallows didn't flutter their wings at all when gathering mud. It seemed unlikely that barn swallows were simply less careful about their personal hygiene, so Butler surmised that the difference in behaviour might be due to the major difference between the social biology of the two species. Barn swallows nest singly or in very small groups, whereas cliff swallows are highly gregarious, often nesting in colonies of a hundred or more pairs,

the nests packed closely together. The nests in these colonies are valuable real estate, and an empty one is immediately usurped by a pair so that it doesn't have to build its own. One member of the pair therefore always perches at the nest site, guarding it from nest stealers, while the other bird gathers mud. If the female of the pair is the one gathering mud, she is open to copulation attempts from other males— so she flutters her wings over her back. In a set of ingenious experiments, Butler showed that birds that did not flutter their wings were immediately mounted by other males. It appears that males, identical in plumage to the females, also flutter their wings so that they can get mud in peace.

Above: Cliff swallows gathering mud.
RICHARD CANNINGS

Prince George, are among the northernmost examples of this species in the world. Sedge meadows east of Cluculz Lake often have two distinct bands of sedge ringing the pond—two sedge species adapted to different water depths. Tamarac Lake, on the south side of the road, is named after the eastern larch species that is one of the few deciduous conifers in the province. In the fall, tamarack needles turn bright gold, joining the aspen in adding colour to the dark green boreal forest. Black spruce add further diversity in a boggy marsh on the north side of the road just past Tamarac Lake. Beyond Tamarac Lake the highway travels through a landscape dominated by gravels, silts and sands deposited beneath a large, melting ice sheet. Narrow gravel ridges (eskers) are separated by equally narrow depressions filled with sedge marshes and big spruce; the uplands are forested by smaller spruce, lodgepole pine and trembling aspen.

About 20 kilometres southwest of Prince George, the highway descends to the Chilako River. The Chilako is a small river winding through lush black cottonwood and white spruce forests, about 10 kilometres as the raven flies south of the Chilako's junction with the Nechako River (about 20 kilometres as the canoe paddles along the meandering river). These rich riparian woodlands are important oases in the boreal forest, providing large trees that serve as homes to many animals, including marten, fishers and barred owls. The Chilako is a muddy river, carving its path through deep, silty sediments laid down on the bottom of a large glacial lake; you can see the depth of these sediments as the highway descends from the west; it follows the course of Beaverley Creek as it climbs to the plateau on the east side of the valley.

Boreal snaketail dragonfly.
ROBERT CANNINGS

East of the Chilako River, the terrain is gently rolling, with broad vistas in most directions but few mountains in sight. Mt. Baldy Hughes, only 1131 metres in elevation (the highway is at 750 metres here), stands out on the southern horizon with its communications tower. The forest is an ever-changing mix (though the ingredients seem never-changing) of lodgepole pine, white spruce and trembling aspen. The highway descends to Prince George around the south end of Cranbrook Hill, then travels across a flat plain (part of the Nechako delta) through lodgepole pine woods, increasingly broken up by malls, big box stores, cemeteries and golf courses.

> ### Prince George to Tête Jaune Cache:
The Rocky Mountain Trench and Its Antique Forests
From Prince George south to the Tête Jaune Cache junction, Highway 16 follows the arrow-straight trough of the Southern Rocky Mountain Trench. As explained on page 44, the trench is a massive crack that appeared about 60 million years ago. Although the Rocky Mountain Trench continues northward into the Yukon, it has a distinct break near Prince George. South of Prince George, the trench is a simple block fault, meaning that the earth opened up and the bottom fell out of the trench like a trap door. The Northern Rocky Mountain Trench was formed in a different manner, when the northward-moving Pacific Ocean plate pulled the land on the west side of the trench more than 425 kilometres northward relative to the land on the east side. Geologists call this type of movement a strike-slip fault, similar to the San Andreas Fault in California.

After winding through downtown Prince George, Highway 16 crosses the Fraser River on the Yellowhead Bridge. The bridge spans the river just below the mouth of the Nechako, one of the great confluences in British Columbia; the Nechako drains most of the central plateau, and the upper Fraser drains the central Rockies and eastern Cariboo Mountains. The northern edge of the city is framed by high bluffs along the Nechako River. The silts, sands and gravels forming these bluffs were laid down in a large glacial lake that formed at the end of the Pleistocene. This lake—dubbed Lake Fraser by geologists—extended from Williams Lake in the south to

Goatsbeard. RICHARD CANNINGS

the big bend of the Fraser River in the north and west to Vanderhoof.

The highway climbs back onto the Fraser Plateau and continues eastward, past the airport and around the north side of Mt. Tabor. Ten kilometres past the Mt. Tabor ski area there is a wildlife-viewing pull-off on the north side of the road, the Grove Burn observation site. A large fire burned 25,000 hectares of forest here in 1961. The willow, aspen and birch that grew up on the burned-over area offered ideal winter food for moose and for years many could be seen from the viewing tower here. The trees are too high now, both for viewing and for optimal moose habitat, but trails cut in spokelike fashion from the viewing tower provide some new growth for moose food as well as the possibility of a sighting.

About 4 kilometres to the east of the Grove Burn pull-off, the highway crosses the Willow River, which flows through a narrow canyon. The Willow River has an important chinook salmon spawning run of about two thousand fish annually. The Canadian Institute of Forestry has built a trail leading from the Willow River Rest Area with interpretive signs about local forest ecology.

The spruce forests at Vama Vama Creek were clear-cut in 1981 and replanted the following year to lodgepole pine. Once the forest was opened up, the shallow-rooted spruce trees became susceptible to widespread blowdowns; subsequent harvesting to salvage blowdown trees in 1988 and 1992 greatly enlarged the clear-cut. A large area south of Purden Lake, along the Bowron River Forest Service Road, was clear-cut between 1980 and 1986 to salvage trees killed by spruce bark beetles. Harvesting did little to control the outbreaks, and eventually a series of clear-cuts had expanded into a single block of about 50,000 hectares—certainly the largest single clear-cut in the world.

Spruce beetle outbreaks are a natural component of the environment here—John McLean, a fur trader in the Prince George area, noted a large outbreak in 1836. Many of the trees affected in the 1980s were probably given a boost of sunlight and growth 150 years ago when the mature trees around them died off.

The Bowron River is one of the larger tributaries of the Fraser and another important salmon river. About twenty thousand sockeye salmon spawn in the Bowron and use its lakes as nurseries, and up to ten thousand chinook spawn in the river as well. The sockeye spawn in the Bowron in late August.

As the highway swings around the north side of the Cariboo Mountains, the climate becomes even wetter. Beyond the Bowron River Forest Service Road, there are stands of subalpine fir and spruce, but these quickly give way to western redcedar and western hemlock. You have entered the Interior Cedar–Hemlock Zone once again (last seen at Moricetown along the Bulkley River). These forests were infested by hemlock loopers in the 1980s, and large patches of dead trees—predominantly hemlock but also some redcedar—are visible, as are growing blocks of clear-cuts made to salvage the timber. Spruce and subalpine fir reappear repeatedly down the trench, especially in the cooler valleys of creeks flowing out of the Cariboo Mountains.

These wet forests rarely succumb to forest fires and therefore can grow beyond old-growth forests into antique forests. Most of the Interior forests have a major fire every few centuries, but these wetter forests have likely stood here for more than a thousand years. Insect outbreaks have thinned their ranks on occasion, but there have been large trees here for more than a millennium. One of the best indicators of the age of a forest is not the size of the trees but the diversity of lichens growing on them. Many of the lichens on these trees are very slow growing and slow to spread and do not show up in forests less than three hundred years old. The wet forests along the Fraser River between Prince George and McBride are among the most

Gold dust lichen on western redcedar trunks. RICHARD CANNINGS

diverse in lichen species, and therefore among the oldest forests in the country. One of these lichens is gold dust lichen, which grows on the trunks of large redcedars that look for all the world as if someone had spray-painted them. You can explore these old forests along the Ancient Forest Trail, located on the east side of the highway, 6.6 kilometres southeast of the Slim Creek Rest Area.

As you near McBride, the forest becomes drier and you re-enter the Sub-boreal Spruce Zone. The valley bottom is a broad patchwork of large farm fields. An isolated population of long-billed curlews nests in these fields; like the Vanderhoof curlews, these big grassland sandpipers have moved into the McBride area since the valley bottom forests were cleared and planted to grains. The highway crosses the Fraser River at McBride, providing the first look at the river since Prince George and one of the only glimpses you will have until you reach Highway 5. You are now on the eastern slope of the valley, the slope that catches the warm afternoon sun, and the forest changes abruptly to Douglas-fir and aspen. Trembling aspen dominates here because of large fires that destroyed the older forests in the 1920s. These large aspen monocultures are also susceptible to outbreaks of insects, especially tent caterpillars and satin moths. Aspen have an advantage over conifers in that they can withstand defoliation, but occasionally tent caterpillars will maintain an outbreak for several consecutive years, stressing the aspens to the point that many do die.

As you cross the Fraser River you get a good sense of the straight-line design of the Rocky Mountain Trench, its sloping walls smoothed by huge rivers of ice that filled the valley during the Pleistocene. The structure gives a repetitive quality to the mountains along the western wall—every peak has a small cirque on its east face, every cirque has a snow field and every snow field has a small creek draining down the trench wall to the Fraser.

The highest major chinook salmon spawning grounds on the Fraser River are at Tête Jaune Cache, though a few adventurous fish conquer Rearguard Falls, as explained in Chapter 4. At Tête Jaune Cache, the Fraser pours out of the Rockies and Highway 16 meets Highway 5; both routes follow the river to Yellowhead Pass.

Tent Caterpillars

Tent caterpillars have cyclic populations. Every eight to eleven years, tent caterpillar numbers increase to astronomic proportions for a couple of summers, then disappear over the next few years before mushrooming again a decade later.

In the year of the decline, the caterpillars first appear healthy but soon become lethargic and then begin to die by the thousands. The cause of death, and perhaps the driving force of the entire cycle, is a disease agent called the nuclear polyhedrosis virus. Viral bodies on leaves are eaten by the caterpillar and replicate in the nuclei of the caterpillar's cells. Within a week or so, millions of viral bodies are produced, and the caterpillar literally bursts, leaving a limp cadaver on the leaf and a huge number of viruses to spread the disease to other caterpillars. When most of the caterpillars are dead, the viruses have very few hosts in which to replicate and outside their hosts are slowly destroyed by ultraviolet light. A few survive in shaded areas and after ten years or so begin to build up in the caterpillar population again as the moths start to multiply—and so the cycle goes.

SIX

The Tsawwassen and Patricia Bay Highways

HIGHWAY 17

THIS IS one of British Columbia's shortest highways yet one of its most travelled. Linking Vancouver with Victoria, it is traversed by thousands of businesspeople and tourists each day. It begins at an interchange on Highway 99 just south of the George Massey Tunnel under the south arm of the Fraser River, and its entire mainland route is across the un–British Columbian flatness of the Fraser delta. The ferry trip from Tsawwassen to Swartz Bay takes you across the Strait of Georgia and through the postcard scenery of the Gulf Islands. The final leg is a short drive through the farmland of the Saanich peninsula to Victoria.

The Fraser Delta

The Fraser River is the largest river in British Columbia, extending 1368 kilometres and draining a watershed of 234,000 square kilometres. With a mean outflow of 3678 cubic metres per second (the equivalent of 8 million tanker trucks of water per day), the mighty, muddy Fraser dumps a lot of silty sediment at its mouth. The delta extends from New Westminster to the outer banks of Lulu Island, a length of 30.5 kilometres and a total area of 572 square kilometres.

Facing page: Active Pass. RICHARD CANNINGS

It is advancing about 8.5 metres per year into the Strait of Georgia along an active front 22.5 kilometres long from Tsawwassen north to Vancouver. The deposits of the delta are on average 115 metres thick. The pattern of deposition at the mouth of the Fraser has been radically altered in the past century as dykes and jetties have trained the water flow away from the delta, and channels are constantly being dredged for river traffic.

These deposits are rich farming soil, though they often become inundated with winter rains, and the entire delta is dyked to keep high tidal surges off the land. Much of this land was salt marsh until the dykes were built and the land drained. Waterfowl are still abundant here in winter, flying in from the tidal flats to use the fields for resting and feeding. In recent years, the numbers of swans has been increasing. Both trumpeter swans and tundra swans can be seen along the highway, especially in the fields just north of the interchange with Highway 99 and the fields near the water slides at Tsawwassen. The Fraser delta is also one of the best wintering grounds for hawks and eagles in Canada. You can almost always see red-tailed and rough-legged hawks perched on roadside fenceposts in winter or soaring overhead on their broad wings, looking for mice in the fields below. Northern harriers course over the fields, tilting on their long, narrow wings and tail (watch for the white patch at the base of the tail) and listening for mice with their sharp ears.

At Tsawwassen the highway angles west and travels over the tidal flats on a long causeway, offering a great opportunity to see the wildlife of the flats without having to don rubber boots and go for a long walk at low tide. These mud flats, and the waters just off-shore from them, are part of the Fraser River estuary, and estuaries are among the richest environments on the planet. Most open ocean environments are rather sterile, since any nutrients in them eventually sink into the deeps and stay there. Estuaries provide a constantly renewed source of nutrients through the organic materials carried by the river, and they concentrate this bounty through a process called entrainment. As the river's fresh water flows out over the salt water, it pulls the upper layers of the heavier salt water along with

Western Sandpipers

Motorists racing to catch the Tsaw-wassen ferry in the evening in early August are likely to drive by one of the most amazing wildlife spectacles in the province. As the evening tide comes in, covering the vast mud flats of the Fraser Delta and Boundary Bay, flocks of tiny sandpipers are forced into smaller and smaller areas. Small flocks coalesce into larger groups, and as the last flats are covered, wheeling flocks of up to thirty thousand birds flash in the last rays of the sun.

Almost all these birds are western sandpipers, which breed on the Arctic coast of Alaska and winter on the shores of South America. Weighing only 23 grams and measuring only 15 centimetres long, these birds can fly up to 1500 kilometres between stops. Such flights burn a lot of fat, and the sandpipers must spend about four days refuelling before continuing.

Almost the entire world population of western sandpipers visits the Fraser Delta on the way north in spring and again on the way south in late summer. About a million birds pass through on their way north in April, adorned with their fresh, rust-spangled breeding plumage. The first returnees are seen in late June, the rusty feathers fading, to be replaced by grey winter feathers. These early birds are adults, which abandon their young on the breeding grounds as soon as they can fly short distances and fend for themselves. By late July, most of the adults have passed through and the first of the juveniles are arriving.

Juveniles form the huge flocks of late summer. These birds, grey and white except for a fresh, rusty shoulder, have flown all the way from Alaska by themselves. Like most young migrant birds, they are born with an innate sense of which direction to go and how long to keep flying.

It was once thought that they fed primarily on tiny shrimplike amphipods called *Corophium*, but recent research has shown that about half their daily food intake is in the form of biofilm, a mucous-like layer on top of the mud, rich with microbes and nutrients. At the height of spring migration, the birds can consume 20 tonnes of this, well, snot-like material every day on the Fraser Delta.

Above: RICHARD CANNINGS

it, creating a deep countercurrent of saline water into the estuary. Most silt and detritus sinking into the salt water below the brackish wedge is thus carried back toward the river mouth and deposited on the bottom.

In spring and late summer, the mud flats are often covered with vast flocks of tiny sandpipers refuelling on their migratory journey. Tens of thousands of dunlin, another small sandpiper, spend the winter here before returning to their breeding grounds in the High Arctic. From late March through early May, thousands of Brant geese stop over to feast on eelgrass in the intertidal zone, gathering energy for the flight to Alaska and beyond. These small geese forsake British Columbia on their return flight in fall, travelling nonstop from Alaska to their wintering grounds in Baja California. Brant populations declined along the Pacific coast in the 1960s but have recently stabilized at around 125,000 birds.

The headland south of the jetty is Point Roberts, part of Washington State (the ferry terminal is just north of the U.S. border). Point Roberts was once an island, but the growth of the Fraser River delta attached it to the mainland about a thousand years ago. Most of the great blue herons that feed on the Fraser Delta nest in a large colony (about three hundred pairs) on Point Roberts.

The Strait of Georgia and the Gulf Islands

Once the ferry is under way, it begins to cross the Strait of Georgia. The first 16 kilometres of this voyage is through the silty waters of the Fraser River plume. The fresh water coming out of the river rides on top of the heavier salt water, and you can usually see distinct lines of colour change where the most recent push of river water has overridden a previous plume. These cycles of discharge occur because of the tides—at high tide the sea pushes the fresh water of the Fraser back upriver, then releases the river flow again as the water level drops to low tide in the strait. During spring freshet in May and June, the Fraser plume extends across the strait to Galiano Island, turning the inland sea into a brackish tidal lake.

REST STOP

Tsawwassen Ferry Terminal

SINCE YOU USUALLY have to wait for some time to board the ferry at Tsawwassen, it is a good idea to get out and take a closer look at the edge of the Fraser Delta and its bird life. On the south side of the terminal is a rocky breakwater that is usually covered with double-crested cormorants. These large black seabirds are fish-eating specialists. You can often see them sitting on the rocks or pilings with their wings outstretched, presumably drying them out after a series of dives.

Take a close look at the wooden pilings around the ferry dock—they are covered in barnacles and mussels below the tide line, and you can often see black turnstones running up and down the sloping timbers, probing the mussel shells for a meal. These sandpipers blend in surprisingly well with the dark wood, and you often cannot see them until they fly a short distance, spreading their startlingly black-and-white wings and giving loud, whistling calls. A large flock of gulls and terns gathers on the north side of the ferry terminal; in late summer this flock is often dominated by Caspian terns, large white birds with black caps and long scarlet bills.

Above: Black turnstone with larger surfbirds and smaller dunlin.
RICHARD CANNINGS

> There must be some copious river here, for we sailed two leagues
> through water more sweet than salt.
> JOSÉ MARÍA NARVAEZ, off the Fraser Delta, 1791

Between the Tsawwassen ferry terminal and Active Pass, there is usually little wildlife to see on the water, though occasionally a pod of killer whales crosses the bow. On a clear day, the glacier-covered volcanic cone of Mt. Baker (3285 metres) is visible on the eastern horizon. If you want to relax inside the ferry or eat a meal in the cafeteria, the eastern leg of the trip is the best time to do it.

If at all possible, try to be out on the deck by the time you reach the Gulf Islands at Active Pass, because there is almost always a wildlife spectacle waiting there. The Gulf Islands are a significant barrier to the daily tidal flow in from the Strait of Juan de Fuca. At maximum flow the sea level on one side of the pass can be almost a metre higher than that on the other side, creating a riverlike flow through the pass. Although nowhere near the strongest tidal flow in British Columbia, the currents through Active Pass can move at rates of about 6 knots.

The effect of these strong currents, which flow through Active Pass four times a day (twice from the west, twice from the east), is to constantly bring up cold, nutrient-rich waters from the sea floor. These nutrients feed plankton, which attract fish, and the fish attract seals, sea-lions and seabirds by the thousands, especially in winter. As you approach the Georgina Point lighthouse on the northeasterly tip of Mayne Island, you can often see hundreds of Pacific loons gathered on the water, diving to feed on the abundant herring. The loons are often joined at either end of the pass by Brandt's Cormorants, which migrate north from California and Mexico after their nesting season to spend the winter in Canada—quite the opposite of most migrant birds in Canada. They are similar to the Double-crested Cormorants you might have seen at Tsawwassen, but in early spring they grow impressive fine white plumes on their necks. You will also see a few of the smaller Pelagic Cormorants, which in spring have a large white patch on their flanks.

Active Pass is perhaps most spectacular in April, when spawning herring are moving through in large schools and shrimplike zooplankton are burgeoning. The cormorants and loons are in their spring finery, and the zooplankton attracts thousands of handsome Bonaparte's gulls, small gulls with black heads and white wing flashes. Bald eagles also gather in the pass in winter and spring, and a few can be seen here all year long. If you look closely in the trees on Mayne Island and above the cliffs of Galiano Island, you should be able to count twenty or thirty eagles.

At the west end of Active Pass, you can often see sea-lions in the water or hauled up on rocks off Helen Point on Mayne Island. There are two species of sea-lions in B.C. waters—the large brown Steller's sea-lion, with a bearlike head and a roar like a Formula 1 car, and the smaller dark California sea-lion, with a high forehead and a bark like a circus seal (since all circus seals were California sea-lions).

The other big mammals that you might be lucky enough to see from the ferry are killer whales, or orcas. Three pods of these magnificent animals roam the Gulf Island waters in summer and early autumn, pursuing salmon as they return to the Fraser River. In 2012, there were 88 killer whales in this population, down from a high of 98 in 1995. The reasons for this decline are not known for certain but likely include high contaminant levels in the whales and their food chain and the serious decline in salmon stocks over the past few decades, especially of chinook salmon, the whales' preferred prey. These pods provided many of the first killer whales that were captured for display in large aquariums; 47 were taken from this area between 1967 and 1973.

The ferry route takes you quite close to some of the Gulf Islands, especially in Active Pass. Rainfall here is about 80 centimetres

Bonaparte's gull. RICHARD CANNINGS

Killer whales, or orcas, follow migrating salmon into the Strait of Georgia every summer. RICHARD CANNINGS

per year, 50 centimetres less than in downtown Vancouver, and the result is a very different habitat. Instead of western hemlock rain forest, the islands have a Douglas-fir forest with open grasslands on the south-facing slopes, a Garry oak savanna.

After Active Pass, the ferry travels through a wider channel between Prevost Island on the north and North Pender Island on the south, then passes Beaver Point on the southeastern tip of Saltspring Island. Beaver Point is part of Ruckle Provincial Park. The next small island to the south of the ferry route is also a park; Portland Island was presented as a gift to Princess Margaret during her visit to British Columbia in 1958, then returned to the province to become Princess Margaret Marine Park in 1967. The tiny island on the west side of Portland is Brackman Island, which became a provincial Ecological Reserve in 1989 to preserve a prime example of the Gulf Islands ecosystem.

The Saanich Peninsula

The ferry docks at Swartz Bay, a small harbour near the northern end of the Saanich Peninsula, and Highway 17 continues south for 30 kilometres to Victoria. Most of the route is inland, away from the sea, but it does skirt the edge of Tsehum Harbour just south of the ferry terminal. This shallow bay is typical of thousands of small bays along the coast, with mud flats at low tide. Buffleheads, small black-and-white diving ducks, frequent the bay during the winter, and great blue herons fish in the shallows all year round.

You quickly reach the town of Sidney and pass the Victoria airport on the west side of the road. The airport is one of the best spots in North America to see Sky Larks, a Eurasian species that was introduced into southwestern British Columbia in 1903. Although the mainland populations quickly died out, the Vancouver Island population grew to over a thousand birds until urbanization and fragmentation of habitat resulted in a rapid decline after 1970. There are now fewer than a hundred Sky Larks on the Saanich peninsula.

About 10 kilometres south of Sidney, you pass a broad, flat valley to the east of the road. This is the Martindale Valley, centred on Martindale Road and bounded by Island View Beach Road on the north. A rich agricultural area in the summer, it becomes a mecca for waterfowl in winter, when its fields are flooded with rains, and several thousand American Wigeons and Mallards, hundreds of Canada geese and many trumpeter swans arrive to feed. Birders can regularly see over a hundred species of birds in this small area on a midwinter day, making it one of the richest winter birding sites in Canada.

The highway climbs above the Martindale Valley, passing Bear Hill Park to the west, then reaches Elk Lake. The lake was presumably named after the Roosevelt elk, the coastal subspecies of this large deer, which was once widespread in southwestern British Columbia but is now restricted to Vancouver Island. Elk Lake is a rich lake, though its natural ecosystem has been upset by a myriad of introduced species, including rainbow and cutthroat trout, small-mouth bass, brown and black bullheads, pumpkinseed sunfish and, most serious of all, bullfrogs.

Bullfrog Invasion

The bullfrog is the largest frog in North America—adult females are the size of a dinner plate and weigh up to 500 grams. They are easily recognized by their brownish colour and large eardrum (much bigger than the eye) and the mating call of the male—a loud, deep *bwu-u-um, bwu-u-um* or *jug-o-rum*. The females lay huge, floating masses of eggs, which hatch into tadpoles that remain in the pond for at least two years before transforming into small frogs.

Bullfrogs are not native to British Columbia and were probably first brought here because many people prize their large legs as food. Unfortunately, they have become part of the natural ecosystem on southern Vancouver Island and in the Lower Mainland, where they are voracious predators, eating everything from young ducks and mice to fish and other frogs. They have been implicated in the almost complete disappearance of the Oregon spotted frog.

RUSS HAYCOCK

The south end of Elk Lake is called Beaver Lake; the lakes were separate until Colquitz Creek was dammed in the 1870s to create a water supply for Victoria. The rich fish fauna of the lakes supports a wide variety of fish-eating animals, including otters, osprey, mergansers and loons.

SEVEN

The Chilcotin Highway

HIGHWAY 20

HIGHWAY 20 is one of the best-kept secrets in British Columbia. Beginning inauspiciously at a junction with Highway 97 in the industrial outskirts of Williams Lake, it soon crosses the Fraser River and begins to traverse the Chilcotin Plateau. After more than 300 kilometres of prairies, lakes, rivers and mountain skylines, it gradually ascends to the high mountain forests of Tweedsmuir Provincial Park. Then, in 10 kilometres, it drops precipitously to the coastal forests and glacier-topped peaks of the Bella Coola Valley, ending abruptly at a small dock at the edge of the Bella Coola estuary.

▶ **Williams Lake to Anahim Lake:** The Chilcotin Plateau

The Chilcotin Plateau is the portion of the Fraser Plateau west of the Fraser River. Its eastern edge lays open several major geological stories, the most obvious of which is the great Miocene lava flows that covered the plateau 12 to 20 million years ago. On the west side of the plateau are three large shield volcanoes: the Itcha, the Ilgachuz and the Rainbow ranges. These mountains, like the huge volcanoes of Hawaii, erupted with immense lava flows, unlike the explosive

ash eruptions of Mt. St. Helens, Mt. Mazama and the other Cascade volcanoes. The lava flowed over a plateau that already had a subdued relief after millions of years of erosion. When the lava cooled, it formed a flat skin over the plateau that can be seen where major rivers such as the Fraser and Chilcotin cut its surface.

As the highway leaves Highway 97, it immediately crosses Williams Lake Creek, the small stream that flows from Williams Lake 10 kilometres west to the Fraser River. The large sawmill on the northwest side of the road processes trees from all across the Chilcotin. The road gradually ascends through a dense forest of young Douglas-firs, then begins the descent to the Fraser River. About 10 kilometres from Williams Lake, you can see a large limestone bluff in front of you, on the north side of the highway. This is a spectacular outcrop of the Cache Creek Terrane, rock formed in tropical seas in the Permian period, 260 million years ago. As explained on p. 26, the Cache Creek Terrane was sandwiched between Stikinia and Quesnellia when the former collided with North America about 180 million years ago.

As the highway reaches the Fraser River, it turns south along a narrow bench high above the river. You can see more limestone bluffs across the river, as well as silt benches like the one the highway is travelling on. These benches formed in the late Pleistocene as glacial silt filled narrow lakes along the sides of large valley glaciers that were stagnating as the thinner upland ice melted. The highway then crosses the Fraser and immediately begins to ascend to the plateau surface on the west side of the river. The valley bottom here is one of the northernmost extents of hot, dry grasslands in the province, and you can often see southern valley birds such as Lazuli Buntings singing from the shrubs along the road. Grassland butterflies, such as the two-tailed and Oregon swallowtails, also reach their northern limit here.

At the major switchback just south of the bridge, you can see Doc English Bluff, another of the big limestone bluffs along this section of the Fraser. Since many plants cannot grow on limestone soils, the plant communities on these bluffs are very different from those on

Facing page: A narrow strip of dry grassland runs up the Fraser River north to Williams Lake. RICHARD CANNINGS

surrounding slopes. One plant species, the Carolina whitlow-grass, is found in British Columbia only on Doc English Bluff.

As you swing back to the north, you will be facing the columnar cliffs of plateau basalt that underlie most of the Chilcotin. A few more kilometres and you are on the plateau itself, driving through the grasses of Becher's Prairie, one of the northernmost outposts of extensive dry grasslands in British Columbia. Its mix of pothole lakes, grassland and forests give it a tremendous biological diversity. The open Douglas-fir forests, especially those at the edge of the plateau along the Fraser, are home to flammulated owls and common poor-wills, two small, nocturnal, insect-eating birds that are not found any farther north in the world. Northern species such as great gray owls nest in the lodgepole pine and trembling aspen woodlands here.

Only 2 kilometres after reaching the plateau, you will pass a large communications tower on the north side of the road. This is a loran tower, one of three such facilities in western North America, which send out signals used by ships at sea for navigation, a technology quickly being replaced by satellite-based systems. From this point a distant butte, called the Dome, is visible on the north-western horizon—it is a volcanic plug. Beyond the small community of Riske Creek, the highway begins to climb up the South Riske Creek valley. Black terns often course over the marshy reservoir of Becher Lake on summer days. This valley provides a dramatic example of the differences between north- and south-facing slopes, with thick spruce forests to the south of the highway (facing north) and open grasslands to the north. The highway soon reaches the top of the plateau and levels out in a forest of young lodgepole pine. A rest

Western Kingbird. STEVE CANNINGS

Vertical columns of basalt form the skin of the Chilcotin Plateau, the result of massive lava flows that covered central British Columbia in Miocene times, about 20 million years ago. RICHARD CANNINGS

area above Hanceville provides a view of the Chilcotin River valley, though you cannot see the river itself.

The highway descends to the valley at Hanceville, where basalt lava flow terraces are conspicuous on the south side of the river. The dry slopes north of the highway are forested with open stands of Douglas-fir. Junipers, both the small tree form of Rocky Mountain juniper and the low, spreading common juniper, are scattered under the larger trees. This pattern continues all the way to Alexis Creek and beyond, with some spectacular views of plateau basalt cliffs.

About 7 kilometres west of Alexis Creek, the Chilcotin River flows through Bull Canyon. Compare the glacial blue hues of the river here with its clear brown colour at Redstone, 25 kilometres farther west. The Chilko River meets the Chilcotin just west of Bull Canyon. The Chilko, the largest tributary of the Chilcotin, brings in large quantities of fine glacial flour sediments from the icy peaks of the Coast Mountains, while the upper Chilcotin drains the pine and spruce forests of the Chilcotin Plateau, bringing only brown tannin pigments to the mix.

Disappearing Grasslands

The grasslands of the B.C. Interior are one of the province's rarest and most threatened ecosystems and have been disappearing at an alarming rate over the past few decades. Intensive agriculture and urbanization have played an important part in this loss, but in many parts of the Interior one of the most worrisome threats is forest encroachment—you can't see the grassland for the trees.

Many B.C. grasslands were maintained for centuries by periodic fires that swept away young trees. Fire suppression has stopped that natural cycle, and since 1960 around 37 per cent of the grasslands on the Chilcotin Plateau have been invaded by lodgepole pines and Douglas-firs. These invasions occur at intervals, usually during a wet summer that follows several dry years. Many of the young trees on Becher's Prairie, for instance, germinated in 1982 and 1983. Once a new clump of trees is established, encroachment continues steadily out from the shaded north side. Range managers are experimenting with several techniques, including fire, to reverse this trend of grassland and loss.

Facing Page: Douglas-fir and trembling aspen woodlands along the edge of Becher's Prairie near Riske Creek.

SYDNEY CANNINGS

Beyond Bull Canyon the highway leaves the river for a 20-kilometre cutoff through rolling hills forested in Douglas-fir. When it reaches the Chilcotin again at Redstone, the river has changed character completely—instead of a large blue river, it is now a small brown stream. Two rivers join the Chilcotin between here and Bull Canyon—the Chilanko and the much-larger Chilko River—hence the dramatic change in size. This is the last you will see of the Chilcotin on the trip west.

For the next while, the highway follows the Chilanko River. The landscape is quite flat through this section, the sandy soils forested with lodgepole pine and covered by creeping growths of kinni-kinnick, stonecrop and juniper. About 20 kilometres from the bridge, you come to the rock hill of volcanic rock that gave Redstone its name; it is best viewed from the west.

REST STOP

Chilanko Marsh

JUST PAST CHILANKO Forks, a Wildlife Viewing sign directs you to the Chilanko Marsh Wildlife Management Area, about 3.5 kilometres from the highway on the Puntzi airport road. This is a classic Chilcotin marsh and a great place to stop about halfway across the Chilcotin Plateau.

Chilanko Marsh is alive with beavers, muskrats and many species of waterfowl. You can see eastern kingbirds and Wilson's warblers along its willow-lined shores and mountain bluebirds and sharp-tailed grouse in the surrounding open lodgepole pine woodland. If water levels are lower in spring and late summer, large numbers of migrating sandpipers and plovers often stop to refuel along the muddy shores. If you are lucky, you may spot one of the most majestic of marsh birds, the sandhill crane.

Facing page: Sandhill crane. RICHARD CANNINGS

The upper Chilanko drainage is full of small ponds and marshes that make it a haven for wildlife. Beyond Le Blanc Lake, the highway climbs to a very flat section of plateau—sand and silt deposits laid down on the bottom of a large lake that covered this area at the end of the Pleistocene. The flat plateau affords good views of the Chilcotin Ranges of the Coast Mountains to the south and west. Lodgepole pine continues to be the dominant tree—and will be for another 150 kilometres until you are beyond Anahim Lake—and the main understorey shrub is the grey-green soopolallie, or soapberry.

The community of Tatla Lake is framed on the north by grassy, south-facing slopes of silt deposits laid down in the glacial lake mentioned above. These slopes have the westernmost patches of bluebunch wheatgrass, the characteristic bunchgrass of the southern

Interior of British Columbia. Large Douglas-firs tower over the grasses from here to the Klinaklini River (also known as the Kleena Kleene); beyond the river the climate becomes too cold for this temperate montane species.

Just west of Tatla Lake, you cross an inconspicuous but important divide, leaving the Chilcotin drainage for a series of watersheds—the Klinaklini, Dean and Bella Coola—that flow directly through the Coast Mountains to the Pacific Ocean. Perhaps "directly" is not completely accurate; the upper Klinaklini flows north and east from the Pantheon Range almost to Tatla Lake, then turns abruptly northwestward to One Eye Lake, where it begins a broad turn to the south and finally empties into the head of Knight Inlet. The dark spire of Perkins Peak (2850 metres) is a prominent landmark south of the highway up the Klinaklini Valley.

Past the One Eye Lake road, the highway swings west between a rocky hill and small alkaline lake into a marshy valley. The hay fields of Kleena Kleene are filled with foxtail barley, a native grass indicative of alkaline soils. The highway climbs onto sandy hills covered in small lodgepole pines and kinnikinnick. The forest floor is littered with trunks of larger pines, killed by a mountain pine beetle outbreak in the late 1970s and another outbreak about twenty-five

Foxtail barley is a typical grass around alkaline Chilcotin ponds and meadows.
SYDNEY CANNINGS

years later. In the dry climate and sandy soils of the western Chilcotin Plateau, lodgepole pine is a climax species. Elsewhere in the province, it is replaced over time by climax forests of spruce or fir. The highway leaves the main Klinaklini Valley and continues northwest along the aspen-lined McClinchy River, one of the Klinaklini's main tributaries.

The highway levels out by the birch-willow meadows of Caribou Flats, then goes over a low pass to the Dean River drainage. The sand and gravel soils here are often arranged in ribbon-link ridges called eskers, laid down by small rivers flowing underneath the large glacier that covered this area during the Pleistocene. From Nimpo Lake you can see the Ilgachuz Mountains rising from the plateau in the north. This range, topped on its north side by Far Mountain (2408 metres), is one of three shield volcanoes that were active during the Miocene, spewing lava across the Chilcotin Plateau. The other two volcanoes are now the Itcha Mountains and Rainbow Range. Today the Ilgachuz are home to the northwesternmost herd of bighorn sheep in the world and are also the southern limit of Arctic tundra species such as the American golden-plover and brown lemming.

After you cross Pelican Creek north of Anahim Lake, you have a better view of the Ilgachuz in the northwest, with a more distant view of its sister range—the Itchas—to the east and occasional glimpses of the spectacular Anahim Peak (1892 metres) to the northwest. Anahim Peak is at the eastern edge of the volcanic Rainbow Range and was an important source of obsidian—volcanic glass—for indigenous peoples. The obsidian was used to make arrowheads, spear points and other sharp tools.

▶ Anahim Lake to Bella Coola: A Steep Descent to the Pacific

The highway now begins a very gradual climb across the southern edge of the Rainbow Range, westward to Tweedsmuir Provincial Park and Heckman Pass (1550 metres). The forest is at first pure lodgepole pine—most of it killed by the mountain pine beetle epidemic that swept through British Columbia in the first few years of the 2000s. West of Green River, a mixed forest of lodgepole pine and Engelmann spruce was burned by two large forest fires in 2009 and 2010. The pass itself is a broad area of bogs and fens, the sedges dotted with the white tufts of cottongrass seedheads. Heckman Pass is unlike most passes through British Columbia mountains—instead of a narrow defile between towering peaks, it is simply the edge of the Interior Plateau. From that edge, the road plunges over "The Hill" into the deep, glacier-carved Atnarko Valley. The Atnarko, and later the Bella Coola, River guides the highway through the mountains.

The road descends, moderately at first, along Young Creek. At the Young Creek bridge, the forest is typical of Interior subalpine zones—a mix of lodgepole pine, Engelmann spruce and subalpine fir. The road continues for 3 more kilometres, then descends very steeply for 10 kilometres. The forest changes rapidly to Douglas-fir and Douglas maple, then to large western redcedars and Douglas-firs at the bottom of the hill. You are now in the Atnarko Valley, with no sign of a plateau in sight.

The Atnarko flows clear and green from a series of lakes upstream, providing important spawning habitat for pink salmon and to a lesser extent for coho, chum and chinook salmon. Serious flood events on the Atnarko in 2010 and 2011 damaged the pink salmon spawning beds at the height of the spawning season, and the population may have been significantly impacted. Grizzly bears are common in this valley, attracted by the annual bounty of easily caught fish. The highway continues down the Atnarko Valley through magnificent Douglas-firs, past local areas of lodgepole pine woodlands on rocky outcrops and dry, sandy riverine terraces. The Fisheries Pool picnic site provides a nice rest area along the clear green waters of the Atnarko, as well as an opportunity to see fish and bears.

The highway and river bend north around the south ridge of Mt. Walker, then meet the Talchako River coming in from the south. Together, the two rivers form the Bella Coola, which takes on the milky colour of the glacialfed Talchako. Burnt Bridge Creek marks the route of the Grease Trail, a trading route used by the coastal Nuxalk and Interior Carrier peoples for millennia; Alexander Mackenzie followed this trail in 1793 on his trip overland to the Pacific from eastern Canada.

The Bella Coola Valley has a broader floodplain than its two tributaries, and hay fields appear around the community of Firvale. The high peaks of Table Mountain (2677 metres) and Stupendous Mountain (2700 metres) tower over the valley to the southeast, and Nusatsum Mountain (2600 metres) looms to the southwest. With its precipitous slopes and open, grassy forests, this end of the Bella Coola Valley is excellent mountain goat habitat; with luck you might see some at a mineral lick beside the highway at Assanany Creek.

After the highway crosses the Bella Coola River, the forests show signs of higher rainfall, with extensive red alder growing on the gravelly roadsides. Sitka spruce, a purely coastal species, is now common along the valley bottom, its long branches spreading like great arms from the tall trunks. The highway winds around a high gravel ridge at the mouth of the Nusatsum Valley and enters the wide lower Bella Coola Valley and the farm fields of Hagensborg.

The deep Bella Coola Valley is surrounded on all sides by spectacular peaks, including the well-named Stupendous Mountain. SYDNEY CANNINGS

Just before you reach the village of Bella Coola, the forest becomes draped in long, cream-coloured Methuselah's beard lichen. This hair lichen is the longest lichen in the world; some strands are more than a metre long. The highway goes through Bella Coola, then continues to the south side of the Bella Coola estuary and ends at a small government dock on the shores of North Bentinck Arm. The estuary is a rich tidal sedge marsh bordered by patches of sweet gale. From the dock you can continue your journey by boat or turn your vehicle around and head for the Hill once again.

EIGHT

The Stewart-Cassiar Highway

HIGHWAY 37

HIGHWAY 37, or the Stewart-Cassiar Highway, is one of the two great northern roads of British Columbia, winding through 725 kilometres of mountain valleys and plateaus between the Skeena Valley and the Alaska Highway in southern Yukon. The southern traveller may find that this journey will redefine what "northern British Columbia" means to them, or even what "north'" means. For much of the length of the highway, virtually half the length of the province, it is the only road traversing otherwise roadless wilderness. The human population is sparse; the largest settlement is Dease Lake, a regional centre with a population of only 650 souls. Northern wildlife is rich—moose and wolves may be seen, and grizzly and black bears are especially abundant. And winding through the Skeena and Cassiar Mountains, the scenery is always astonishing.

The road begins in the lush forests of the Skeena River valley and follows the Kitwanga River north into the Nass River drainage. North of Meziadin Junction, the highway follows the Bell-Irving River, and then crosses a low pass into the Ningunsaw River valley in the Iskut River watershed. Leaving the Ningunsaw River, but paralleling the Iskut, it climbs abruptly into the truly northern spruce forests at Bob Quinn Lake. At the headwaters of the Iskut, the gorgeous triplet of Kinaskan, Tatogga and Eddontenajon Lakes split the Spatsizi Plateau to the east from the Klastline Plateau and the massive volcanic edifice of Mount Edziza to the west. The highway then descends, twisting into the valley of the Stikine River. Approaching the town of Dease Lake, the highway leaves the south behind entirely, crossing the low pass into the Arctic drainage of the Dease and Liard Rivers. It then follows the Dease Lake valley north into the Cassiar Mountains and, at Boya Lake, leaves those mountains behind as well and debouches onto the Liard Plateau, a broad, flat, boreal plain.

➤ Kitwanga (Gitwangak) to Meziadin Junction:
The Valleys of the Skeena and the Nass

With the snowy summits of the Seven Sisters (2755 metres) at your back, you cross the Skeena River and begin the journey north. In the summer, the northern bank of the Skeena may be lined with anglers fishing for its abundant salmon (see Chapter Five, page 123).

This region is in the rain shadow of the Coast Mountains and transitional to the drier, more continental Sub-boreal Spruce Zone to the east—spruce trees here are hybrids between the coastal Sitka spruce and the interior boreal white spruce. This is the Interior Cedar-Hemlock Zone, characterized by great snowfalls in the winter and warm summers—and climax forests dominated by western redcedar or western hemlock. However, for much of the southern stretches of the road the forest is young and mixed, a reflection of past fires and recent extensive logging.

The moist road verge and the highway's sparse traffic make the Stewart-Cassiar the ideal bear-watching road. This is true especially in June, when billions of tasty dandelions carpet the cleared shoulders. Most of the bears seen are black bears; but perhaps one in ten will be a grizzly bear. The fortunate visitor will see a Kermode bear.

The highway passes by the small communities of Gitwangak and Kitwanga, and then follows the valley of the Kitwanga River northward. The Kitwanga River supports runs of all five Pacific salmon species, as well as steelhead. The river's sockeye salmon population

Towering black cottonwoods and hybrid spruce dominate the lush riparian forests along the Cranberry River. SYDNEY CANNINGS

was the mainstay of the Gitanyow people but has declined perilously in recent decades. The Gitanyow have voluntarily stopped their harvest of sockeyes and now monitor the state of the population. In odd-numbered years, the small but numerous pink salmon return to the Kitwanga in great abundance—sometimes almost 400,000 come home from the sea. About 6 kilometres past Gitanyow is Kitwancool Lake, a shallow, productive lake that is the sockeye salmon nursery of the Kitwanga system.

At the north end of Kitwancool Lake, the upper Kitwanga River swings west to its headwaters in the Hazelton Mountains. The northbound traveller crosses an unnoticed watershed boundary, entering the Nass River system as the highway slides in beside the Cranberry River. This was part of the route of the *Genim Sgeenix*, the "Grease Trail" of the Nisga'a people—each spring the Nisga'a harvested eulachon (see p. 126), extracted their bountiful oil and packed it overland to Gitanyow and Gitwangak to trade with the peoples of the interior. Over the last fifty years, however, the harvest at the mouth of the Nass has declined about 90 per cent, and the Nass population has been designated as Special Concern.

At Cranberry Junction, you can choose to turn left on the Nass Forest Service Road, which leads south to New Aiyansh and then down the Kitsumkalum Valley to Terrace. If you are approaching the Stewart-Cassiar Highway from Prince Rupert, this route is a good alternative for the beginning of your journey, though it is rougher and not recommended for low-clearance vehicles.

North of Cranberry Junction, the Stewart-Cassiar joins the Nass River itself on its journey north, but you rarely see the river through the thick forest. As it approaches Meziadin Lake, the highway crosses the rugged gorge of the Nass River on a narrow bridge. Here the river flows over the black shales of the sedimentary Bowser Basin. The Nass itself continues north into Spatsizi country to what has become known as the Sacred Headwaters, where the melt waters of snow-covered ridges flow into three great river systems—the Nass, the Skeena and the Stikine.

The sedimentary layers in the mountain faces around you are younger than, and overlay the older rocks of, Stikinia. These rocks had their origin far to the south of today's highway, in a large basin west of the Rocky Mountains. As the early mountains began to rise, erosional sediments collected in a large marine basin centred at about the latitude of Kamloops. Later, the whole interior portion of British Columbia was extruded north, almost like toothpaste being squeezed from its tube. The land eventually moved north 500 to 800 kilometres, sliding along strike-slip faults to both the east and to the west. Today, this mountainous region is still referred to as a basin by geologists—the Bowser Basin, referring to the rocks around Bowser Lake, which lies west of the highway north of its southern crossing of the Bell-Irving River.

North of the Nass crossing, the highway enters an area of exceptionally great snowfall. The high snowfalls are the result of the broad Nass Basin allowing Pacific winter storms free access to the interior, where they collide with cold Arctic air. Western redcedar and lodgepole pine both drop out of the forest here—you will not see redcedar again on this highway, but lodgepole pine will reappear in the boreal forest to the north.

The waters of the Ningunsaw River are filled with chalky grey glacial silts.
SYDNEY CANNINGS

Meziadin Lake is the rearing ground for much of the Nass River sockeye. Each year, 100,000 to 150,000 sockeye swim upriver to this spectacular lake. Two other species of salmon—chinook and coho—also spawn in the Meziadin system, and the lake also hosts rainbow trout, Dolly Varden, and mountain whitefish. The sockeye here not only spawn in creeks, but also along some of the lake's gravelly, wave-washed beaches. If you are travelling the highway in late summer or early fall, watch for them spawning in Hanna and Tintina Creeks.

➤ Meziadin Junction to Dease Lake:
From the Nass to the Stikine and Beyond
At Meziadin Junction, you can choose to take a relatively short side trip on Highway 37a to Stewart, B.C., and Hyder, Alaska, on

tidewater at the head of the Portland Canal. This highway leads you through the soaring Coast Mountains in a grand fashion, past the tumbling blue ice of the Bear Glacier.

After the junction, the main highway climbs over a low pass into the valley of the Bell-Irving River, one of the main northern tributaries of the Nass. The massive snowfalls bring a subalpine look to the valley forests, with tree clumps and forest openings of alder and willow thickets. Subalpine firs love the snow's abundant moisture and grow to world record size here, with some reaching 60 metres in height.

After the highway parts ways with the Bell-Irving, it follows its tributary, Snowbank Creek, north to Ningunsaw Pass, the low divide between the Nass and the Stikine drainages. Large wetlands span both sides of the highway in the area of the pass—home to beaver, moose and waterfowl, including migrating trumpeter swans. Ningunsaw is a native word meaning "bank beaver," referring to the beavers that choose to burrow in the banks of a river rather than build a stick lodge in a dammed pond. The slopes above the pass are ribboned with numerous avalanche paths covered in Sitka alder thickets, testament to the tremendous amount of snow that falls in these mountains. The glacier-fed waters of the Ningunsaw River flow into the Iskut River, which in turn joins the Stikine River.

The lush, low-elevation forests along the highway are dominated by western hemlock, with white spruce and black cottonwood along the river's edge. Along the roadside is an understory of cow parsnip, goatsbeard, thimbleberry and devil's club, all indicative of the cool, moist climate.

At Ogilvie Creek, the highway swings north, away from the westerly-flowing Ningunsaw, and climbs up to Bob Quinn Lake, where it rather suddenly leaves behind western hemlock and enters the true boreal spruce forest—the Boreal White and Black Spruce Zone. You have entered the land of long, cold winters, where snow lingers into May and comes again to stay in October.

At Bob Quinn Lake, you also enter the headwater valley of the Iskut River. The headwater lakes of the Iskut—Natadesleen,

The south-facing slopes of Todagin Mountain are prime winter range and lambing habitat for Stone's sheep. Because of this, they have been protected in the Todagin South Slope Provincial Park. Mountain goats are also common on the more precipitous slopes and ledges. SYDNEY CANNINGS

Kinaskan, Tatogga and Eddontenajon, are all famous for the native rainbow trout that thrive in them. These trout have been isolated for millennia by Cascade Falls, downstream of Natadesleen Lake.

About 4 kilometres north of the south end of Kinaskan Lake, the highway enters the exposed volcanic island arc of Stikinia (visible in the hill to the east), which south of this point has been covered by the younger Bowser Basin sediments. About 5 kilometres up the road, you will see your younger sedimentary friends in the Bowser Basin one last time in the high ridges that tower over the northern side of the Todagin River valley. The layered sandstones and shales can easily be distinguished—the resistant sandstones remain as cliffs, whereas the more easily eroded shales form the angled ledges.

Spatsizi Plateau Provincial Wilderness Park lies some distance to the east of the highway, beyond the valley of the Klappan River. Because the region is in the rain shadow of the mountains, it receives relatively little snow, so large populations of woodland caribou and Stone's sheep can thrive there. It is also one of the southern outposts for a number of birds and mammals associated with subarctic alpine regions, such as gray-cheeked thrush, Smith's longspur, and Arctic ground squirrel.

After leaving the village of Iskut and the Skeena Mountains behind, the highway climbs over a plateau-like pass at Forty Mile Flats. Near the top of the pass, watch on the right for a small, rough Tsaybe Mountain road leading back to the east. If you have a vehicle with good clearance, you can make the journey into the alpine and be rewarded with a view of Mt. Edziza to the west (see sidebar). As the highway begins its long, twisting descent into the valley of the Stikine River, watch for the Morchuea Lake turnoff to the west of the highway. A short drive in takes you to a productive plateau lake dotted with lilypads and northern waterfowl such as lesser scaup and surf scoters. Forty kilometres away on the southwestern horizon is the snow- and ice-capped summit of Mount Edziza.

At the highway bridge over the Stikine, the river is flowing through a rather gentle valley, but about 20 kilometres downstream it enters a

Mt. Edziza

Mt. Edziza (2787 metres), Canada's highest volcano, is part of a massive volcanic complex 40 kilometres long and 20 kilometres wide. The volcanic activity began about 7.5 million years ago, as the Pacific plate slid northward along the Queen Charlotte Fault to the west. The shearing effect of this movement on the western edge of the continent stretched, thinned and fractured the crust in this region, allowing magma to come to the surface. The plate continues to slide northward and even today the crust here is being stretched 2 centimetres per year. Eruptions in this complex occurred in five separate periods—the stratovolcano of Mt. Edziza itself was built in a series of eruptions that ended about 900,000 years ago, but the latest period of activity began only about 10,000 years ago. The most recent pumice from the region is undated, but believed to be younger than 500 years old. Mt. Edziza was the main source of obsidian (volcanic glass) for First Nations tool makers in the region and was traded as far away as Alaska and northern Alberta.

Lower Gnat Lake. SYDNEY CANNINGS

narrow defile with high, vertical rock walls—the Grand Canyon. The
ancient course of the river was blocked by lava flows from Mt. Edziza,
and the river has been forced to carve a dramatic, new course to the
north. The churning rapids and falls through the canyon prevent the
passage of any seagoing salmon to the reaches above.

At the top of the hill, you enter Gnat Pass, a gorgeous high valley
lined with sedge marshes, fens and small lakes. Although the slopes
above the pass are forested, the lower benches and valley bottom
have only scattered spruce trees and are dominated by thickets of
willow and birch. On the valley bottom is a shrub carr, a common
feature of the northern landscape. With such an abundance of willows, beaver are common here—look for their dams and lodges
throughout the wetlands.

Across the Gnat Lakes, you can see the flat terraces created when
sediments were deposited beside a valley glacier here at the end of
the ice ages. As you approach the highway summit north of the Gnat
Lakes, there is an unofficial pull-off on the west side of the road, right
beside a beautiful sloping, spring-fed fen. This is a fen rich in nutrients—and therefore rich in wildflowers, especially orchids.

The Stewart-Cassiar Highway 179

Just south of the village of Dease Lake, you cross the Tanzilla River as it rushes downhill toward the Stikine and then almost immediately crosses two unseen natural boundaries. Crossing beneath the road at about the "Welcome to Dease Lake" sign is the King Salmon Fault, where the ancient island arc of Stikinia meets up with the seafloor rocks of the Cache Creek Terrane (see p. 26). That geological boundary is hidden here by glacially deposited sediments, which also separate the Pacific-bound water of the Tanzilla from the northbound waters of Dease Lake. As you enter the village, you cross the Arctic continental divide and enter the watershed of the great Mackenzie River.

➤ Dease Lake to the Alaska Highway:
The Cassiar Mountains and Liard Plateau

From Dease Lake, a gravel road leads west for 100 kilometres to Telegraph Creek along the lower Stikine River. If you feel adventurous and take this side trip, you can see the columnar basalts formed during the eruptions of Mt. Edziza along the Stikine. Because Telegraph Creek is in the rain shadow of the Coast Mountains, the steep, south-facing slopes on the north side of the Stikine are covered in bunch grasses and other steppe plants, much like those in the dry interior of the province hundreds of kilometres to the south.

White bog orchids are plentiful in the springy turf of rich fens in Gnat Pass.
SYDNEY CANNINGS

Because it is in the Arctic watershed, Dease Lake is home to northern fish such as northern pike and Arctic grayling; lake trout, lake whitefish and burbot also swim through the depths.

Because you are traversing the region where exotic Pacific island

Serpentinite from the Cache Creek Terrane in a road cut near Dease Lake. This rock originates deep in the Earth's mantle, but as it is uplifted closer to the surface, water invades it and converts minerals like olivine and pyroxene into serpentine—the name comes from its resemblance to a snake's shiny skin. SYDNEY CANNINGS

arcs and ancient ocean floor collided with the leading edge of western North America, you will cross a number of important geological lines in the next hour or so of driving. At about the north end of Dease Lake you roll from the Cache Creek Terrane onto the ancient island arc of Quesnellia. For the next while, the highway follows the meandering course of the Dease River as it flows north toward its meeting with the Liard River. The lakes and wetlands along the winding river are excellent moose habitat.

About 15 kilometres north of the lake, the highway swings to the west and you cross a narrow slice of the Yukon-Tanana Terrane—you will see much more of this piece of the Earth's crust along the Swan Lake valley, south of Teslin.

The highway swings to the north again just before crossing the Dease River, and at this corner you cross the Cassiar Fault and enter ancient North America. However, the old sedimentary rocks of the North American continental shelf are not visible here because they are overlain by a younger granitic batholith. The modern landscape changes as well as you cross the Dease River, since the road now enters the Cassiar Mountains proper. Even though it is part of ancient North America, the Cassiar Terrane is given its own name and separate status because it has been displaced 500 to 800 kilometres north from its original position in southern British Columbia, along the strike-slip fault of the Northern Rocky Mountain Trench.

If you are travelling in the late autumn or early spring, look for migrating trumpeter swans in the open water along the Dease River.

The road turns north away from the Dease River and you see, for the first time on this trip, ancient North America. The mountains directly in front of you have a band of light-coloured marble running through them, made up of shallow-water sediments at the western edge of the young North American continent. These were laid down just as the Pacific Ocean was opening up for the first time. After some time, the rifting ocean grew wide enough that the margin collapsed into deep water; the darker sediments you see on top are the first (that is, oldest) deep-water deposits in the young Pacific Ocean.

After you pass Simmons and Cook Lakes to the west, the road swings to the north again, with Vines Lake on the east side. The Cassiar Terrane (ancient North America) is to your east, but directly in front of you is a dark ridge, with a light-coloured peak in the background. This mountain and the others around it record the power and relentlessness of the tectonic forces that shaped western North America. The dark rocks are ocean-floor basalts and deep-water sediments of the Slide Mountain Terrane. As North America moved westward relative to the Pacific, the ocean floor was peeled off and pushed up on top of the pale limestones that lay along the edge of North America. As the pushing continued, both crustal pieces were folded and raised into these mountains.

Cassiar was the company town for an asbestos mine that was active from 1953 to 1989. Asbestos is altered serpentinite from the Earth's mantle, here coming from the bottom of the Slide Mountain ocean. Cassiar held a tiny piece of asbestos in a small slice of serpentinite in a huge swath of oceanic crust—it was only discovered when

Boya Lake and the Horseranch Range. HANS ROEMER

geologists were told by First Nations people that the local goats bed-
ded down in wool made from rocks!

The Cassiar Mountains are also the world's largest source of
nephrite jade. This jade (the historical jade of Chinese sculpture) is a
tough silicate of calcium and magnesium. Gold is in these hills, too.
Prospectors moving north after the Cariboo Gold Rush discovered
placer gold here in 1874, and the largest all-gold nugget in British
Columbia's history—72 ounces—was taken out of McDame Creek
in 1877. Look along the highway outcrops for orange fractures with
white-quartz veins—these veins are the source of the placer gold in
the creeks.

The tidy, symmetrical shape of subalpine fir drops out of the forest north of Simmons Lake as you are entering the snow-shadow
zone east of the mountains.

The road re-enters ancient North America as it follows McDame
Creek downhill. The mountains at Good Hope Lake are like paint-
ings, with pale grey or buff limestones streaked with darker shales.
One layer of red or pink is particularly eye-catching—this, the
Stelkuz Formation, is a late-Precambrian shale that can be used as a

REST STOP

Boya Lake

BESIDE THE DEASE River here is a wide area of glacial kettle terrain, where erosion debris from the Cassiar Mountains once covered a stagnant valley glacier that was melting in place at the end of the Pleistocene. Where the massive blocks of ice melted, they left hollows in the debris—hollows that filled with water and became a shallow lake with many intricate bays. The stunning aquamarine colours of Boya Lake are caused by the white marl (calcium carbonate) mud on its bottom, which reflects the colours of the sky, refracted by the water. The marl is derived from the underlying calcareous bedrock in the region.

Both Arctic terns and osprey patrol the lake, looking for fish. Trails skirt the lakeshore to the north and south of the campground. The moist, calcium-rich soil along the southern lakeshore hosts a number of common and not-so-common wildflowers. Butterwort is one of them—this striking little purple flower has a basal rosette of slimy, yellowish leaves that really do look buttery, but their purpose is not to feed insects but to capture any small ones that land on them. Two other common purplish wildflowers along the trail are alpine sweetvetch and showy locoweed. Alpine sweetvetch has long plumes of drooping flowers; it is a favourite food of grizzly bears and one often sees divots throughout northern forests where they have scooped up the tasty roots. The northern trail passes through areas of limestone seepage where orchids and primulas bloom.

Above: Common butterwort. HANS ROEMER

marker by even non-geologists, since it is repeated on mountain after mountain. You soon leave the Cassiar Mountains behind you and enter the broad valley of the Dease River once again.

North of Boya Lake, you enter the broad, flat plain of the Liard Basin. Here the biota of the eastern boreal forest slips through the Liard's broad, low gap between the Rocky and Mackenzie Mountains. You may have seen the soft, pale-green foliage of tamarack trees along the road just south of Boya Lake, but now scattered stands begin to appear regularly along the roadside. This is an eastern boreal tree that is a pioneer species in cold peatlands, or a pioneer after forest fires; in British Columbia, it is confined to the far north and northeast. Tamarack is an Algonquian word meaning "wood used for snowshoes," and the tree has other close connections to winter as well—it is tolerant of winter cold snaps down to at least −65°C.

For many kilometres along this stretch, you drive through the Tisigar Lake forest fire, which burned 11,000 hectares of forest in 2011. The warm, relatively humid summers in the Liard Basin spawn numerous thunderstorms that commonly ignite fires in the region, though this one is uncommonly large.

Just north of the Yukon border at kilometre 720, you cross Albert Creek; this small stream arises in a chain of shallow lakes only a few kilometres upstream. In contrast to the cold mountain streams you have crossed many times on this highway, Albert Creek is warm, fed by the surface water of its lowland, headwater lakes and is home to a

The soft green foliage of the tamarack turns golden in the autumn and falls, just like the leaves of many broad-leaved trees. SYDNEY CANNINGS

The Canada Whiteface is one of the subarctic dragonflies that fly over mossy fens at Blue Lakes near the north end of Highway 37. DENNIS PAULSON

dragonfly at the northern edge of its range, the boreal snaketail. As dragonfly watchers will tell you, you can take the dragonfly out of the tropics, but you can't take the tropics out of the dragonfly. So despite its name, the boreal snaketail does not appreciate cold water but lives in streams that are warm enough to wade in with comfort. Most northern dragonflies shun cold, flowing water and live in shallow, still waters that can warm up in the long days of the short summer.

NINE

The East Kootenay Highway

HIGHWAY 93

L IKE MOST north-south routes in British Columbia, Highway 93 takes advantage of one of the many northwest-trending valleys in the province. Highway 93 follows the Southern Rocky Mountain Trench, which extends from just south of the U.S. border in Montana to Prince George. The highway tracks this valley north to Radium Hot Springs, where it turns east into the Rocky Mountains themselves, using the Kootenay and Vermilion River valleys to reach Vermilion Pass on the border of Banff National Park and Alberta. For most of its length, Highway 93 shares the road with Highway 95; the latter continues on past Radium Hot Springs to meet Highway 1 at Golden.

▶ **Roosville to Radium:** The Southern Rocky Mountain Trench
The overriding theme of this route is the Southern Rocky Mountain Trench, a huge geological feature that stretches from Prince George to just south of the Montana border. It is a linear crack in the Earth's surface, formed about 60 million years ago when pressures from colliding tectonic plates in the west subsided, allowing crust that had been pushed up over other rocks to fall back (more details are given on p. 44).

Highway 93 begins at Roosville, on the U.S. border just north of Eureka, Montana, and travels north through a small side valley of the Kootenay. This valley is now occupied by a series of small creeks, but at the close of the Pleistocene it was carved by the Elk River, deflected south from its former mouth at Elko by a large glacier lying where Lake Koocanusa is today (see p. 99 for a discussion of Lake Koocanusa and the Libby Dam).

This section of the Rocky Mountain Trench has open forests of ponderosa pine, Douglas-fir and western larch. A large area of grasslands in Montana barely crosses the border, extending only about 10 kilometres north to Tobacco Plains, largely out of sight from the highway behind the low ridge west of the highway. The valley is bounded on the east by the Galton Range. About 5 kilometres north of the border, the slopes of the Galton Range show signs of a recent fire—the grass and shrub habitat of the McDonald Burn. In winter these steep, grassy slopes are a good place to spot bighorn sheep. This is also elk country, so watch for the large ungulates grazing near the highway, especially at dusk. Heavily browsed saskatoon and antelope-brush indicate the presence of elk and deer.

About 10 kilometres north of the border, the highway enters the Grasmere Valley; the grasslands of Tobacco Plains are visible off and on through the trees to the west. The valley here is filled with hay fields, where white-tailed deer graze in spring. North of Grasmere the dry forests have antelope-brush on the warmer, west-facing slopes and Douglas-fir on the cooler, east-facing slopes. Many sites from here to Elko have been enhanced for elk and deer habitat in recent years. The dense young growth is thinned from the forests, the understorey is burned in spring and then the new growth is reburned after four or five years. This process opens up the forests, which have been choked with young growth since fire-suppression policies were put in place a half-century ago. In this relatively dry climate, the forests have a natural fire cycle of about twenty-five years.

You swing westward north of Grasmere to cross the Elk River near its mouth on Lake Koocanusa. This course travels between the Elk's former route to the Kootenay west of Elko and its route south

Elk

Elk are one of the largest members of the deer family, second only to the moose in size. They are properly termed *wapiti* in North America, the Shawnee name (meaning "white rump") for the species; in Britain they are called red deer, though the European subspecies is considerably smaller than its North American counterpart. *Elk* is the Germanic word for moose. Elk are grazers and browsers, preferring open forests and grasslands, and the East Kootenay is an ideal environment for them.

In the early 1980s, there were about thirty thousand elk in the Southern Rocky Mountain Trench. Because of a number of factors, including harsh winters, overhunting, overgrazing of winter range and an increased number of wolves and cougars in the area, the population dropped to about sixteen thousand by 1997. Since that time, restrictions on hunting, habitat restoration projects, increased harvest of wolves and cougars, and a series of mild winters have allowed the population to bounce back to about twenty thousand animals.

Above: STEVE CANNINGS

of the border as the glaciers were melting. The white silt bluffs along the Elk River were laid down in a lake alongside the glacier in the Kootenay Valley; the driftwood to the west of the highway is a result of the flooding of the Kootenay River by the Libby Dam.

The topography is rather flat for the most part, since you are travelling on the floodplain of the Elk and Kootenay Rivers. The mountains ahead of you, grey sheets of upthrust limestone, are the

Lizard Range of the Rocky Mountains above Elko. As mentioned in the discussion of Highway 3 (p. 101), much of the Lizard Range was flipped completely upside down as it was thrust eastward during the building of the Rocky Mountains.

At Elko, Highway 93 turns northwest and follows Highway 3 to Cranbrook. From Cranbrook it takes a short northeast jog to cross the Kootenay River at Fort Steele, then resumes the journey up the trench. Just north of Fort Steele, you pass a series of wetlands along the Kootenay River west of the highway with the euphonious name of Bummers Flats, which is the site of an important habitat enhancement program of the Canadian Wildlife Service, B.C. Environment and Ducks Unlimited. The highway continues north through ponderosa pine forests to the wetlands south of Wasa Lake, another patch of important waterfowl habitat.

North of Wasa you cross the Kootenay River and reach Skookumchuck Flats, the bottom of an ancient glacial lake. These grasslands are valuable habitat for about twenty pairs of long-billed curlews, large, curve-billed sandpipers that nest in shortgrass prairies across western North America. As in most grasslands in British Columbia, recent fire-suppression policies have allowed the spread of young trees into these grasslands, reducing the extent of this rare habitat.

At Johnson Flats, north of the Skookumchuck Pulpmill, the understorey has been burned to open up the forest to counteract the expansion of the forest, improving habitat for many species of wildlife, including deer and elk. At this point you are close to the northern limit of extensive grasslands in the Rocky Mountain Trench, especially for grassland shrubs such as antelope-brush. The forest reflects the slightly cooler and moister conditions as you go north, with lodgepole pine and western larch appearing in numbers on the hillsides and spruce in valley bottom wetlands.

You soon cross the Kootenay River for the last time just south of Canal Flats. The flats were built as a gravel floodplain by the Kootenay where it leaves the Rocky Mountains and enters the trench. They are a very low pass between two of the largest rivers in the

Rockies—the Kootenay and the Columbia. The name Canal Flats derives from a short-lived canal that was dug in the 1880s between the two great watersheds here. Only two ships ever used the canal before it fell into disuse. These days the flats are used primarily as a convenient area for large log sorts.

Travelling north, the highway swings onto the west side of the valley, climbing through western larches and an old burn to a viewpoint over Columbia Lake, the headwaters of the river of the same name. This is the northern limit of ponderosa pines in the valley and one of the last places you will see bluebunch wheatgrass. A stop at the viewpoint gives you a good opportunity to get leisurely, close-up views of this bunchgrass, as well as to scan the warm, west-facing slopes across the lake, which are valuable winter range for bighorn sheep and deer.

You descend to the floor of the trench at Dutch Creek, site of a remarkable wall of silt and stone, a remnant of lake bottom sediments deposited here against the wall of the last large valley glacier. The Dutch Creek Hoodoos, as they are called, are also the site of a small colony of white-throated swifts, which feed by rocketing through the air with their large mouths wide open, scooping up insects over grasslands and open forests in the dry valleys of western North America.

Beyond Dutch Creek, you cross the Columbia River for the first time and drive past Fairmont Hot Springs, a highly developed resort community centred on a hot spring complex known for its rare plants. It is the only site in Canada where southern maidenhair fern grows, attracted by the limestone soils and mild temperatures immediately surrounding the springs. Another unusual species here is the giant helleborine, an orchid found at only a handful of sites in British Columbia.

The highway continues along the east benches of the valley, through open Douglas-fir forests dotted with junipers and rabbitbrush. About 6.5 kilometres north of Invermere, you cross Stoddart Creek; the hillsides east of here are important winter range for about 140 bighorn sheep.

Facing page: Dutch Creek Hoodoos tower over the highway. RICHARD CANNINGS

Just south of Radium Hot Springs is a viewpoint over the wetlands along the Columbia River. In a province full of high-gradient rivers racing to the sea, the combination of the Columbia River and the almost flat bottom of the Rocky Mountain Trench produces a large area of winding river oxbows and marshy lakes that is unique in British Columbia. The large size of this wetland complex—20,129 hectares stretching 180 kilometres from Columbia Lake to north of Golden—and the fact that it has formed in such a deep, north-south valley make it critically important habitat for migratory waterfowl. Over a thousand tundra swans feed in these marshes each year in their migration between Arctic breeding grounds and winter grounds in central California. The wetlands are also important winter range for moose and other large mammals.

If you continue north through the trench to Golden on Highway 95, the climate continues to become gradually moister and cooler, a change reflected in the vegetation. The dry grasslands peter out at Edgewater, along with the accompanying rabbit-brush. Large hay fields and pastures border the marshes below the highway. The forests here are dominated by Douglas-fir and trembling aspen, and spruce and cottonwood are common in the valley bottom. By the time you reach Golden, the annual precipitation is almost 50 centimetres per year, compared with only 38 centimetres near the south end of the trench at Cranbrook.

➤ **Radium Hot Springs to the Continental Divide:**
Kootenay National Park

Highway 93 provides an especially scenic route into the heart of the Rocky Mountains through Kootenay National Park. You enter the Park on the outskirts of Radium Hot Springs. The park was founded in 1920 as part of an agreement between the federal and provincial governments—the province gave the land to the federal government for a park in return for a promise of federal funds to build a new highway between Banff and Windermere.

The public centrepiece of the park is the hot springs, called Radium Hot Springs because they are slightly radioactive, similar to

REST STOP

Olive Lake

THIS PICTURESQUE LAKE is a natural stopping point in Sinclair Pass, with a picnic site and boardwalk nature trail. Not only is the boardwalk accessible to disabled visitors, but the informative signs are molded in three-dimensional bronze so that visually impaired people can learn about the distinctive bark of local tree species or the small brook trout inhabiting the lake. The boardwalk extends over the lake in two places so that you have a good chance of seeing the colourful trout.

the famous springs at Bath, England. The springs arise from a deep geological fault, the Redwall Fault, that extends several kilometres into the Earth. Just around the corner beyond the springs you are confronted with the high red cliffs that give the fault its name. Like several groups of rocks in this western edge of the Rocky Mountains, the sedimentary rocks at the Redwall Fault have been tilted so that they now stand in a vertical position. The red colour comes from oxidized iron—rust—in the rocks. The highway goes through a tunnel in these cliffs, appropriately called the Iron Gates Tunnel.

The highway climbs quickly to Sinclair Pass (1486 metres) at Olive Lake. You descend for a few kilometres through shale and wave-washed sandstone outcrops, then come out on a tremendous view of the Kootenay Valley. Across the valley is the Mitchell Range, its lower slopes clothed in lodgepole pine. Patches of dead pines, killed by mountain pine beetle, are often visible from the viewpoint. The forest in the valley bottom is a beautiful and unusual mixture of ponderosa pine, which prefers hot, dry locations, and spruce, which thrives in cool, damp conditions. Western larch grows along the highway here as well—the only place in the four large Rocky Mountain national parks where this splendid tree is found. The greyish-green shrubs spangled with small yellow flowers in summer are shrubby cinquefoil.

Dolly Varden Campground is named after a colourful fish found in the Kootenay valley. The Dolly Varden char has since been split into two species; the Interior species found here is called the bull trout. The bull trout is a large, predatory fish that eats other types of trout, and its populations have been declining significantly over much of its range. It is considered a threatened species in the United States and is vulnerable in British Columbia, largely because of habitat loss and degradation caused by hydroelectric dams, logging and road construction combined with overfishing.

The highway crosses the Kootenay River, turning east to follow the Vermilion River. On the northwest side of the road just past the bridge, you pass a small kettle-hole lake called Kootenay Pond, formed in a hole left by a huge chunk of ice that was covered in gravel as the glaciers retreated from this valley. When the ice chunk melted, it left a deep hole in the gravel deposit, which is now filled by the pond.

These mountain goats are at a mineral lick in Kootenay National Park.
RICHARD CANNINGS

The Vermilion River is first visible far below in Hector Gorge on the south side of the road. On the north, the high rocks of Mt. Wardle (2830 metres) provide ideal habitat for mountain goats. These animals are often seen along the highway at whitish rock cuts, where they lick the soil to get calcium and other essential minerals that are difficult to obtain from eating plants alone. A few kilometres on there is another mineral lick, marked by a sign on the east side of the road. This lick is more of a mud puddle that has high concentrations of nutrients such as sulfur, and attracts moose that slurp up the murky water.

Black Swifts

The shady cliffs of Marble Canyon provide an ideal nesting site for black swifts. These enigmatic birds look like large, dark swallows but are more closely related to hummingbirds. Very few nests of this species have ever been found, and all have been on sheer cliffs moistened by the spray of a waterfall, or in one case, the Pacific surf.

Black swifts feed on high-flying insects and spend most of the summer days coursing over mountain peaks, scooping up swarming ants in their large mouths. A bird may fly up to 80 kilometres away from its nest to gather food for the single nestling, which is fed only once a day at dusk. At summer's end the swifts gather in flocks and fly down the spine of the Rockies into the cloud forests of Central America for the winter.

The Vermilion River valley was burned by a large forest fire in the summer of 2003, the worst year in British Columbia's history for wildfires. Lightning strikes on the same day in late July set fires in the Verendrye Creek and Tokumm Creek watersheds. These fires quickly grew and merged into one giant fire that covered more than 12 per cent of Kootenay National Park before being contained a month later.

The highway crosses the sky-blue Vermilion River as it cuts through a small gorge of grey rocks. If you are wondering why such a blue river was given such a red name, watch the west side of the river about 15 kilometres farther up the valley. These rusty banks are outcroppings of ochre, an iron-stained clay. Ochre is the star attraction of the Paint Pots, a group of three cool springs that well up in a rich orange clay bed. These ochre beds were sacred to the Ktunaxa people, who used the ochre as a dye for face paint and rock pictographs.

Northern Hawk Owl. STEVE CANNINGS

The springs are reached by a 1.5-kilometre trail that leaves the north side of the road just after it turns east for the final ascent to Vermilion Pass.

As you climb higher, you pass Marble Canyon, a spectacular narrow chasm cut by Tokumm Creek along a weak fault. Technically, the rocks here are not marble but dolomite. Marble is metamorphosed, or recrystallized, limestone (calcium carbonate), whereas dolomite is magnesium carbonate. The canyon, 60 metres deep in places, is well worth a short walk from the highway.

Just beyond Marble Canyon, the highway climbs into the Vermilion Pass Burn, 2500 hectares of silver snags that burned when a lighning-set fire raged through here on July 9, 1968. The conifer forest has been replace by a verdant growth of fireweed and other flowers and grasses and supports a large wildlife population. An important part of that wildlife is a cyclic population of voles, or meadow mice, that feed owls and hawks. Two owl species in particular—the northern hawk owl and the breal owl—are often seen in this burn when the mouse populations peak.

The Stanley Glacier is visible on the south side of the highway through the burn. Like most glaciers in Canada, it has been quickly receding in the last few decades and has now melted into separate sections. It is named after Lord Stanley, as in the Cup.

And finally, you reach Vermilion Pass, the continental divide, at 1640 metres elevation. Water falling on the east side of this pass flows into the Bow River and thence into the Saskatchewan, eventually emptying into Hudson Bay. You have followed the path of water falling on the western side, which flows into the Kootenay and Columbia Rivers and finally into the Pacific Ocean. Ahead of you are the towers of Castle Peak in Banff National Park.

TEN

The Okanagan and Cariboo Highways

HIGHWAY 97

HIGHWAY 97 is one of the great north-south routes in western North America, beginning in the high Cascades of California and winding north through Oregon and Washington to the Canadian border just south of Osoyoos. In British Columbia it travels through the dry grasslands and lush orchards of the Okanagan Valley, then jogs westward through the Thompson Valley to Cache Creek. There it resumes its long northward path, over the Cariboo Plateau to the spruce and pine forests of Prince George, through the Rocky Mountains and onto the northern plains at Dawson Creek. It then begins its most famous section, the Alaska Highway.

➤ **Osoyoos to Monte Creek:** The Okanagan

The B.C. portion of this immense journey begins at the Osoyoos-Oroville border crossing in the Okanagan Valley. The Okanagan has a deserved reputation for being a special valley in British Columbia. Although it is neither the hottest part of the province nor the driest, its very warm, dry summers combined with mild winters allow many species to thrive that are found nowhere else in Canada.

Facing page: The Okanagan River below McIntyre Bluff runs its natural course—the only unchannelized section of this river in Canada. RICHARD CANNINGS

You can look south from Osoyoos and see the golden, grassy hills of the Columbia Basin spreading out; look north and the valley is narrower and more thickly forested. The Okanagan is a natural meeting place, a place where northern forests meet southern deserts, where Pacific storms meet Interior skies.

From the border north through Osoyoos, you travel along fertile benches planted with peaches, apricots, cherries and other fruit trees. The cool but not cold winters and long hot summers of the Okanagan are ideal for fruit trees. The large propellers you can see in some of the orchards are air movers, started up on cold April nights when late frosts could kill the blossoms of apricots and other early varieties.

Across Osoyoos Lake to the east are large vineyards planted on the sandy soils that in natural situations support antelope-brush habitat. Antelope-brush was considered by C. Hart Merriam, an early American ecologist, to be an indicator plant of the Upper Sonoran Desert in his influential classification of North American ecosystems. This desert stretches from the south Okanagan to the plateaus of northern Mexico. Antelope-brush is still used as an indicator species, but mostly by the wine industry as an indicator of good growing conditions for Merlot and other heat-loving grape varieties. In the past decade, vineyards have replaced hundreds of hectares of native shrub steppe, now considered one of the most endangered ecosystems in Canada.

REST STOP

The Osoyoos Desert Centre

THE OSOYOOS DESERT Centre has informative displays and guided walks through the dry grasslands in spring and summer. Turn west at 146th Street and drive a short distance to the centre. You can walk along a 1.5-kilometre boardwalk to see antelope-brush, mariposa lily, brittle prickly pear cactus and other dryland plants or watch mountain bluebirds feed their nestlings in nearby nest boxes. The centre is conducting experiments on grassland restoration, an integral part of conservation plans in the Okanagan Valley.

Facing page: Brittle prickly pear cactus. STEVE CANNINGS

North of Osoyoos Lake, the floodplain of the Okanagan River lies to the east of the highway. The river was channelized in the 1950s for flood control, but the oxbows of the old meandering river channel still wind back and forth across the valley bottom. The wet pastures, still seasonally flooded despite the channel, provide nesting habitat for bobolink and long-billed curlews. The fields also have abundant voles, or meadow mice, which are food for several species of owls that roost and nest in the water birch woodlands along the old river channels. This is the only site in the Interior of British Columbia that has a regularly nesting population of barn owls, attracted by the voles and the low winter snowfall.

As you travel north toward Oliver, you can see more vineyards on the sandy benches on the west side of the valley. These benches are kame terraces, formed about twelve thousand years ago as melt waters carried sand out of the western ridges and deposited it in deep banks against the sidewalls of the huge glacier still present in the valley bottom.

Barn Owl

About 4 kilometres north of Oliver, the highway turns to cross the Okanagan River. The river is in its natural channels here, since this is the main spawning grounds of the Okanagan sockeye salmon run. This spawning site is one of only two significant sockeye spawning grounds left in the entire Columbia River system. In some years, more than 100,000 sockeye return here to spawn; the young salmon that hatch from these eggs spend a year in Osoyoos Lake before heading seaward over and through the eleven major dams on the Columbia. A few chinook salmon make it this far as well, but their numbers are so small that the Okanagan population is considered Endangered by the Committee on the Status of Endangered Wildlife in Canada.

McIntyre Bluff is a massive block of metamorphic rock, as are all the cliffs opposite it on the east side of the valley from here north to Vaseux Lake. These rocks are probably the oldest rocks in British Columbia, laid down as sedimentary rocks on the continental shelf of a smaller North America anywhere from 2 billion to 360 million years ago, then melted and reformed as crystalline gneisses and schists when the terrane Quesnellia collided with North America about 180 million years ago. The rocks remained buried deep in the Earth's crust until about 50 million years ago, when the pressure of terranes colliding with the west coast of North America

Cliff Dwellers

The spectacular cliffs on both sides of the valley around Vaseux Lake are home to a fascinating community of animals—reptiles, invertebrates, mammals and even birds that use the cracks and crevices to escape the heat of the summer sun or to find ideal winter temperatures for hibernation. Snakes and lizards are perhaps the most obvious inhabitants. Western rattlesnakes, racers, gopher snakes and the rare night snake are all found here, as are western skinks. Black widow spiders and northern scorpions hide under the rocks by day; the scorpions emerge at night to hunt for crickets and other nocturnal insects.

One of the most interesting mammals is the spotted bat, discovered here for the first time in Canada in 1979. Spotted bats are relatively large, with a wingspan of 35 centimetres, huge pink ears and a black body with white spots—somewhat like a tiny flying skunk. Spotted bats are the only North American bats that produce sonar clicks audible to the human ear. If you ever hear a persistent *tsip-tsip-tsip-tsip* overhead in the summer night sky in south-central British Columbia, it is probably a spotted bat searching for large flying insects to eat. The low pitch—and thus long wavelength—of the sonar clicks is adapted to reflect strongly off the large size of the prey the spotted bat is searching for.

Several birds are also found on these cliffs. The canyon wren probes for spiders and insects with its long curved bill, while white-throated swifts rocket by overhead.

Above: Racer. RICHARD CANNINGS

finally relaxed, allowing much of the upper strata in southern British Columbia to slide seaward. This stretching cracked open the Okanagan Valley (and the Southern Rocky Mountain Trench; see p. 44) and exposed these beautiful gneiss cliffs.

At the end of the Pleistocene glacial period, about twelve thousand years ago, a large block of ice filled the valley at McIntyre Bluff, blocking the flow of melt water from the Okanagan watershed to the north. That water was forced to flow north into the Shuswap Valley and from there through the Thompson River to the Fraser, rather than south through the Columbia, as all Okanagan water flows today.

Vaseux Lake is one of the smallest lakes in the Okanagan chain but one of the richest in biodiversity. At the narrowest point of the valley, it is the most natural valley bottom site remaining in the Okanagan and has been a focus of conservation efforts for the past eighty years. It was initially declared a federal bird sanctuary in 1923 to preserve a small flock of wintering trumpeter swans that had been decimated by lead poisoning. The swans feed on the roots and stems of water plants in shallow water and are susceptible to ingesting lead shot that has settled on the muddy bottom. There are still swans wintering on the lake annually, both tundra and trumpeters. They usually feed near the mouth of the Okanagan River channel at the north end of the lake. When the lake is ice-free, it is also popular with Canada Geese and many species of ducks. But because it is small, shallow and relatively protected from wind, the lake usually freezes over in the last half of December and remains frozen until February.

In the village of Okanagan Falls, the highway doglegs westward for a few hundred metres and crosses the Okanagan River at its outlet from Skaha Lake. There is another small dam here at the site of the rapids that gave the town its name. The highway then climbs up a gravelly kame terrace on the west side of the valley to avoid the steep western shores of Skaha Lake en route to Penticton. The large, dark gangly shrubs on the grassy slopes here are antelope-brush; Skaha Lake marks the northern limit of any sizable stands of this plant, though a few individuals can be found as far north as Westbank.

Bighorn Sheep

The Vaseux Lake area is famous for its herd of California bighorn sheep. About six hundred of these animals normally range along the rugged cliffs from Penticton south to Osoyoos Lake, about half that number concentrated near Vaseux Lake. An outbreak of pneumonia in the winter of 1999–2000 killed more than half the herd, but small numbers can still be seen on the cliffs and grassy benches on the east side of the valley from late September through June.

A wildlife fence stretching from the canal south of the lake to the vineyards on the north prevents the sheep from crossing the highway, where many were killed each year.

Bighorn sheep are the common wild sheep of western North America from central British Columbia south to Mexico. The adult males have massive curved horns; the females and young males have shorter, thinner horns. Males use the horns in displays and spectacular head-butting contests in a continuing battle for dominance in the herd. Most of the females mate with the dominant male.

Females give birth in May, keeping to the steep cliffs and narrow ledges at that time of year to protect the lambs. When the low-elevation grass dries out in July, they move upslope to higher meadows until September, when they return to the valley bottom to avoid the deep winter snow.

Above: STEVE CANNINGS

Vaseux Lake gneiss cliffs. STEVE CANNINGS

As the land levels out, you will see a small kettle lake nestled in the pine forest on the west side of the highway. This lake formed when a large block of ice became buried in the gravel and sand that filled the valley as glaciers melted in the highlands. Later, the ice melted, leaving a kettle hole in the landscape, which partially filled with groundwater.

REST STOP
Vaseux Lake Wildlife Centre

PULL IN AT the Vaseux Lake Wildlife Centre at the north end of the lake. A kiosk presents information on the natural history of the area and a boardwalk takes you through the riparian woodlands along old river oxbows to a waterfowl-viewing blind that looks out over the marshes at the river outlet. Watch for trumpeter and tundra swans and a wide variety of other waterfowl in fall, winter and early spring. Painted turtles sun themselves on logs on warm summer days, and colourful songbirds such as Bullock's orioles and black-headed grosbeaks are common in the birch woodlands.

From Okanagan Falls north, much of the bedrock on the west side of the valley is volcanic. At the White Lake Road junction, there is a good view to the west of Mt. Parker (1422 metres), a layer cake of lava deposits laid down about 50 million years ago. The rock formations on this mountain were made even more obvious when a forest fire cleared the trees in 1986.

As the highway approaches Penticton, you will see good views of the valley. The granitic Skaha Bluffs are visible on the east side of the lake; these cliffs have become a very popular rock-climbing destination. Penticton is built on alluvial fans that spread out from three creek valleys—Shingle Creek on the west, Penticton Creek on the northeast and Ellis Creek on the southeast. These fans cut the lake in two, separating what is now Skaha Lake from the rest of Okanagan Lake.

The highway drops back to lake level at Penticton, skirting the south end of the airport along the natural sand beaches of Skaha Lake. After crossing the Okanagan River channel, it turns north to follow the river. The former channels of the river are visible as winding oxbows on either side of the present canal, which was constructed from 1954 to 1958 for flood control.

Leaving Penticton northbound, you cross the Okanagan River channel one last time—its source is regulated by a dam a few hundred metres upstream at the southwest corner of Okanagan Lake. This part of Penticton was once a large marsh, full of muskrats, waterfowl, Red-winged Blackbirds and other animals. Its last vestiges were filled during the 1980s to construct a gated adult community called, ironically, Redwing Estates.

At the north end of this development the highway begins to travel along the shores of Okanagan Lake. This is a large fiord lake, its bottom carved out of the valley by a huge glacier that flowed through the Okanagan Valley during the Pleistocene. It is 120 kilometres long and up to 200 metres deep in places. Okanagan Lake is big enough and the winters warm enough to prevent it from freezing over most of the time. Once every decade or so, a cold spell will send sheets of ice out for several hundred metres from shore, and every fifty years or so, it will freeze completely. But most winters it is completely ice-free, and thousands of waterfowl feed along its shores.

American coot. RICHARD CANNINGS

From October through March, watch for large flocks of coots—comical black waterfowl with white beaks—which dive underwater to feed on submerged plants. Coots are not ducks but are related to cranes and rails, and they do not have webbed feet but curiously lobed toes to help them swim. Coots are the favourite winter food of bald eagles in the southern Interior of British Columbia, and one or

The white bluffs along the southern shores of Okanagan Lake are formed from silt deposited on the bottom of Glacial Lake Pentiction. STEVE CANNINGS

two eagles often perch on the large, dead-topped pine on the west side of the highway at the southwestern corner of Okanagan Lake, eyeing the coots below.

Across the lake to the east is a low hill with "penticton" written in white letters on its western slope. This is Munson's Mountain, the southernmost of several extinct volcanoes that were active in the Okanagan Valley 50 million years ago, fuelled by the rifting that created the valley itself. Some other mountains of this type are Giants Head in Summerland, Mt. Boucherie in Westbank and Dilworth Mountain in Kelowna.

The outstanding feature of this section of the highway is the white silt bluffs, locally called clay cliffs, that line the south end of Okanagan Lake from Penticton to Summerland on the west side of the lake and to Naramata on the east side of the lake. These bluffs are formed from silt deposited about twelve thousand years ago on the bottom of a large glacial lake named Glacial Lake Penticton. If you have ever seen a glacial lake, you'll know that these lakes have a very milky blue look to them, especially in summer when the glaciers are melting. This milky colour comes from very fine silts in the water—often called glacial flour—created by the glacier as it grinds over bedrock like a millstone grinds flour. Glacial Lake Penticton was in place for at least a hundred years until the ice dam south of Vaseux Lake opened, allowing water to resume its present drainage south to the Columbia River and draining the lake.

If you look carefully at the silt bluffs, you can see fine layers of sediment. These are called varves and indicate annual cycles in silt deposition; one varve is laid down per year.

The silt benches on either side of the lake were covered with bunchgrass and sagebrush for thousands of years, forming a rich, brown, loamy soil. The orchards and vineyards you see across the lake in Naramata are planted on this rich soil. The highway crosses the delta of Trout Creek, its sand beaches accessible at Sunoka Provincial Park. The large cottonwoods of Trout Creek are an important nesting area for Lewis's woodpeckers, an odd, crowlike woodpecker with a bright pink underside. These birds don't gather food in the usual manner of woodpeckers but instead fly around like giant swallows, catching large insects in the air, then returning to a high perch. A few Lewis's woodpeckers overwinter here as well—one of the only wintering sites in Canada—when they switch to eating fruit and nuts from local orchards and gardens.

Trout Creek drains the second-largest watershed in the Okanagan system, but the lower sections have been more or less sterilized by dyking and clearing of streamside trees in an attempt to control flooding. The lack of shade combined with reduced water flow from upstream diversions creates late-summer water temperatures of 27° to 30°c. These temperatures are well above the lethal limit for salmon and trout, and the creek's kokanee run is essentially extinct.

As the highway crosses the northwest corner of the delta, a large landslide slump is visible beneath the silt bluffs; the silts are susceptible to slides, especially when saturated with irrigation water or heavy rain. Above the bluffs rises the rock face of Giant's Head, the remnant of an extinct volcano, which has been carved by glaciers into a classic roche moutonée, its northern slopes rising gently to steep cliffs on the south side. This term is French for 'sheep rock'; the shape of the rock resembles a resting sheep. This shape also indicates that the valley glaciers here came from the north, smoothly eroding the north side of the mountain as they climbed over it, then plucking out the southern side. After a short stretch along the lakeshore, the road climbs to the Summerland benches and stays high above the lake until Peachland.

North of Summerland, a series of high rock bluffs is visible above the road. Watch carefully for mountain goats on these slopes, especially in the section south of Okanagan Lake Provincial Park. Golden eagles also use cliff ledges here to build their huge stick nests. The steep, grassy slopes above the highway in this section are part of Antler Saddle, one of the most important local wintering grounds for mule deer. A high wildlife fence was constructed in 1998 to reduce the number of deer killed each winter—more than five hundred were killed in 1996–97 alone.

Across the lake you can see Okanagan Mountain Provincial Park, one of the few wilderness areas left in the valley. The character of the valley changes significantly here; the side benches disappear, along with the areas of open grassland and sagebrush; instead, ponderosa pine forests grow down to the lakeshore. Grasslands reappear north of Kelowna, but these lack the sagebrush of the very dry grasslands of the south Okanagan. The lake makes a sharp dogleg to the northeast around Okanagan Mountain.

The highway drops back down to lake level just south of Peachland at Antlers Beach and almost immediately crosses Peachland (Deep) Creek on a small bridge at the creek's outlet. Peachland Creek is a major spawning site for kokanee, the land-locked form of sockeye

REST STOP

Hardy Falls

TURN NORTH JUST west of Peachland Creek and walk in to Hardy Falls, about 500 metres upstream on a good trail. The shady canyon and cooling spray from the falls make this an ideal break on a hot summer day, and the spawning kokanee are an added attraction in September and October. Watch for American dippers at the falls—these small grey songbirds build their moss nests right beside the cascade. Vaux's swifts, swallowlike birds that have been described as "cigars with wings," nest in the hollow cottonwoods along the trail, and veeries, reddish-brown thrushes with a beautiful cascading song, sing from the dense shrubbery.

Facing page: American dipper. STEVE CANNINGS

salmon, and is well worth a stop in September and October, when the bright red fish fill the creek. Fish-eating birds such as gulls, mergansers, loons and osprey wait offshore as the kokanee come in to spawn.

At the north end of Peachland, the highway climbs away from the lake again up saskatoon-covered Drought Hill (named after a local family, not the weather), another important wintering ground for mule deer. At the junction with Highway 97c (the Coquihalla Connector), rabbit-brush is prominent in the cloverleaf—this silver-grey shrub has brilliant yellow flowers in late summer and early fall. A small lake on the west side of the road just north of the junction is noted for its population of painted turtles and several are hauled out on logs in the pond most summer days. The sedimentary rocks opposite the north end of the Gorman Brothers sawmill are about 50 million years old and are noted for their fossils and coal deposits.

Northeast of the sprawling malls and fast-food outlets of Westbank, Mt. Boucherie (754 metres) rises between the highway and the

lake. This is an old volcano that erupted in the Eocene period, about 50 million years ago, when the Okanagan Valley was forming. The signs of a forest fire are clearly visible on the north side of the mountain, where much of the thick growth of young Douglas-firs was burned in 1992. The sandy soils along the highway just north of Mt. Boucherie once had a small population of antelope-brush, the northernmost site for the species, but most was ploughed under when the highway was widened.

You descend to the lake for the last time to cross it on the floating W. R. Bennett bridge, built in 2008. Across the bridge is the urban sprawl of Kelowna; the small channel of Kelowna Creek is a reminder of the processes that formed the flat, alluvial sediments that the city is constructed on. The rocky hills to the north of Kelowna, including Knox Mountain on the west and Mt. Dilworth on the east, are old volcanic structures similar in age to Mt. Boucherie. The highway takes you steadily away from Okanagan Lake and into a smaller valley that parallels the main valley north to Vernon.

As you pass the airport on the north end of Kelowna, look in the trees on the far side of the runway for a group of large stick nests. These belong to a small colony of great blue herons that have taken up residence next to the busy runway. The dry grasslands east of the airport show long, parallel ridges that were lateral moraines of the valley glacier—linear heaps of gravel and other deposits that collected beside the glacier as it stagnated at the end of the Pleistocene.

Just north of the airport, you pass Ellison Lake, the smallest and shallowest of three lakes in this side branch of the Okanagan Valley. Water from this lake flows north into Wood Lake, then to Kalamalka Lake and finally through Vernon Creek to Okanagan Lake just west of Vernon. The shallow waters of Ellison Lake are popular with many species of waterfowl, including a small population of wood ducks that nest in the large cottonwoods at the south end of the lake. A pair of bald eagles nests there as well, likely attracted by the abundant duck population and the easy fishing opportunities.

Wood Lake has a healthy fish population, and fish-eating birds such as mergansers, loons and grebes are commonly seen. Wood Lake was once about a metre higher than it is today, but in 1909 a canal was built between it and Kalamalka Lake, and the level immediately dropped to that of Kalamalka. A narrow strip of land separates the two lakes at the village of Oyama. Wood Lake used to experience regular algal blooms that clouded its waters, but in 1972 a distillery opened that pumped thousands of litres of water from Okanagan Lake into Wood Lake. This extra flow flushed nutrients from Wood Lake into Kalamalka Lake, helping to clear Wood Lake but causing greater algal growth in Kalamalka. The distillery has now closed, however, and biologists are watching the lakes with interest to see if they revert to their former patterns of algae production.

Despite being connected to Wood Lake by the Oyama Canal, Kalamalka Lake is very different. Whereas Wood Lake is a highly productive lake with relatively low clarity, Kalamalka is famous for its clear, turquoise colour.

The large gravel terrace at the southeast corner of Kalamalka Lake originated from a large postglacial outflow from Cougar Canyon, the narrow valley immediately east of the lake. About halfway up Kalamalka Lake, the ponderosa pine forests along the road give way to the open grasslands of the Vernon Commonage.

Many of the birds found here are more typical of a prairie landscape than mountainous British Columbia. One of the characteristic birds of this grassland is the clay-coloured sparrow, found wherever small patches of rose and snowberry dot the landscape. Another

Swan Lake is the most important site for waterfowl in the Okanagan Valley.
RICHARD CANNINGS

drab sparrow (and most grassland sparrows are rather drab) here is the grasshopper sparrow, named for its buzzing, insectlike song. In the skies above, Swainson's hawks patrol the grasslands, looking for mice and large insects. They are best distinguished from the commoner red-tailed hawks by their two-tone wings—light in front and dark behind. In 1925, seventy-five of these hawks feasted on an infestation of crickets here, but numbers such as this have not been seen for many years. Swainson's hawks migrate to the Argentinian pampas for the winter, returning to Vernon each April to breed.

From the northern part of Kalamalka Lake, there is a good view to the east up the Coldstream Creek valley. The mountains in the distance are the Monashees, and during parts of the Pleistocene ice flows from the Monashees flowed down from what is now Mabel Lake through the Coldstream valley and into the Okanagan. As you pass the Okanagan University College (Vernon Campus), look up to the west and you'll see a white building on a grassy hill—this is the Allan Brooks Nature Centre, which provides good interpretation of the natural history of the north Okanagan as well as a stupendous view of the Vernon area.

Long-billed curlew

Once through Vernon, the highway swings across wet meadows, which are quickly disappearing under malls and big-box retail outlets. You soon reach the south end of Swan Lake, a shallow, marshy lake fed and drained by B.X. Creek. Swan Lake is a haven for waterfowl of all kinds—thousands of ducks gather here during spring and fall migration, and many stay through the summer to nest on its marshy shores. Great blue herons stand motionless on the banks, looking for small fish such as the introduced pumpkinseed. These magnificent birds have built their nests in a grove of cottonwoods in the northern part of Vernon, just east of the McDonalds restaurant. Swan Lake almost always freezes over in winter, so its waterfowl must leave for open water at that time, which is usually not far away on Okanagan Lake.

At the north end of Swan Lake, the highway splits in two; one branch goes north to Salmon Arm and Sicamous (branching again north of Enderby), and the other goes northwest through Falkland to Monte Creek and Kamloops. We'll take the Kamloops route here, since that's the way to the Cariboo and beyond on Highway 97.

As the highway skirts the north end of Swan Lake, look in the fields to the north for long-billed curlews—big sandpipers that have taken to these fields as substitutes for their normal short-grass prairie habitat. The grain crops grown in the Vernon-Armstrong area are one of the best indications that the climate has changed markedly as you've travelled north from Osoyoos. The grapes and apricots that thrive at the south end of the Okanagan are marginal crops here, and large acreages of wheat and barley would be almost unthinkable at Osoyoos.

Although the valley looks subdued in relief here, it is actually the deepest part, measured by the depth to bedrock. As you drive across the valley floor, you are travelling on postglacial deposits of sand and gravel about 550 metres deep—the bedrock on the valley floor is about 180 metres below sea level.

The highway angles over the north end of a low ridge, then swings down into the main Okanagan Valley again—Okanagan Lake is visible in the southern distance. Just past the historic O'Keefe's Ranch is a small pond on the north side of the highway. This pond is a wonderful spot to take a quick look at some of the more interesting marsh birds that summer here, including the yellow-headed blackbird and the ruddy duck. The male ruddy duck has a bright reddish-brown body and white cheeks, but its most striking feature is a big sky-blue bill. The males try to impress the drabber females by striking their bills against their breasts in a strange rhythmic performance that forces bubbles out of the breast feathers to create an amazing sound as well as visual display.

You are very close to the northern end of the Okanagan watershed here—a few kilometres to the northwest is the Salmon River, which drains into Shuswap Lake, part of the Thompson and Fraser systems. Near the end of the Pleistocene, when there was still a lobe of stagnant ice in this part of the Okanagan Valley, large quantities of sand and gravel were carried out of the Salmon Valley by a river that dropped those deposits against the Okanagan ice mass. The deposits created the large, flat terrace that lies just north and east of the highway as you leave the Okanagan and go over the low pass to the Salmon River. Small kettle lakes are common in these gravel deposits.

A few kilometres farther on, you pass over a seemingly insignificant pass and enter the Salmon River drainage. Any water you now see is flowing into the Shuswap system, thence to the

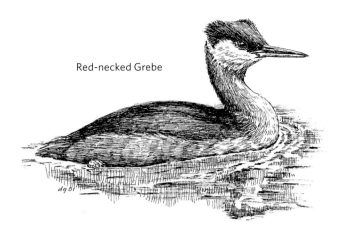

Red-necked Grebe

Thompson and on to the Fraser, rather than into the Okanagan-Columbia drainage you have been in since the start of this journey. The Salmon River flows into Shuswap Lake at Salmon Arm and, not surprisingly, gets its name from the salmon spawning runs it hosts (see Highway 1, p. 11).

The highway follows the Salmon River up a rather narrow valley with dense Douglas-fir forests on the slopes to the south. At the Una Rest Area, a forest fire has cleared the woodlands on the north side of the road, leaving a shrubby habitat. Beyond Falkland the valley opens up into a broad expanse of hay fields, the river winding against a backdrop of high bluffs on the north side of the valley. These bluffs were formed by lava flows during the Miocene period about 25 million years ago.

Further volcanic activity, albeit much more recent, can be seen in a double layer of tephra (volcanic ash) in the road bank between Westwold and Monte Lake. The lower layer is ash from Mt. Mazama (Crater Lake), Oregon (6600 years ago), whereas the upper layer is from an eruption of Mt. St. Helens about 3400 years ago. Monte Lake is a good place to spot red-necked grebes in spring and summer. These waterbirds with brick-red necks and silvery-grey cheeks build their floating nests in the bulrushes along the lakeshore and dive to feed on small fish and aquatic insects.

North of Monte Lake, the Duck Meadow wetland provides more wildlife-viewing opportunities. In 1989, when this habitat was purchased by the Nature Trust of British Columbia, it was a hay meadow; since then a joint reclamation project with the Nature Trust, Ducks Unlimited and the provincial government has returned it to a rich marsh environment, benefiting ducks, blackbirds, harriers, herons, rails and other wetland species. Beyond Duck Meadow the highway begins its descent into the South Thompson Valley, moving from a forest of Douglas-firs to a pure ponderosa pine woodland just past the Barnhartvale road. A steep descent to the junction with Highway 1 brings you out of the lower treeline into the Bunchgrass Zone. Highway 97 now turns west and piggybacks onto Highway 1 to Cache Creek (see Highway 1, pp. 11 to 47).

Cache Creek to Prince George:

The Cariboo Highway

The town of Cache Creek is located at the junction of Cache Creek and the Bonaparte River. Highway 97 turns north here to follow the course of the Bonaparte. Here in its southern stretches, the Bonaparte acts as a true oasis, creating a rich riparian habitat of cottonwood and other deciduous trees and shrubs in the dry sagebrush hills. A few kilometres north of Cache Creek, you pass through the village of Stuctwesemc and cross the Bonaparte on a small bridge. On the hills to the west, recent fires have raised the lower treeline somewhat, clearing ponderosa pines and Douglas-firs and expanding the grassland.

Yellow-headed blackbirds are characteristic summer residents in the rich marshes of the B.C. interior.
STEVE CANNINGS

These colourful rocks along the Bonaparte River were formed when ancient hot springs rose through a fault along the valley bottom. RICHARD CANNINGS

As explained in Chapter 1 on Highway 1 (p. 11), the Bonaparte River flows down a major geological boundary, and the rocks on either side of the valley are very different. To the west lie the limestone hills of the Marble Range; to the east are volcanic rocks of the Nicola group. About 3 kilometres north of the Bonaparte River bridge, you begin to see volcanic breccia bluffs above the highway and many boulders amid the sagebrush that have fallen from these cliffs. In some places these crumbly rocks have formed tall spires or hoodoos, the result of water erosion. One of the common summer flowers along the roadside is salsify, its yellow flowers and round seedheads making it look like a large dandelion.

The valley is still broad enough here for large fields of alfalfa watered with pivot irrigation as well as the ubiquitous black shade cloth covering ginseng plantings. At the junction of Highway 99 (marked more prominently by signs for the historic Hat Creek Ranch), you can clearly see different terrace levels on the west side of the valley, artifacts of flow patterns during deglaciation. There is still

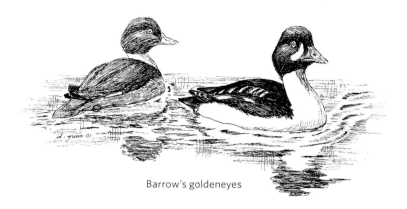

Barrow's goldeneyes

plenty of big sagebrush along the highway, but that ends abruptly about 4 kilometres north of the Highway 99 junction. At the same spot, bright reddish-orange rocks are obvious on the west side of the valley. This colourful outcrop is a gossan, a deposit of rocks rich in iron oxides.

Rabbit-brush now replaces the sage for the next few kilometres, but the highway is climbing into the lower treeline and soon will leave the grasslands behind. Scattered ponderosa pines appear on the lower slopes. The highway turns northwest here and crosses the Bonaparte River for the last time, enters a smaller valley and begins its serious ascent to the Cariboo Plateau. The south-facing slopes are still dotted with grassland shrubs such as chokecherry and rabbit-brush, but the north-facing slopes are cloaked with Douglas-fir. You pass a series of small lakes, all ideal breeding grounds for Barrow's goldeneyes.

The road levels out somewhat and the valley opens as you approach Clinton. A round lake, more alkaline than the ones you have been passing, lies in grassy fields north of the rodeo ground. The limestone mountains of the Marble Range rise above Clinton to the west. Once through the town, the highway begins to climb again through the ponderosa pines and rabbit-brush, and within 5 kilometres you reach the rim of the Cariboo Plateau at the Big Bar Rest Area.

Six kilometres north of 70 Mile House, you pass Loch Lomond, a broad, shallow lake lined with rushes. Many of the boulders in and around the lake are encrusted with sunburst lichen *(inset)*, which grows only on rocks that receive periodic doses of bird and mammal droppings. You will notice that as you leave the lake to the north, the roadside boulders quickly return to the normal dark-red basalt coloration. RICHARD CANNINGS

The view from the rest area looks out over the level surface of the plateau to the north, dropping to the deep valleys to the south. The forest here is more or less pure Douglas-fir, although ponderosa pines make a brief reappearance a short distance north at the Chasm road but vanish for good within another few kilometres.

The Cariboo Plateau is floored with a thick layer of basalt, rock that is formed when thick lava flows pour over the surface, then quickly cool. As basalt cools it forms columns perpendicular to the surface. These columns are not obvious over most of the plateau, since they are covered with soil and trees, but many road cuts and cliffs give you a good view of the basalt, the skin of the plateau. Basalt boulders, broken off by the glaciers as they scoured this surface during the Pleistocene (and perhaps by road construction

Black terns

crews as well), are common along the highway from Meadowlake Road north to 83 Mile.

One of the characteristics of the Cariboo Plateau is an abundance of small lakes and ponds, and you pass several of these ponds in the vicinity of 70 Mile House. These shallow ponds attract dabbling ducks such as teal, wigeon and pintail and are also the northernmost breeding grounds for the Great Basin spadefoot toad.

Beyond Loch Lomond the plateau rises in elevation and contains numerous hollows and gullies filled with marshy lakes and ponds. Spruces line wet meadows in some hollows, and large Douglas-firs are scattered through the upland forest. Most of the uplands are dominated by lodgepole pines with soopolallie beneath. At 83 Mile the highway crosses a cattail-lined creek, then climbs steeply to Begbie Summit, a volcanic butte with basalt columns in the road cuts on the south side. The summit, at 1237 metres elevation, is the highest point on the Cariboo Highway.

A large beaver pond a few kilometres to the north is home to lesser scaup—white-sided diving ducks with black heads—whereas smaller, tree-lined ponds farther on attract bufflehead—small diving ducks with large white face patches. Watch for small but handsome Bonaparte's gulls flying over some of the larger lakes in this

REST STOP

100 MILE MARSH, on the west side of the highway as it enters 100 Mile House, has a good trail around the small lake. Watch for yellow-headed blackbirds, ruddy ducks, American coots and other waterfowl. Muskrats are common as well, and listen for the loud, whistled whinny of the sora rail.

Facing page: Sora rail. RICHARD CANNINGS

section—these black-headed gulls build their nests in spruces around the lakeshores. The forest continues to be mostly of lodgepole pine here, with trembling aspen in newly cleared areas, but as the highway begins to descend to the Bridge Creek valley just south of 100 Mile House, the north-facing woodlands change to a mixed forest of Douglas-fir, lodgepole pine and white spruce.

The highway climbs out of the Bridge Creek valley to the plateau again, and just north of 100 Mile House is another marsh on the west side of the road, appropriately named 101 Mile Marsh. It is owned by the Bridge Creek Estate but managed by Ducks Unlimited, which has dug a channel in the south side of the wetland to provide fresh water for cattle away from the marsh itself. Watch for black terns hawking for insects over the bulrushes like big, graceful swallows.

Oxeye daisy. RICHARD CANNINGS

Patchy grasslands reappear a short distance to the north, with the familiar Cariboo pattern of spruce in the creek bottoms, Douglas-fir on the uplands and grass on the south-facing slopes. About 30 kilometres north of 100 Mile House, you reach Lac la Hache, a large plateau lake. Lines of aspen mark water courses through the grassy slopes to the east. Old-growth Douglas-firs surround Lac La Hache Provincial Park near the north end of the lake. A forest fire here in the 1960s burned several hectares and left fire scars at the bases of the large firs, which are well adapted to ground fires with their thick bark.

North of Lac la Hache, the highway begins to descend the San Jose River valley. This river at first flows through a narrow, spruce-lined valley, then meanders across broad meadows as it makes its way to Williams Lake.

A section of the San Jose valley at 130 Mile has been enhanced for wetland habitats by Ducks Unlimited. Common Loons and yellow-headed blackbirds are prominent beneficiaries, while yellow-bellied marmots romp in the dry grasslands along the road. American Kestrels are often seen in these grasslands—these small falcons perch on power lines, watching the grass below for mice and large grasshoppers. The grasslands peter out at 140 Mile as the highway goes through a section of forest, but the landscape opens again a short distance beyond to small lakes in grasslands, with Rocky Mountain juniper scattered across the slopes. Columbian groundsquirrels are common here in the meadows. At 150 Mile House, the highway begins its descent to the Williams Lake valley, the last oasis of southern valley flora and fauna on this route.

Williams Lake has a rich marsh and wet meadows at its east end. This marsh was once home to one of the very few western grebe colonies in British Columbia, but the birds abandoned the site in the early 1970s, probably because of increased disturbance by boaters. The deciduous woodlands around the lake are still one of the northernmost points in the province for southern valley specialty birds such as Gray Catbird and Bullock's Oriole. Another species at the northern edge of its range here is the spotted bat (p. 205), which roosts in the yellowish bluffs on the slopes of Fox Mountain, overlooking the northeastern edge of town (above the obvious cliffs of Signal Point).

At Williams Lake you can turn west onto Highway 20 and explore the magnificent Chilcotin Plateau (p. 157). We will continue

Alders and Willows—A Case of Flycatcher Evolution

The San Jose valley was the site of an interesting study in bird evolution in the late 1960s, when Robert Stein looked at the Traill's flycatchers nesting along the river. This species was known to have two different song types—northern birds sang *fee-bee-o* to announce their territories, whereas southern birds said *fitz-bew*. Although birds from each population were essentially identical except for minor differences in size and shape, Stein wondered whether they were actually two closely related species rather than one. The San Jose valley was ideal for the study in that birds sang *fee-bee-o* at Lac la Hache and *fitz-bew* at Williams Lake. And what did

they do in the middle? They mated entirely with their own types and are now known as two different species—the northern alder flycatcher and the southern willow flycatcher.

Traill's flycatcher

American kestrels are the commonest hawk seen along roadsides through the Cariboo grasslands. STEVE CANNINGS

north on Highway 97 as it climbs out of the valley along Missioner Creek, then back down Minton Creek to the Hawks Creek (Deep Creek) valley. On the northeastern slopes of Hawks Creek, you can see light grey rock outcrops; these are limestones of the Cache Creek Formation (p. 26), created as coral reef deposits in a distant tropical sea. The forests here are mostly Douglas-fir, with circular mats of juniper in the understorey. As the highway swings away north from the creek, you catch a glimpse of the Fraser River valley for the first time. The road goes through a narrow defile, past small, marshy Egg Lake (presumably named for its shape), then out into the open again near Soda Creek, where there is another view of the mighty river to the west. A fire on the eastern slopes has burned most of the forest except for some Douglas-firs. Basalt bluffs line the Fraser River valley to the west.

The Fraser bends to the west at Soda Creek and the highway continues north up McLeese Creek. You soon pass Duckworth Lake on the east side of the highway, then reach McLeese Lake on the west side. McLeese Lake is home to an interesting fish with an oxymoronic name—the giant pygmy whitefish. This species is known from only one other lake in British Columbia—Tyhee (Mclure) Lake near Smithers—and likely evolved initially in a lake system lacking other whitefish competitors.

Turning north again around McLeese Lake, the highway finally meets the Fraser River just south of Marguerite, where there is a small ferry for those wishing to visit the western side of the river. Grassy slopes to the east are dotted with grey rabbit-brush bushes, perhaps the last you will see of this habitat as you go north.

Silver-leafed wolf willows line the riverbank, their tiny yellow flowers sweetening the June air with beautiful scent.

Between Alexandria and Australian, the Fraser River winds through deep deposits of sand and gravel laid down in more actively eroding times at the close of the Ice Age. The highway travels on the surface of several of these very flat terrace deposits until it enters more rolling plateau country north of Australian. Away from the warm, dry river valley, the forest immediately changes to a mix of spruce and trembling aspen.

As you approach Quesnel, you can see Dragon Lake off to the east. In 1956 this lake was poisoned by fisheries biologists to "rehabilitate" it, or kill all its fish so that rainbow trout could be reintroduced to a lake with no competition. Subsequent study of the poisoned fish showed that one of the species eliminated from the lake was a whitefish known nowhere else in the world. Thus, the Dragon Lake whitefish has the dubious honour of being discovered after it had become extinct. The Dragon Lake "rehabilitation" also killed off a rare stock of the giant pygmy whitefish.

As you enter Quesnel, you cross the Quesnel River, an impressively large stream that has spawning runs of all the Interior salmon species—sockeye, coho, pink and chinook. The Quesnel drains a significant part of the Cariboo Mountains, one of the highest-precipitation—both snowfall and rainfall—areas of the province. The Quesnel has one of the highest potentials for salmon production of all B.C. rivers, but most of the salmon spawning grounds were destroyed in the 1800s by placer miners searching the gravel for gold.

North of Quesnel the highway turns northeast, partly to avoid a large bend in the Fraser and partly

Prickly rose. RICHARD CANNINGS

REST STOP
Scout Island

THE SCOUT ISLAND Nature Centre is just off the highway at the eastern entrance to the town of Williams Lake. Trails around the island lead through a wide variety of habitats from grassy fields with fox dens to rich cattail marshes full of turtles and birds to riparian woodlands and their songbirds. The centre itself is open most days during the summer and has information about the natural history of the Cariboo.

Above: Williams Lake from the Scout Island causeway.
RICHARD CANNINGS

to find an easy crossing over the Cottonwood River. This section of highway, from Quesnel north to Prince George, is one of transition from the drier, relatively warm forests of the Cariboo Plateau to the moister, cooler forests of the Fraser Plateau and Basin. Douglas-firs are common along the first few kilometres north of Quesnel, but beyond that they become quite rare. When the highway returns to the plateau surface, white spruce are the dominant conifer, with trembling aspen, white birch and cottonwood flourishing in

This volcanic bluff on the east side of the highway north of Marguerite shows obvious basalt column formation. RICHARD CANNINGS

disturbed areas. Moose are often seen between Quesnel and Hixon, and red paintbrush, white oxeye daisy and orange hawkweed flowers brighten the summer roadside.

About 15 kilometres north of Quesnel, you descend to the aptly named Cottonwood River, its banks lined with towering cottonwoods that dwarf other trees in the area. Riparian habitats such as this are tremendously important for wildlife in these central and northern forests where plateau forests are too cool to support large trees. A rock cut with basalt columns just past the railway crossing north of the Cottonwood reminds you that you are still on the Cariboo Plateau, with its skin of cooled lava.

A short distance north of the Cottonwood River, you pass Hush Lake on the west side of the highway. Along the southern shore is a stand of black spruce—the southern outpost of this classic boreal species on this highway. From here to the Arctic tundra, most of the forested bogs are dominated by this spindly tree with its knobby crown. It also coincides with the appearance of "eastern" bird species that are characteristic of the boreal forest—blackpoll warblers and white-throated sparrows both reach their southwestern limits here as well. The forest here is noticeably moister than that farther south—the dominant shrubs are cow parsnip, red elderberry and black twinberry, whereas the cream flowers of false Solomon's seal are common in grassy areas.

About 10 kilometres north of Hush Lake, you descend to the Ahbau Creek valley and the small community of Cinema. The moist pastures here merge into a broad black spruce bog at their northern end. Northern harriers course over the sedges and sphagnum on summer evenings, listening for voles with their owl-sharp ears. Beyond the large Dunkley sawmill and the community of Strathnaver, the highway parallels the valley of Naver Creek, then drops down to cross it at Hixon, almost immediately crossing the smaller Hixon Creek as well.

North of Hixon the highway climbs quickly again to the plateau; a rest area on the west side of the road has a sign proclaiming it the Nuxalk-Carrier Grease Trail used by Alexander Mackenzie to cross British Columbia to the Pacific Ocean near Bella Coola in 1793. Mackenzie left the Fraser River near this point and turned west to follow the aptly named West Road River across the Chilcotin Plateau. The forest changes to lodgepole pine in the sandy soils south of Stoner, with kinnikinnick spreading across the forest floor. You get more glimpses of the Fraser as the highway skirts a bend of the river just north of Stone Creek, then heads up Red Rock Creek to the flatlands of the Fraser Plateau. Once on the flats, it goes due north, past black spruce and dwarf birch bogs before angling northwest to meet the Fraser one last time, this time crossing it and entering Prince George.

Highway 97c: The Coquihalla Connector

After leaving the Highway 5 freeway at Merritt, you immediately begin to climb out of the Nicola Valley. The grasslands at first are dominated by sagebrush, but as you gain elevation this grey shrub is replaced by rabbit-brush. Watch for mountain bluebirds along the fenceposts throughout this grassland. After 7 kilometres of climbing, you reach a broad, high valley in the plateau and turn southeast. These high grasslands are dominated by fescues rather than the bluebunch wheatgrass common at lower altitudes.

Except for the rolling hills and ponderosa pine–Douglas-fir woodlands scattered through it, this valley is reminiscent of the Canadian prairies, dotted with rich marshes and small lakes. The first large lake you pass is Garcia Lake, down in the valley to the west of the highway; the next two are Corbett Lake and Courtney Lake, both on the east side. Both are noted fishing lakes, and Corbett is aerated to keep oxygen levels elevated to avoid winter kill of its introduced rainbow trout population.

About 5 kilometres south of Courtney Lake, the highway turns east to climb the high plateau. It starts by climbing a small ridge, then descends into the Pothole Creek valley, part of the Quilchena Creek watershed that drains into Nicola Lake. You are still in aspen parkland habitat, with grasslands on the south-facing slopes and some large, red-trunked ponderosa pines and old, flat-topped Douglas-firs. The highway then begins to climb seriously, crossing over a minor divide into the Similkameen River drainage at Shrimpton Creek.

The forests are soon typically subalpine, with a dense growth of lodgepole pines and occasional patches of mature Engelmann spruce and subalpine fir. A few kilometres before Elkhart Lodge, you reach the undulating surface of the plateau. Most of the roadside rocks here are granitic, part of the Okanagan batholith that is prominent on Highway 3 east of Princeton. Three kilometres east of the Sunset Main exit, you can see a cottongrass fen on the south side of the highway. Fens are similar to bogs but have a water flow through them; bogs develop where water flow is more or less stagnant.

Beyond the Bear Creek Road exit, you cross Pennask Creek and begin to climb to the final summit. The rock cut on the south side of the highway above Pennask Creek is a serious problem, since rainfall on the newly exposed rock produces a bright orange mix of acids and metals that drain into the creek, where they are toxic to fish. The highways ministry is currently working on ways to fix this unforeseen problem. To the north you can see Pennask Lake, one of the most renowned fishing lakes in southern British Columbia.

Pennask Summit (1744 metres elevation) marks the high point of this highway, indeed one of the highest points on any highway in

Mountain Pine Beetle

In the late 1990s, a series of mountain pine beetle infestations across the Interior of British Columbia began to spread and coalesce into a major attack on the lodgepole pine forests of the province. These tiny beetles—each about the size of a grain of rice—burrow into the bark of the pines, lay their eggs, and let their larvae eat through the cambium layer so vital to the trees' survival. They prefer mature trees, and in the 1990s British Columbia had a bumper supply of older lodgepole pines, the legacy of rampant forest fires in the 1800s. Fuelled by warm, dry summers that stressed the trees and energized the beetles, and with no early winter cold snaps to kill off the larvae, the beetle infestation spread rapidly. In 1999 there were about 165,000 hectares of affected forest, but within ten years that had swelled to 17.5 million hectares, an area about five times the size of Vancouver Island. The growth of the infestation peaked in 2005 and has declined every year since, primarily because the beetles are running out of trees to eat.

So what does this mean for our forests and wildlife? Fortunately, the lodgepole pine fills a temporary niche in forests; it germinates in the bright sunshine of areas cleared by fire or logging, then dies after a relatively short life of a hundred years or so. In the shade of these lodgepole forests, spruce and fir seedlings germinate and grow into young trees ready to take over dominance of the forest after the demise of the pines. These fir and spruce form the climax forest in most of the British Columbia Interior, and the beetles are accelerating the succession to the new regime. That said, the extent of the recent pine beetle infestation was unprecedented and will likely have a strong effect on every aspect of the forest ecosystems in the affected area, from water tables to bird species composition.

British Columbia. The forests here are predominantly subalpine fir, with Engelmann spruce and some lodgepole pine. Open the window if you are driving by in summer—a subalpine fir forest offers a wonderful session of aromatherapy at no extra cost to the traveller.

This upper section of the highway suffers from frequent dense fog, especially in the winter months. If the day is clear, you can see the Monashee Mountains on the northeast horizon; Little White Mountain is the treeless bump on the skyline just southeast of Kelowna.

You descend very quickly (unless you are driving in dense fog, of course) to the huge embankment of the Brenda Mines tailings pond. This open-pit mine produced copper and molybdenum from 1970 to 1990, when it was closed because reserves were depleted.

From Brenda Mines the highway continues its rapid descent along the south slope of the Trepanier Creek valley, through a mix of young lodgepole pine and Douglas-fir forests. At one point you go under a wildlife overpass built to allow animals, especially mule deer, to cross over the highway. A large population of mule deer migrates out of the high plateau in fall to spend the winter at lower elevations in the Okanagan Valley, where snow depths are more amenable to them. One of their favourite wintering sites is Mt. Drought (980 metres), just ahead of you.

As you near the valley floor, you can see both local species of ceanothus shrubs on the roadside—the low, matlike buckbrush, with its evergreen leaves, and the higher-growing red-stem ceanothus. Both shrubs have sprays of white flowers in late spring. After crossing Trepanier Creek, you are back in the low-elevation ponderosa pine forests as the highway skirts the southern slopes of Mt. Drought. You get wonderful views of Okanagan Lake making its big bend around Okanagan Mountain and Squally Point before meeting up with Highway 97 on its way through the Okanagan Valley.

ELEVEN

The John Hart Highway

HIGHWAY 97

THE JOHN HART HIGHWAY, named for a former premier of British Columbia, connects central British Columbia with its northeastern plains. It begins at Prince George, traverses the Rocky Mountains and ends on the prairies at Dawson Creek. Not far north of Prince George, it crosses the Continental Divide at Summit Lake, and then follows the Crooked River north to McLeod Lake and the Northern Rocky Mountain Trench. Crossing the Parsnip River in the trench, it climbs up the moist, windward side of the Rockies into Pine Pass, following the Pine River into the true boreal forest to Chetwynd. At Chetwynd, it meets the northern prairies and heads east across the plains to Dawson Creek.

▶ **Prince George to the Parsnip River:**
Crossing the Continental Divide
Prince George lies in a large, flat-bottomed bowl at the junction of two major river valleys: the Fraser and the Nechako. Meandering back and forth over time, the rivers have cut down into the thick ice-age sediments that overlie the sedimentary and volcanic rocks of Quesnellia. Before the Pleistocene, the two rivers flowed north into

the Peace River, but about 750,000 years ago, they began to flow south through the young Fraser Canyon. Near the end of the Pleistocene, however, glaciers blocked the Fraser, forming Glacial Lake Prince George, and for a short time its waters flowed once again over the low divide into the Peace River. The cliffs of sand, silt and gravel to the east of the highway are the sediments of that glacial lake. The Nechako River, whose name means "big river" in the Carrier language, is much smaller at Prince George than it was before it was first dammed in 1952. Most of its water is now sent westward through a tunnel in the Coast Mountains to the Kemano power plant. The flow has not only been reduced, but now the water in the Nechako is also warmer. Both of these factors have caused problems for the fish in the river, particularly the white sturgeon and the sockeye and chinook salmon. In the last fifty years, the Nechako sturgeon population has plummeted from about 5000 to fewer than 600—and almost all of the remaining fish are older than thirty years. The sturgeon are either not producing babies or their babies are dying, but an entire generation is missing. Elsewhere, sturgeon need strong spring freshets to spawn, and the Nechako simply cannot provide those any longer.

Several sockeye salmon populations migrate up the Nechako, entering the river from mid-July to early October. Overall, these runs have also declined substantially since the mid-1990s; scientists believe that the main culprit is warm water temperatures during the adult migration. Chinook stocks, though much smaller than sockeye populations, seem to be stable.

Leaving the suburbs of Prince George, the highway passes through farming country interspersed with a mixed sub-boreal forest of white (hybrid) spruce, trembling aspen, paper birch, and lodgepole pine. In 2011, the aspens in the area were heavily infested with aspen leaf miners. Just south of kilometre 28, you cross the Salmon River on its way to the Fraser; about 500 to 2000 chinook salmon spawn in this stream each summer. Its headwaters form part of the Continental Divide between the Pacific-bound Fraser River and the Arctic-bound Peace River.

Facing page: The Crooked River meanders northward, its waters destined for the Arctic Ocean. SYDNEY CANNINGS

The Continental Divide is not marked by a high mountain range here; it is merely an imaginary line meandering across a subdued landscape. It is not marked well on the highway, either—it is honoured only by an old sign off a road to the east, just south of Summit Lake Road near kilometre 48. At this point, the Giscome Portage Trail, an important link in the route to the Omineca Gold Rush of the early 1870s, also meets the highway.

Leaf Miners

The aspen leaf miner is a tiny white moth native to North America. Leaf mining is a popular way to make a living among some small moths and sawflies. For small caterpillars, eating a leaf from the inside out is a great way of eating as much as you want and not having to worry about getting eaten yourself. Mined leaves are filled with pale, sinuous tunnels that give infested aspen groves a silver colour rather than the normal deep green. The moths overwinter as adults and fly in great clouds on the first warm days of spring, when the leaves are in bud.

Occasionally, the aspen leaf miner population reaches outbreak proportions. In the far northwest, an outbreak began in Alaska in 2000 and has since spread through the Yukon and much of northwestern British Columbia. Initiation of outbreaks is associated with a series of warm, dry summers. The end of the outbreak is difficult to predict; presumably the natural control agents of the species—diseases, parasitoids—will be able to overwhelm them at some point, perhaps with the aid of a hard frost in early fall or a cool, wet summer or two. Ongoing infestation doesn't usually kill the trees, but can result in a loss of growth and branch die-back.

The willow blotch miner is another small moth of the boreal regions that mines leaves, attacking most willow species. In this case, the mined leaves turn a blotchy brown, making it appear that the shrub is dying.

Top: Aspen leaf tunneled by a leaf miner caterpillar. SYDNEY CANNINGS
Bottom: Willow blotch miner damage. SYDNEY CANNINGS

Cattails border a floating fen near Summit Lake. SYDNEY CANNINGS

The land around and beyond Summit Lake is awash in glacial features—eskers and meltwater channels wind across the landscape, and a vast field of drumlins (small, teardrop-shaped hills) trends southwest to northeast to southwest, indicating the direction of ice flow at the end of the Pleistocene. Many of the kettles (depressions left behind by melting ice blocks) have filled with water and are now ponds or fens. For example, just south of the south entrance to Summit Lake Road is a rich boreal marsh, with cattails, shrubs and dead trees; across the highway is a floating fen: a mat of willow, marsh cinquefoil, bog buckbean and sedges, with some willows, separated from the highway by a man-made ditch filled with cattails and hardhack.

At the end of the Pleistocene, large glaciers dammed the Fraser River downstream of Prince George. The dam created Glacial Lake Prince George, whose waters reached the Summit Lake area and drained north into the Peace River watershed. This temporary exchange of the two drainages allowed two fishes of the Great Plains—white sucker and brassy minnow—to colonize the Fraser.

At the north end of Summit Lake (about kilometre 57), Teapot Mountain stands above the glacial plain. This is a column of volcanic

REST STOP
Bear Lake, Crooked River Provincial Park

THE SANDY FOREST floor becomes a nice beach when it meets the warm waters of Bear Lake, a favourite swimming destination in the region. The forest in the day-use area changed dramatically when beetle-killed trees were felled, but young pines now flourish in the open meadows. White spruce, subalpine fir, and Douglas-fir also occur; Douglas-firs are near the northern edge of their range here. If you are visiting in the late summer, you will want to bring some sort of container, because the sandy ground is thick with dwarf blueberries and saskatoons.

Square and Hart Lakes promise good angling for rainbow trout, Dolly Varden or Rocky Mountain whitefish, but Bear Lake has a more interesting fish: the brassy minnow. This small, unassuming species hails from the Missouri River, and occurs naturally in British Columbia in only two or three areas: the Summit Lake/Bear Lake region, the lower Fraser Valley, and possibly the south Peace region. How did it get here? It seems that it entered the Peace drainage through a series of transient, proglacial lakes in Alberta at the end of the Pleistocene and was then able to swim into the Fraser system shortly afterwards when that river was dammed by ice and flooded back up to this level. The minnows have vanished from a number of the small lakes around here and now seem to be restricted to Bear, Huble and Summit Lakes. Red-necked grebes breed in the quiet bays of Bear Lake and probably raise their young on brassy minnows.

Above: Dwarf blueberries. SYDNEY CANNINGS

Beginning in mid-October, trumpeter swans arrive from their northern breeding grounds to spend the winter on open sections of the Crooked River. GAIL ROSS

basalt—a remnant of one of the sources of the lava that covered the plateau in Miocene time.

As you approach Bear Lake/Crooked River Provincial Park from the south, the land is dominated by sand deposits, laid down at the end of the Pleistocene along the shores of Glacial Lake Prince George. Sandy soil is perfect for lodgepole pines, but as you drive north, more and more dead pines appear, victims of the mountain pine beetle outbreak of the 1990s and 2000s. The beetles preferentially attack mature trees, so act as renewal agents in the forest.

The Crooked River is a slow stream winding its way north through a series of shallow lakes. It is relatively small today, but flows through the channel of a much larger predecessor that drained the Nechako and upper Fraser watersheds at the end of the Pleistocene. At kilometre 112, there is a rest stop beside the Crooked River—watch for river otters, beaver and muskrat. Beginning in

Whiskers Point, McLeod Lake. SYDNEY CANNINGS

mid-October, trumpeter swans arrive from their northern breeding grounds to spend the winter on open sections of the river.

The largest lake that Crooked River flows through is McLeod Lake; Whiskers Point Provincial Park makes another welcome stop: you can stroll through the riparian forest of white (hybrid) spruce, with abundant thimbleberry and soopolallie in the understory. Along the lakeshore, black cottonwoods tower over red osier dogwood and willow shrubs—look for bald eagles and ospreys perched on the treetops. The long, shallow lake is an ideal breeding site for common loons, which nest on the many small islands.

The Crooked River and McLeod Lake also follow an important geological boundary—running down the middle of the lake is the McLeod Lake Fault, which separates ancient North America to the northeast (where you stand) from land with a more complex geological history to the southwest. Across the lake, the exotic Slide Mountain Terrane (in the foreground) and Quesnellia (in the background) have been forced on top of the former western edge of the continent. But it's more complicated than that, because the fault is part of the strike-slip fault system of the Northern Rocky Mountain Trench, which it joins beneath Williston Lake to the north. All the land across the lake has been squeezed by tectonic forces about 75 kilometres north relative to the land you are standing on.

The Crooked River continues north through Tudyah Lake into Williston Lake, the reservoir behind the Bennett Dam on the Peace River. Beyond Tudyah Lake, the highway leaves the Crooked River drainage and swings eastward to cross the Parsnip River above its drowned valley.

➤ The Parsnip River to Dawson Creek:
Crossing the Rocky Mountains and Meeting the Prairies

The arrow-straight valley of the Parsnip River forms the southern end of the Northern Rocky Mountain Trench; from this point this major lineament is followed by Williston Lake, and then the Finlay and Kechika Rivers all the way north to the Liard River Basin. North of that valley, it continues on as the Tintina Trench in the Yukon. This is a strike-slip fault, along which different parts of the earth's crust slide by one another, and it is the child of tectonic movement of the North American and Pacific plates. North America is moving west relative to the Pacific, movement which has created the mountain ranges of the west, but the Pacific plate is also moving north relative to North America. The Northern Rocky Mountain Trench and its branches are the breaking lines in the Earth's crust that translate this northward movement into the North American crust.

The black cottonwoods lining the Parsnip River are near the northeastern edge of their range here. Just north of Mackenzie, they meet their eastern boreal cousins, the balsam poplars. Like many east-west pairs of animals and plants that were separated during the ice ages, these two meet along the spine of the Rockies as far north as this latitude; north of here, balsam poplar sweeps across northern British Columbia, the Yukon and into Alaska. The reason for this is that the eastern slopes of the Rockies became ice-free much sooner than the land in heavily-glaciated central British Columbia, allowing eastern species to colonize northern British Columbia before their western counterparts.

Leaving the trench behind, the highway follows the valley of the Misinchinka River into the heart of the Misinchinka Ranges, which are more subdued than their classic Rocky Mountain cousins to the south. South of the latitude of Prince George, the Rockies are dominated by thick layers of resistant quartzites and limestones that create the dramatic, castellated Park Ranges of Jasper and Banff. Farther north, these layers become much thinner and, in the Misinchinka Ranges, the dominant rocks are schists, which are much softer than quartzites and limestones and are not up to the task of creating precipitous slopes and towering cliffs.

This is the wet, windward side of the mountains and snowfall is deep here during the winter. The forested slopes across the Misinchinka River from the highway are important wintering habitat for woodland caribou. This high-snowfall region is one of the northernmost areas where woodland caribou use tree lichens for winter sustenance. North of here, Caribou depend on ground lichens in the winter and so seek out windswept ridges or areas of light snowfall.

As you climb into the pass, you enter a subalpine forest dominated by Engelmann spruce and subalpine fir. Pine Pass, the high point on the highway, is south of Azouzetta Lake, but the true watershed divide between the Misinchinka and Pine Rivers is just north of the lake. Numerous avalanche slopes around the lake speak of the impressive snow depths here.

REST STOP
Bijoux Falls Provincial Park

BIJOUX IS THE French word for "jewels," and the 40-metre-high falls sparkle like diamonds as they cascade over ancient sedimentary rocks that once made up the continental shelf of North America. In the forest shade, the spiny stalks and maplelike leaves of devil's club remind you that you are indeed in a wet forest. Clumps of foamflowers grace the rocky shores, and Steller's jays, noisy representatives of western forests and British Columbia's provincial bird, almost always make their presence known. Take a good look—on the other side of Pine Pass, Steller's jays, Townsend's warblers, MacGillivray's warblers, black cottonwoods, and their other western brethren will have vanished behind you. If you are lucky during your stop, you will see an American dipper visiting its globelike nest tucked in behind the sheet of falling water.

Facing page: Bijoux Falls. SYDNEY CANNINGS

Azouzetta Lake lies along a thrust fault that divides the Misinchinka Range from the distinctly different Murray Range. The dramatic slopes of the Murray Range across the lake are Upper Cambrian limestones, slates and argillites of the Lynx Formation—the twisting folds in the rocks within the formation tell us of the tremendous forces that have pushed them into the sky. These are the rocks at the heart of the Park Ranges to the south—this formation takes its name from Lynx Mountain, a sister peak to Mt. Robson, and it makes up the entire summit massif of that great mountain. On the northwest side of the fault, the rocks you are standing on are older than the ones you are gazing at; the younger rocks that correspond to the Lynx Formation have long since eroded away from this sheet, their sediments carried down the ancient Peace River.

The folded rocks of the Murray Range in Pine Pass. SYDNEY CANNINGS

In the fall, Pine Pass is an excellent place to witness the annual migration of hawks and eagles from their breeding grounds in the northern forests and mountains; look for such species as northern harriers, sharp-shinned hawks, red-tailed hawks and golden eagles. These birds follow the Rockies' ridge tops, using the updrafts along the cliffs for lift in their long journey.

About 10 kilometres north of Azouzetta Lake, you get close-up views of the limestones of the Lynx Formation in the vertical road cuts on the east side of the highway. Descending into the deep valley of the Pine River, you enter the true boreal forest of the northern North American interior: in British Columbia, ecologists call this the Boreal White and Black Spruce Zone.

You may still be in British Columbia, but you have entered an eastern world more similar to Winnipeg than Prince George in terms of its biota. In these forests, birders from southern British Columbia are thrilled to find eastern birds such as black-throated green warblers, ovenbirds, rose-breasted grosbeaks, and Baltimore orioles. It is amazing that these winged creatures, which fly thousands of kilometres between their wintering and breeding grounds, hardly ever stray over the low mountains you have just driven over in the last hour or two.

Above the rich riparian forests, trembling aspens begin to appear on the dry, south-facing slopes. Not only is it drier on this, the lee side of the Rockies, but warm, dry Chinook winds often blow down the slopes in the winter, taking the snow with them. The result is that the snowpack is considerably less here than it is along the Parsnip River. In 2011, the willow shrubs along the road here had been invaded by willow blotch miners (see sidebar, p. 240), tiny moths whose larvae tunnel in the leaves and turn them a dead, orange-brown colour.

As you approach Chetwynd, you leave the Rockies behind and enter the foothills, which slope off to the high plains to the east. The geology becomes simpler—all the rocks around you are reasonably young sedimentary rocks of Cretaceous age, their flat layers have never been folded or broken, and you are firmly on ancestral North America. At about kilometre 269, there is a pull-off on the south side of the road at Jack Pine Point with an excellent view of the valley. About 3 kilometres east of here the first grassy breaks appear on the south-facing slope above the highway road cuts. Although these grasslands are still well within the foothills, they are biologically similar to the Peace River grasslands farther east and have prairie butterflies like Uhler's Arctic fluttering over them. The first name for Chetwynd was, in fact, "Little Prairie." Now, however, the little prairies have largely disappeared under the plough or under pavement, so these small grassy slopes are important to the survival of prairie species in the region.

In the well-watered riparian forest along the Pine River, white spruce and balsam poplars tower over an understory cloaked in red osier dogwood and thimbleberry. SYDNEY CANNINGS

At Chetwynd, you can choose two alternate routes on your north-ward journey: Highway 29 North leads past Hudson's Hope and the Peace River valley; Highway 29S heads to Tumbler Ridge and its dinosaur finds.

East of Chetwynd, the Hart Highway leaves the Pine River valley, climbs up onto the high plains, and makes its way through a mixed, mostly young boreal forest of trembling aspen, lodgepole pine (many dying from mountain pine beetle infestation) and some white spruce. Some agricultural fields interrupt the forest, and these interruptions come more and more frequently as you travel east. To the south is the high mesa of Mt. Wartenbe.

At East Pine, you cross the Pine River one last time, this time over a high bridge that gives a good view of the river canyon. The Murray River enters the Pine just upstream, greatly increasing its flow. After winding your way out of the Pine River canyon, you will find the road much straighter as you enter the true plains and pass through small farming communities such as Groundbirch and Progress. At Arras, the highway crosses the Kiskatinaw River (which you will cross again if you are continuing up the Alaska Highway) and passes by the headwaters of Dawson Creek. The creek arcs north but then swings south, and you rejoin it at the end of the Hart Highway, in the community of Dawson Creek.

TWELVE

The Alaska Highway

HIGHWAY 97 AND
YUKON HIGHWAY 1

THE ALASKA HIGHWAY is the legendary road of the north. From Dawson Creek, British Columbia, it travels through the Rockies into the Yukon, then stretches northwest into Alaska, where it ends at the Richardson Highway in Delta Junction, 2252 long kilometres from its starting point. This guide book treats only the Canadian portion of the highway, which ends at the Alaska border, 1874 kilometres from Dawson Creek.

From Fort St. John north, the trip is largely through wilderness, with only the occasional small community or remote lodge appearing beside the road. The largest city en route is Whitehorse, Yukon, with 26,500 residents. The highway first travels north into the muskeg plateau of northeastern British Columbia. At Fort Nelson, it begins a long, westerly journey across northern British Columbia and the southern Yukon. Along the way, it crosses two ranges of the Rocky Mountains, stops by Liard River Hot Springs and follows the Liard River to Watson Lake, Yukon. From Watson Lake it traverses the northern end of the Cassiar Mountains, crosses the Continental Divide and meanders through the magnificent Southern Lakes region of the Yukon to Whitehorse. From Whitehorse, it continues

west to the St. Elias Mountains, the highest mountains in Canada, and follows their eastern flanks north to the Alaska border, just past the community of Beaver Creek.

▶ Dawson Creek to Fort Nelson: The Boreal and Taiga Plains

The plateau country around Dawson Creek and Fort St. John is an isolated extension of the Prairies to the south. Summers are warm but short, winters cold and long: Fort St. John's average daily high in July is 21.2°c, and its average January daily low is –18.4°c. In the rain shadow of the Rockies, the climate is relatively dry, and much of its precipitation comes in summer thunderstorms.

As you leave the town of Dawson Creek, the highway travels through farmland, with scattered copses of trembling aspen surrounded by silvery wolf willow shrubs. This isn't a real willow—in fact, "wolf" before a plant name often alerts you to the fact that this is an impostor—but a member of the Oleaster family, a close relative of the introduced Russian Olive of southern British Columbia.

The highway crosses the Kiskatinaw River over a spectacular canyon, then continues to the Peace River, where you descend a long and winding hill, cutting through the coarse sedimentary rocks of the Upper Cretaceous Dunvegan Formation at the top, then down and down over 200 metres through the finer siltstones and mudstones of the Fort St. John Group.

The Peace River has a long history on this young side of the continent; its course certainly predates the latest uplift of the Rocky Mountains. In fact, up until about 750,000 years ago, the Nechako River and the upper Fraser River watershed were the headwaters of a larger Peace River, draining north into the Parsnip through the Crooked River. But at that time the Peace did not flow into the Mackenzie River—instead, it emptied into a great river that flowed east toward Hudson Bay. The modern Mackenzie drainage didn't capture the Peace until late in the Pleistocene, when the retreating continental ice sheet blocked the eastern drainage and simultaneously opened up a corridor against the mountains.

Facing page: The Alaska Highway winds its way westward through the foothills of the Rockies at Steamboat Mountain. SYDNEY CANNINGS

Wolf willow

At the end of the last ice age, a complex of large lakes covered much of the Peace River country in British Columbia. At different times, these lakes drained either south into the Missouri-Mississippi system or north into the Mackenzie system, allowing Missouri River fish to colonize northeastern British Columbia. Before about ten thousand years ago, a lake briefly covered the Peace River Canyon, which before had been a serious barrier to fish movement. This lake allowed some of the Missouri fish to enter the upper Peace and later, via the Summit Lake connection near Prince George (see Highway 97-Hart Highway), allowed two of these—the white sucker and brassy minnow—to colonize the Fraser. Still, fourteen species of Great Plains fish, including pike and walleye, are found in the lower Peace but absent from the upper river.

The lakes created by ice dams on the Peace at the end of the Pleistocene deposited up to 30 metres of silts on the land they flooded. Although climax forests in this region are dominated by white or black spruce, fires are naturally common and have created a largely young forest landscape. On the lake-bottom silts, a parkland of trembling aspens and grassland dominates; on coarser soils at higher elevations, lodgepole pine forests are common. Now, of course, the aspen parkland has largely been replaced by an agricultural landscape, but copses of aspens are still common and relict grasslands still occur here and there, primarily on steep, south-facing slopes.

The isolation of the Peace River grasslands has led to the evolution of a distinct biota, especially of plants and invertebrates. If you see a large, yellow butterfly with black shoulders fluttering over tarragon on the steep roadside slopes, you are probably looking at a Pike's swallowtail, the local form of the Baird's swallowtail. This striking butterfly, larger and brighter yellow than its southern cousins, was discovered in 1980 by Ted Pike and Felix Sperling, keen-eyed lepidopterists from Alberta.

As it passes Charlie Lake, the highway climbs up a small hill out of the valley; at the top of the hill is the junction of Highway 29, which leads west up the scenic and fascinating Peace River valley and back to Highway 97 at Chetwynd. As you climb gradually in altitude toward the foothills, the forest gets moister and the trees get larger. Many of the mature lodgepole pines have been killed by mountain pine beetles but, in 2011 at least, the trembling aspens in this forest had so far escaped the widespread aspen leaf miner infestation that has swept out of Alaska and the Yukon and into northern British Columbia. However, the roadside willow shrubs show the orange-brown leaves indicative of the willow blotch miner (leaf miner sidebar, page 240).

The highway climbs gradually up the gentle waves of the Rocky Mountain foothills to Wonowon; north of here, the ridge tops begin to give you better and better views of the front ranges to the northwest. At kilometre 200, the highway goes through a rare road cut that exposes the sedimentary layers of the Dunvegan Formation, the same Cretaceous rocks you saw at the top of the hill into the Peace River valley. The Dunvegan Formation, named after the Alberta community on the Peace River, was first described by George Mercer Dawson, the brilliant geologist whose name has been honoured in both Dawson Creek, British Columbia, and Dawson City, Yukon.

Many industrial roads dissect the forest in this region, and the occasional waft of natural gas reminds you of their destinations.

Just north of the hamlet of Pink Mountain, the highway begins a long, gradual descent into the headwater valley of the Beatton River. Pink Mountain itself is the rounded alpine ridge you see to

REST STOP

Beatton Provincial Park

AS YOU LEAVE Fort St. John on your trip north, you may want to take a short side trip on Road 271 to the east to Beatton Provincial Park on the east shore of Charlie Lake. This park is a perennial favourite of birders from southern British Columbia—in the spring and early summer, they get up at dawn to look for Cape May warblers in the tall spruces, but they are more likely to see other eastern birds such as blue jays, black-and-white warblers, ovenbirds, Baltimore orioles, and winter wrens. Thousands of the prairie-loving Franklin's gulls socialize on the lake in early summer before heading east to Alberta to nest. In spring and in fall, large flocks of scoters, goldeneyes and scaups rest and feed here, and in fall, all four species of loons can be seen in migration.

the west. This modest mountain is a key destination for palaeontologists. In 1991, a 23-metre-long ichthyosaur—the world's largest known specimen to date—was discovered in 220 million-year-old rocks on its western slopes. Butterfly and plant enthusiasts also come here from far and wide to seek out Beringian tundra species at or near their southern range limits—butterflies like Eversmann's Parnassian and the Old World swallowtail. During the Pleistocene ice ages, Beringia was the broad, unglaciated land that stretched from Yukon and Alaska across the Bering Land Bridge into Siberia. Many of the animals and plants that inhabited the tundra and steppe of Beringia still live there today, and many of those have closer family ties to Asia than to North America.

In 1971, 48 plains bison escaped from a ranch on the upper Halfway River near Pink Mountain, and more than 1300 of their descendants now range over a large area of the mountains in the region. You can drive 30 kilometres to the top of Pink Mountain on

Baltimore orioles

a rough forestry road that begins along the southern bank of the Beatton River—bear right at the forks.

The upper Beatton River valley is a wide meadow clothed in willows, a good example of a shrub carr. Here, soils can become saturated with meltwater during spring and early summer, which makes it difficult for trees to grow. Heavy, cold air also flows down the surrounding slopes and pools here, significantly reducing the frost-free season and discouraging tree growth.

In the short distance between the Beatton and the Sikanni Chief rivers, the highway crosses the watershed divide between two of the major tributaries of the Mackenzie River system: the Peace and Liard rivers. The climate and vegetation change subtly as well. Arctic air often blankets the low plains around Fort Nelson in winter and spring. In summer, the region's location between the Arctic and Pacific air masses can give it long periods of moist, unstable weather. Patchy permafrost occurs and black spruce peatlands are widespread. As you approach the Sikanni Chief River, black spruce becomes increasingly common, and along the long hill down to the bridge, it is abundant on north-facing slopes.

The highway then follows the broad, straight valley of the Minnaker River north past the ridge of Trutch Mountain to the east. The acidic, treed bogs along the highway are dominated by black spruce; the richer fens are dominated by tamarack, the boreal species of larch. The understories of the bogs are made up of Labrador tea, cloudberry, lingonberry, dwarf blueberry and sphagnum mosses; the fens are clothed with scrub birch, sweet gale, leather-leaf and various fen mosses. In the spring, the incongruously named palm warbler sings its wheezy song from the tops of the black spruce.

At the junction of the Muskwa and Fort Nelson Rivers, the community of Fort Nelson has a truly continental climate: winters are cold and dry, whereas summers are surprisingly warm and occasionally rainy. The average January daily low is −25.6°c, whereas the average July daily high is 23°c.

Fort Nelson to Liard River
Crossing: Over the Northern Rockies

This section of the Alaska Highway not only boasts spectacular scenery, but its Rocky Mountain traverse is one of the best journeys in the province for encountering large wildlife. Black and grizzly bears, caribou, moose, elk, bison and Stone's sheep are all likely to be seen.

Leaving Fort Nelson, you soon pass the junction of the Liard Highway (not covered in this book), the farmlands disappear and you enter wilderness once again. Before long, the highway begins to climb up onto the mesas of the Rocky Mountain foothills; the black, carbon-rich sediments exposed in the road cuts are the marine mudstones of the Buckinghorse Formation, about 100 million years old. As the road begins to skirt the high mesa of Tepee Mountain, it cuts through the sandstones of the Sikanni Formation, and you can see the spectacular

REST STOP
Buckinghorse Provincial Park

THE BUCKINGHORSE RIVER is a tributary of the Sikanni Chief. The campground at the crossing makes a nice stop, with a mixture of white-spruce woodland, riverside meadows and a cobble-boulder stream shoreline. The woodland vegetation is truly northern, populated by such plants as boreal and alpine sweetvetch, narrow-leaved fireweed and marsh grass-of-Parnassus. Bears love to eat the roots of alpine sweetvetch, but shun the larger-flowered boreal species, presumably because it is poisonous. On the opposite side of the river a north-facing black spruce forest is slumping into the river—probably the result of the stream exposing permafrost, which causes the ice-rich soil to melt during the summer and flow downhill.

Facing page: As ice-rich soil melts and flows downhill, a black spruce woodland slumps into the river at Buckinghorse Provincial Park.
SYDNEY CANNINGS

summit prow of Steamboat Mountain ahead, its hard Dunvegan sandstones more resistant than the rock below. Here they have been uplifted about 1000 metres above their elevation at the Peace River crossing. The highway now descends into the valley of the Tetsa River.

Twenty or so kilometres up the valley, the highway begins to follow the Tetsa River more closely. Here it is a typical braided mountain stream, actively bringing down immense amounts of coarse sediments every spring freshet. Its gravel and cobble islands are covered in the yellow flowers of mountain-avens, which burst into fluffy spirals later in the season, and its side channels are dammed constantly by an obviously healthy population of beavers.

As you cross the two bridges over the Tetsa River, look at the slopes around you. The steep, north-facing slopes to the south are

Rain shower on a mesa in the Rocky Mountain foothills near Steamboat Mountain.
SYDNEY CANNINGS

cloaked in stripes of boglike vegetation—sphagnum mosses and Labrador tea—that cover a thin, active soil layer over permafrost. The south-facing slopes to the north have typical, dry boreal forest—white spruce, trembling aspen and soopolallie shrubs.

Keep your eyes on the road now—caribou are often seen between here and Summit Lake and in the MacDonald Creek valley beyond. These are the northern ecotype of mountain caribou—they feed on ground lichens during the winter, either on windswept ridges or in dry, open forests.

Leaving Summit Lake, you pass a rich fen that marks the pass between the watersheds of the Muskwa and the Toad Rivers—although waters flowing either way will end up in the Liard River and ultimately the Mackenzie. At 1295 metres elevation, the pass is the highest point on the Alaska Highway. On the north side of the road is a trailhead to the hoodoos on the slope above—hoodoos are erosional features that are created where the soft sediments on a hillside are almost entirely washed away, but those protected by a cap of rocks or more resistant sediments remain. Soon you are twisting down a narrow limestone canyon—you must drive slowly through here, not only because of the winding road, but also because this is where Stone's sheep often wander across the highway.

You have entered the valley of MacDonald Creek, an active stream choked with cobbles and boulders and braided islands—erosion is obviously pulling down these mountains every day.

Near the bottom of the MacDonald Creek valley, the highway crosses the creek and swings west to join the Racing River. On the steep, south-facing slopes across the valley, periodic fires are set to keep the aspens at bay and maintain the grasslands. Elk, lovers of mountain grasslands, are common here, as are Stone's sheep and deer. You don't follow the Racing River for long and soon cross it and head overland to the Toad River. On the south side of the road is a low-lying fen of black spruce and sedges, a favourite haunt of moose.

After passing the Toad River Lodge, you enter Muncho Lake Provincial Park and continue to follow the river upstream. At kilometre 657, there is a pull-off with a view of Folded Mountain—this is a remarkable example of how solid rock, under extreme pressure, can be folded and warped and folded again. The road stays with the

The Coldest Place in North America

At about kilometre 551, you reach Mill Creek and the turnoff to Tetsa River Provincial Park. This valley isn't remarkably different from the other river valleys draining the east slope of the northern Rockies, but a location along the highway just west of Mill Creek holds the honour of having had the coldest recorded temperature in North America. Here, in the early morning hours of January 7, 1982, the temperature plunged 20 degrees in one hour and went on to drop to -71°c, knocking off the old record of -63°c from Snag, Yukon, by eight degrees. This phenomenon was the result of intense cold-air drainage into the valley on a calm, clear night. The Tetsa River valley is narrowed downstream as well, which prevents rapid dispersal of the cold air. There was a marked inversion—in the alpine above Summit Lake, the temperature was only -38°c!

REST STOP

Summit Lake, Stone Mountain Provincial Park

SUMMIT LAKE OFFERS not only a pleasant campground at the east end of the lake, but also several walks to the surrounding alpine ridges. You can hike to the top of Summit Peak or up to Flower Springs Lake, or you can just take a short break from driving and mosey along the trails, looking closely for arctic and subarctic wonders. This is a mountain ecosystem dominated by limestone and dolomite, so the botanizing is always rewarding. Orchids love the calcium-rich limestone, and even between the gravel campsites you can find one-leaved rein orchids and sparrow's egg ladyslippers—as well as plenty of wild strawberries. Along the first section of the Ridge Trail, you climb an open slope carpeted with reticulated willow, alpine bearberry, Arctic mountain heather and moss campion, among many others. A small arctic rhododendron, the Lapland rosebay, is also common here. Across the highway, the Summit Peak Trail crosses a small creek with a beautiful subalpine bonsai garden along its low terraces, graced with yellow saxifrage and the delicate pink of Raup's Indian paintbrush.

Above: Limestone ridges surround Summit Lake in Stone Mountain Provincial Park. SYDNEY CANNINGS

Toad River upstream through spectacular limestone canyons; this is perfect Stone's sheep country. At kilometre 668, geology and geomorphology is once more the highlight of another roadside pull-off, where a classic alluvial fan is on display.

North of this rest stop, the character of the Toad River changes dramatically to a slow-moving, deep river with attendant marshes, fens and beaver ponds. This is ideal moose country—in fact, the Toad River flows out of Moose Lake just a few kilometres upstream. As the Toad River swings southward, however, the highway turns sharply north to follow the mountain trench over Muncho Pass to Muncho Lake. On the other side of the pass, many more alluvial fans pour out of the mountain canyons.

Muncho Lake is a jade-coloured gem set in a long, straight trench between the Sentinel Range of the Rockies to the east and the Terminal Range to the west. Lake trout, Arctic grayling, bull trout and lake whitefish all inhabit the lake's cold, deep waters. The campground at Strawberry Flats is set on a large alluvial fan of calcareous dolomite

Stone's Sheep

The Stone's sheep in the northern Rockies are a product of ancient hybridization between thinhorn and bighorn sheep. Even though their less-robust form and slender, flaring horns speak of their thinhorn ancestry, their mitochondrial DNA (which records maternal lineage) reveals a closer relationship to bighorns of the southern Rockies. These Stone's sheep probably survived glaciation in a shifting ice-free refuge on the eastern slopes of the Rocky Mountains.

Stone's sheep. SYDNEY CANNINGS

The dolomite rocks of the Sentinel Range make up the eastern wall of Muncho Pass.
SYDNEY CANNINGS

debris; its spruce woodland is open, with paper birch growing in a large shrub form, and mountain death camas and sparrow's egg ladyslippers brightening the scene. Despite the calcareous nature of the soil, Labrador tea grows in the shade here—although one normally associates this plant with acidic, boggy places, it will do just fine in most cold, moist soils.

Farther down the valley, at kilometre 726.7, there is a short (five to ten minutes) loop trail to a major salt lick along the Trout River. Lacustrine silt cliffs line the river valley here, rich in minerals ground by glaciers from the dolomites and limestones above—calcium, magnesium, sulphur, phosphorus and sodium. These minerals are craved by Stone's sheep, moose and caribou, all of which may be seen here.

After you cross the Trout River, the landscape becomes more subdued as the highway leaves the Rockies, eventually turning gradually westward around the final peaks of the Terminal Range. You have entered the Liard Plateau, a broad expanse of rolling hill country that separates the northern Rockies from the Mackenzie Mountains of the Yukon and Northwest Territories. As far as you can see, the forest here is a young fire forest of trembling aspen, balsam poplar and paper

REST STOP
Liard River Hot Springs

THE LIARD RIVER Hot Springs is one of the "must-stops" on an Alaska Highway journey. Regardless of the weather, the steamy water will welcome you and your stiff, car-bound body. But the springs are more than a spa, they are also an amazing natural history experience, an oasis of lush diversity amidst a vast expanse of young boreal forest.

The hot springs, Canada's second largest, are underlain by faulted sedimentary rocks covered with a layer of glacial drift. The precise mechanism of the springs is unknown, but in general, ground water seeps down through the cracks in the bedrock and is heated deep underground. The hot, pressurized water is then pushed back to the surface along natural cracks. The calcium carbonate dissolved in the water precipitates as tufa, forming the terraces of the Hanging Gardens above the main pool. The water enters Alpha Pool between 42°c and 52°c— more springs are believed to bubble out along the stream's course.

To a naturalist, the most exciting thing about these springs is the fact that they do not flow directly into a river, but instead into an extensive archipelago of wetlands. As you walk the boardwalk to the Alpha Pool, look carefully at the sights around you. Brilliant yellow monkey flowers line channels choked with the calcareous algae, chara. The hotwater physa, a small snail found nowhere else in the world, lives in the outlet stream of the Alpha Pool and in the upper Beta Pool. An unusual, thermally adapted form of lake chub eats the chara, and larvae of a southern damselfly, the plains forktail, lurk in the marsh tangles. The pools and marshes also create a rich, warm terrestrial environment around them. Ostrich ferns and other lush vegetation give the scene a tropical look. More than a dozen other plant species grow here because of the warmth, including tender sedge, black snakeroot and Lyall's nettle. The uncommon white adder's-mouth orchid and thirteen other species of orchids thrive in the moist, mineral-rich soils.

The adjacent campground is set within a rich boreal forest of white spruce, paper birch and balsam poplar, with a dense understory of red osier dogwood, rose, cow parsnip, high-bush cranberry, raspberry and alder. Birders wake up to a cacophony of eastern boreal bird song; some species are very close to their northwestern range limits here, including Baltimore orioles and rose-breasted grosbeaks. In the wetlands, solitary sandpipers and lesser yellowlegs scold you from the treetops. Moose are also common visitors to this deluxe feeding ground, so take a walk down the boardwalk at dusk and you may be rewarded by a sight of these stately giants grazing in the mist.

The human attraction to naturally hot water has spelled disaster for the specialized, dependent inhabitants of most hot springs, for if the springs are of any size and consequence, they are soon dammed or piped away to concrete pools in commercial resorts. It is remarkable that the springs at Liard, one of the largest and finest in Canada, were initially spared from development by their remote location and now are respectfully managed by B.C. Parks.

Above: Liard River Hot Springs. JENNIFER HERON

birch, with only scattered patches of mature white spruce. Watch for wood bison grazing along the road verge; they are commonly seen from here all the way to the Yukon border at Contact Creek.

You cross the Liard River on a graceful suspension bridge. French Canadian voyageurs gave it the name *Rivière aux Liards*, referring to the balsam poplars that line its banks.

➤ Liard Crossing to the Stewart-Cassiar Junction:
Hot Springs and the Land of Fire

Along this stretch of the Alaska Highway, you follow the general path of the Liard River upstream, travelling from the hilly Liard Plateau into the dissected but relatively flat basin of the Liard Plain. This section of the highway is not as spectacular as the one you have just travelled through or as the one following it—but one does get a feeling of finally being in the north, when you cross the 60th parallel (seven times!) and enter the Yukon just south of Watson Lake.

After leaving the hot springs—perhaps reluctantly—you travel west through a lush old fire forest of big aspens, with some birch and spruce, and occasional glimpses of the river. About 20 kilometres west, you reach the edge of a forest fire that burned more than 23,000 hectares of the valley in 2009. You will be driving through this burn for about 35 kilometres, but you can see that in many places the fire was quite cool and in other places burned more intensely. The result is a forest mosaic, a typical pattern in a fire landscape.

At the Smith River crossing, there is a 2.5-kilometre side road leading to the spectacular, 35-metre-high Smith River Falls; vehicle access was temporarily closed following the 2009 fire, however. Smith River has the honour of being the coldest official weather station in British Columbia—it dropped to -59°C on January 31, 1947.

As you travel east, the landscape becomes flatter as you enter the Liard Plain. This broad, shallow bowl was the meeting ground for glaciers flowing out of the Cassiar, Omineca and Mackenzie Mountains at the end of the Pleistocene; the coalesced ice sheets filled this basin and flowed through the mountain gap to the east. After they

Wood Bison

Wood bison once roamed freely from the southern edge of the boreal forest in Alberta into the Northwest Territories, the northern Yukon and Alaska. In the 1800s, overhunting reduced their numbers from about 168,000 to only a few hundred; the last one in British Columbia was shot near Fort St. John in 1906.

In 1978, wood bison were designated as Endangered in Canada, but a strong recovery program led to increased numbers and in 1988, they were downlisted to Threatened. In 2008, there were approximately 10,000 free-ranging wood bison in Canada. They were first reintroduced to British Columbia in 1995, when 49 were moved from Elk Island National Park in Alberta to the Nordquist Flats area of the Liard River valley, about 34 kilometres east of the hot springs. This herd has grown slowly to about 140 in 2008, but ranges along the highway corridor, so groups of bison are often seen by travellers. Needless to say, a collision with a bison is a serious affair—drive carefully!

Above: Wood bison. SYDNEY CANNINGS

wasted away, their path was marked by extensive drumlin fields and swarms of eskers, all oriented west to east. Dune complexes and kettle lakes are also common on the larger landscape.

You finally leave the 2009 fire at about kilometre 818, but in less than 5 kilometres you enter a much larger one as you descend into the Coal River valley. The Eg Fire, as it is known, is the second largest forest fire in the British Columbia record books—in 1982 it burned over 182,725 hectares from here all the way to near Lower Post, destroying the unfortunately named community of Fireside in the process. In the intervening three decades, the forest has recovered to produce the woodland of small aspens and pines you see now. The Liard region is the land of the big fires—the largest fire in the province's recorded history occurred just south of here, burning almost 226,000 hectares in the Kechika valley in 1958.

At kilometre 909.4, you reach the Yukon for the first time at Contact Creek. On the north side of the creek is a mature white-spruce forest—something you haven't seen for a long time—and birders may find eastern species such as blue-headed vireos near the northwestern edge of their range here. Don't get used to being north of 60 just yet, since the highway winds in and out of the Yukon five more times before entering it for good south of Teslin.

At about kilometre 967.8, you enter the Yukon once again, although the official Welcome to Yukon sign is three kilometres to the north. Across the road from the sign is Lucky Lake, a popular swimming hole for the local community of Watson Lake. You might want to have a dip here, but you can also walk 2.2 kilometres along a signed nature trail to a canyon on the Liard River. The trail passes through an open lodgepole pine fire forest carpeted with lichens on its floor, but when you get to the river, the riparian white-spruce forest contains some of the largest and perhaps oldest spruce in the territory.

Two blocks farther on is the junction of the Campbell Highway,

At Whirlpool Canyon, the Liard River tumbles over resistant layers of sedimentary rocks of the Hyland Group, more than 500 million years old.
SYDNEY CANNINGS

which leads north and west through Faro and Ross River to Carmacks on the North Klondike Highway. If your destination is the Klondike, this is a superb, less-travelled route up the biologically rich Tintina Trench.

Watson Lake lies on the windward side of the Mackenzie Mountains, and near the bottom of the wide, shallow bowl of the Liard Plain. Because of this, it is considerably snowier than Whitehorse and consistently colder in winter as well—its all-time record low temperature is an impressive −58.9°c. On the plus side, it is usually warmer in the summer than Whitehorse, albeit with more thunderstorms. These factors, plus the fact that the Liard Plain has a broad opening to the eastern plains, give rise to a noticeably different biota than the rest of the southern Yukon—a biota that loves some moisture and that has distinctly eastern roots.

The basin of the Liard Plain has been a dumping ground for sediments from the surrounding mountains for the past 40 million years, and these young sediments are now hundreds of metres deep. The sediments obscure the surface traces of the great Tintina Fault west of the outskirts of Watson Lake. Over hundreds of millions of years and through innumerable earthquakes, the bedrock to the west of this fault has slipped up to 1200 kilometres north relative

REST STOP

Wye Lake

IN DOWNTOWN WATSON Lake, the park at Wye Lake makes an excellent stop—turn north on 8th Street N and you are there. The name Wye Lake refers to the fact that it is near the junction—the Y—of the Alaska Highway and the Campbell Highway (or, in past days, the road to the major military airport at Watson Lake). A boardwalk here crosses a sedge fen and then leads you on a 1.5-kilometre journey around the shallow lake, guiding you with interpretive panels on native plants and birds. Red-necked grebes call from the edge of the sedge beds and, on sunny days, dragonflies abound. In the evenings, little brown bats take over from the dragonflies and feed voraciously on the insects emerging from the water. These bats don't have to commute that far—they roost in a retail store not far away.

Facing page: The Hudsonian whiteface is abundant along the shores of Wye Lake. NETTA SMITH

to land to the east—425 kilometres in the last 100 million years alone. The fault has been quiet for the last 20 million years, but similar movement still goes on along faults in the St. Elias Mountains to the west.

A few kilometres west of Watson Lake, you drop into the Liard River valley for the last time. As you descend, you can see outcrops of 6-million-year-old lava beds inlaid in the Liard Plain's sediments.

After you pass through the community of Upper Liard, you cross Albert Creek, a small and superficially unremarkable stream. But because it is entirely a lowland watershed that drains a series of shallow lakes, this creek is unusually warm for watercourses in the Yukon (see p. 185, Highway 37).

The Liard Plain and oxbows of the Liard River, looking west from the Upper Liard.
JOHN MEIKLE

Ten kilometres beyond Upper Liard, you reach the junction of Highway 37 (see Highway 37, p. 171). This is a chance to choose: some will turn south on another spectacular northern road; others will continue on (as we do in this chapter), farther into the Yukon.

▶ Stewart-Cassiar Junction to Teslin: The Cassiar Mountains

On this leg of the journey, the highway continues across the Liard Plain and then follows the Rancheria River upstream toward its headwaters in the Cassiar Mountains. After crossing the Continental Divide, the highway enters the watershed of the Swift River and follows it back into British Columbia to Swan Lake and beyond. As the Swift River arcs southward, the highway swings north, climbs onto the Yukon Plateau and heads overland to Teslin Lake and the community of the same name.

For the next forty kilometres or so, you pass through the core winter range of the Little Rancheria caribou herd. These caribou, about one thousand in number, spend the summers in the alpine regions of the Cassiar Mountains to the south of the Liard. When the heavy mountain snows arrive in October, however, they descend into

REST STOP

Albert Creek Migration Monitoring Station

IF YOU ARE a birder, a slight diversion is in order here—one of the Yukon's two bird migration monitoring stations is at Albert Creek. If you're travelling during the spring or fall migration, the bird banders would love to have interested naturalists pay a visit during the morning banding session. Turn north on the first road west of the Albert Creek bridge, and after 450 metres turn right again on a secondary road for one kilometre. The riparian and wetland habitats of the Liard River are home to such common birds as alder flycatchers, Tennessee warblers and northern waterthrushes. Some birds, such as western tanagers and Cape May warblers, are at their northern or northwestern limits here; others, like Townsend's warblers, are at their eastern limit. This road, though it can be wet and rough early in the summer, makes an excellent birding and naturalizing stop. Western toads are at the northern edge of their range here, too—they can survive the extremely cold winters because the region's dependably deep snow is an excellent insulator. If you have time to explore a patch of mature spruce forest here, you will find a lush interior carpeted with surprises such as round-leaved bog orchids.

Above: Bird banding at the Albert Creek Migration Monitoring Station.
JOHN MEIKLE

the open lodgepole pine forests along the highway in October to forage on the abundant lichens on the forest floor.

Paper birch is still an important member of the forest here, especially on moister aspects, but it will drop out of the forest scene as you head west into the drier zone in the lee of the Cassiar Mountains. It won't become common again until you approach Beaver Creek, near the Alaska border.

At kilometre 1062, the highway leaves the plateau of the Liard Basin and drops into the valley of the Rancheria River—the sign says "Lower Rancheria River," but "lower" refers to the bridge, not the river. The Rancheria valley is a scenic beauty, with understated mountains sculpted by past glaciation and a clear, winding stream passing through rich riparian forests and broad sedge wetlands. The river holds significant numbers of Arctic grayling and bull trout. The latter species, often mistakenly called Dolly Varden (a closely related species of the Pacific coast and western Arctic), has declined dramatically in watersheds in Alberta and Montana, but still thrives here. It loves cold, clear mountain waters but is sensitive to overfishing.

Soon after crossing the Rancheria, the highway climbs to follow the rim of a canyon where the river cuts deeply through resistant limestones of the Rosella Group. These rocks represent the first sediments laid down along the edge of North America as the Pacific Ocean began to open 570 million years ago.

At kilometre 1084, a pull-off on the south side of the highway offers a beautiful view of the Cassiar Mountains behind the verdant green sedge marshes of the Rancheria. Much of the Rancheria River valley and that of the Swift River beyond are high-quality moose habitat, so scan the marshes—and drive carefully.

On either side of Rancheria Lodge, a layer of columnar basalts is exposed on the valley wall to the north. This is a lava flow from the Pleistocene ice ages; some of the flows in the area were subglacial, but these particular ones appear to have occurred during an interglacial period.

West of the falls, the highway climbs over the Continental Divide. The summit is low and subdued, just a swath of glacial debris and

REST STOP
Rancheria Falls

AT KILOMETRE 1112.8, a pull-off offers a picnic shelter and a 400-metre-long wheelchair-accessible trail to Rancheria Falls. Interpretive signs introduce the surrounding boreal forest and the role of fire in its ecology—the open, spruce-pine forest has grown up following a fire a little more than one hundred years ago. The forest floor is dominated by moss and the boreal stalwarts of bunchberry, crowberry, lingonberry and Labrador tea. If you stop to take a breath, you will smell the fragrance of subalpine fir and, if you look carefully, you will actually see a few young firs growing slowly in the shade of the pines, patiently waiting for their time in the sun.

The falls are undeniably beautiful, but if you cast your eyes downward, a fascinating geological story lies beneath your feet. As you stroll along the boardwalk, you cross the Cassiar Fault, which at this site coincides with the edge of the 100-million-year-old Cassiar pluton and the Yukon-Tanana Terrane. The Cassiar Fault is another of the strike-slip faults that result from the collision of westward-moving North America with the northward-moving Pacific plate. The rocks just upstream have moved 50 to 100 kilometres north relative to the land that you are standing on. The fault here is about 50 metres wide and reveals itself in the deformation of the granite. The granite's stretched, crystalline fabric tells us that the active fault was shearing it just as it was cooling and crystallizing deep underground. The falls may have originated at the fault, which weakened the rock along it, but they have now eroded their way upstream into the gneisses and schists of the Yukon-Tanana Terrane. You are standing at the edge of North America.

Above: Rancheria Falls. SYDNEY CANNINGS

hardly noticeable in this broad mountain trough. Still, it is a significant divide—if you threw a little stick off the upper Rancheria bridge it could float into the Liard and down the Mackenzie River to the Beaufort Sea, a northward journey of 4200 kilometres; a little stick thrown into the Swift River at the bottom of the hill could float down the Teslin and Yukon Rivers to the Bering Sea, a westward journey of 3680 kilometres.

The fish fauna changes over the divide as well, despite the fact that the watershed lakes of the Swift and Rancheria Rivers are separated by a low mound of glacial sediments only 200 metres across. For example, the bull trout and rainbow trout of the upper Liard aren't found in the Teslin drainage, and the chinook salmon of the Yukon drainage are not found in the Liard.

The road slides in beside the Swift River, which in its upper valley is meandering and not especially swift. After it re-enters British Columbia, the highway follows the Swift River downstream as it meanders through mature white and black spruce riparian forest.

On Yukon Time

Most visitors come to the Yukon in the midsummer, when the sun shines until late in the evening and no real darkness falls even after it sets. Even though the southern Yukon is well south of the Arctic Circle and one cannot see the true midnight sun there, the visitor's sense of very late sunsets is accentuated by the Yukon's place at the far western edge of the Pacific Time Zone. "On Yukon time" is a local expression that is the equivalent of "on island time" in the Gulf Islands—a relaxed relationship with time and deadlines. But up until a few decades ago, there really was a Yukon Time, which was set one hour behind the Pacific Time Zone. For practical purposes, this zone was amalgamated with Pacific Time, and the time slot was given to Alaska, which merged its zones into Alaska Time. So in June when you see the sun set at 11:30 p.m. in Whitehorse, it's really only 9:30 p.m. sun time—subtract one hour for Daylight Savings and another for Yukon Time, a time zone that no longer exists.

Just east of Swan Lake, there is a rest stop overlooking the valley wetlands. In the southern distance, Mt. Simpson is the granite core of an ancient undersea volcano that was part of the island arc of Quesnellia. In 2004, a huge forest fire raged through this valley, eventually burning over 110,000 hectares.

After passing through Swan Lake, the Swift River flows southwest, eventually entering Teslin Lake. However, you and the highway head northwest, climbing up in a series of steps onto the Yukon Plateau. You have left the Cassiar Mountains behind. The forest is drier; the trees, smaller than they were east of the Continental Divide.

The Dawson Peaks, which dominate the southern skyline of Teslin Lake, are the basal remnants of an ancient, oceanic volcano of the Cache Creek Terrane.
SYDNEY CANNINGS

Just before the Yukon border, the Morley Lake Forest Service Recreation Site is a hidden gem, with a lovely natural beach on a beautiful northern lake—watch for the inconspicuous road on the east side of the highway. At the Yukon border—the last of seven border crossings!—you cross the Morley River and follow it to Teslin Lake.

As you crest the hill above Teslin and begin descending to the Alaska Highway's longest bridge, there is a pull-off to the east with a gallery of signs interpreting both the importance of salmon to the Teslin Tlingit and the wonders of the Nisutlin River Delta National Wildlife Area. The delta of the Nisutlin, at the head of the bay east of the highway bridge, is home to one of the greatest concentrations of breeding trumpeter swans in Canada and is a vital stopover for thousands of migrating waterfowl as well. Chinook salmon have journeyed 2970 kilometres from the Bering Sea to breed in its tributary creeks, and it is important moose wintering habitat.

Squanga Lake Whitefish

Squanga Lake is shallow and productive and is home to a unique species of whitefish, appropriately named the Squanga Lake whitefish. This fish is closely related to the widespread lake whitefish—which also occurs here—but is smaller, has more gill rakers, differs genetically, and feeds on zooplankton rather than bottom invertebrates. It is also found in two other lakes in the Squanga Creek drainage, as well as Little Teslin Lake, which has no connecting creek. Dezadeash Lake on the Haines Highway has a similar, but genetically different whitefish. An interesting feature that links all these lakes is the absence of the Least Cisco, a small, plankton-feeding relative of the whitefish. It seems that, when this species is absent, lake whitefish may sometimes diverge into two forms—a bottom-feeding form and a plankton-feeding form.

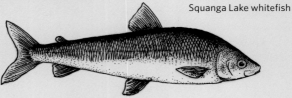

Squanga Lake whitefish

> **Teslin to Whitehorse:** The Southern Lakes

Along this section of highway you pass two of the large lakes that fill the broad, glacially sculpted valleys at the headwaters of the Yukon River—you may think of them as northern but to Yukoners they are known as the Southern Lakes: Teslin, Atlin, Tagish, Tutshi, Bennett, Marsh and Laberge. This is the land of the Yukon Plateau, so the valleys are wide, the views expansive and the modest mountains artistically carved by deep glaciation.

Teslin Lake lies along the Teslin Fault, which is another strike-slip fault that here separates Quesnellia to the east from the Cache Creek Terrane across the lake—the land across the lake has slipped about 130 kilometres north relative to the land you are standing on.

The Teslin Lake territorial campground is 14 kilometres north of Teslin, set on a hillside above the Fox Creek delta. Not only is this a pleasant place to camp, but in August and September it is the site of the Teslin Lake Bird Observatory. The long, straight Teslin valley is an important route for birds in the fall migration and, like they do at the Albert Creek station to the east, workers at this station monitor the migration by mist netting, banding and visually counting southbound birds—and they always appreciate interested visitors.

Just before you reach Johnson's Crossing, the South Canol Road joins the Alaska Highway. This is a quiet but scenic route to Ross River through the Pelly and Selwyn mountains. Past the junction, the Alaska Highway descends through glacial lake-bottom silts to the high bridge across the Teslin River. The bridge is host to an impressive colony of cliff swallows in the summer, and trumpeter swans gather on the river's open water to feed and rest in early winter and again in April.

After climbing the long hill out of the Teslin's valley, you pass through some prime winter habitat for the mountain caribou of the Southern Lakes herd. These caribou were first devastated in number by overhunting during the gold rush and continued to decline after the Alaska Highway was pushed through their range. However, a recent conservation program has turned the trend around and now there are about 1600 caribou that range through these mountains.

A few kilometres past Squanga Lake, you begin to see the pale massif of Mt. White ahead on the south side of the highway. This impressive mountain face is part of the Cache Creek Terrane and was once a carbonate reef in the Tethys Sea, on the other side of the Pacific Ocean (see p. 26).

Jake's Corner is at the junction of three roads—the Alaska Highway swings north and the Tagish Road heads west to Tagish and Carcross. A short distance down the Tagish Road, another road heads south to Atlin, one of the most scenically stunning communities on the planet.

At the junction, the south-facing slopes on the north side of the road are carpeted in grass and pasture sage—you are entering the

To Seed or Not to Seed

If you are driving up the Alaska Highway in June or early July, you will marvel at the acres of wildflowers that line its shoulders. In the Yukon these are, for the most part, native plants—showy Jacob's ladder, field and showy locoweed, boreal sweet-vetch, Franklin's phacelia, golden corydalis and others. Even many of the dandelions are the native horned dandelions. The Yukon is fortunate in having relatively few exotic, invasive species lining its highways. In the past, the Yukon highways department often seeded its new road-cuts with seed mixes containing species from "Outside" but these foreign species occasionally choked out native colonizers. The department is now more open to letting nature take care of the open ground on its own. The flowers that colonize these roadsides are those that naturally thrive in dry, disturbed soil.

Above: Showy Jacob's ladder.
SYDNEY CANNINGS

rain shadow of the Coast and St. Elias Mountains. Arctic ground squirrels are common along the road here, and some individuals represent a rare, black form of this species.

South of the Judas Creek crossing, you enter a region of forested dunes. These originated as sand deposited near the tongues of the retreating glaciers, but were then blown by the wind into dunes. The sandy soil is ideal for lodgepole pines, and kinnikinnick and ground lichens flourish on the open woodland floor. Because of the prevalence of ground lichens in the forests and the relatively shallow snow in this region, both the Tagish Road and this stretch of the Alaska Highway are excellent places to see caribou in the winter.

The delta of Judas Creek at Marsh Lake is a key site for shorebird migration in the spring when the water is low; you can access it via the Judas Creek subdivision road. Most of Marsh Lake's annual water supply comes from melting glacial ice in the Coast Mountains, flowing through Atlin and Tagish Lakes. Because of this, its high-water point is reached late in the summer when glacial melt is at its peak. This contrasts with Teslin Lake, which is fed primarily by snowmelt—its high-water point is reached in late spring.

Marsh Lake also divides the Cache Creek Terrane (here at its northern edge) from the younger rocks of the Whitehorse Trough in the rounded hills to the west. The Whitehorse Trough was a shallow marine basin that lay between Stikinia, the Cache Creek Terrane and Quesnellia as these terranes were being brought together in the Triassic. Early in the trough's history, limestone was laid down in reefs—we'll see a big chunk of that at Whitehorse—and volcanoes spewed out lava. But as the terranes began their slow collision with ancestral North America, the rising mountains on either side of the trough began to erode and, at this latitude, their sediments were laid down on top of the rocks of Stikinia and the Cache Creek Terrane. The rocks of the Whitehorse Trough, now folded and uplifted into hills and mountains, stretch from the Pelly River south to Bennett Lake in northern British Columbia.

The rocky ridges to the east of Marsh Lake are carpeted in abundant three-toothed saxifrage. This is a common, even iconic plant in the Yukon, born of Beringia, but it only just reaches into northern British Columbia. These saxifrages have waxy, spiky leaves that resist drying.

Three-toothed saxifrage.
TERRY MCINTOSH

REST STOP

Swan Haven, M'Clintock Bay

SWAN HAVEN IS the local name given to the western part of M'Clintock Bay. In April and early May, the current at the outlet of Marsh Lake creates an early opening in the ice, and the shallow, open water is a magnet for migrating waterfowl. Trumpeter swans begin to arrive in early April and are soon followed by tundra swans and a host of geese and ducks. At times, over one thousand swans rest here, waiting for their small breeding lakes to open up. Predators are also attracted by the high number of birds—wolves and coyotes may hunt along the ice edge, and bald eagles soar overhead, looking for ducks weakened in migration. An interpretation centre with an observation deck and telescopes is open and staffed during April.

Above: Trumpeter swans. KEN QUONG

As you approach the Marsh Lake Territorial Campground, the highway enters the swampy, sandy delta of the M'Clintock River, which covers the northernmost rocks of the Cache Creek Terrane. This stream is also the uppermost spawning system for chinook salmon on the Yukon River main stem—a journey of two months and 3200 kilometres from the Bering Sea.

If you are travelling along the highway in April or early May, you may want to follow the Wildlife Viewing signs to Swan Haven, turning west just north of the M'Clintock bridge.

Twelve kilometres past the M'Clintock, you finally reach the Yukon River itself. Here it flows through the large Lewes Marsh. The First Nations of the region fished here for chinook salmon, burbot and northern pike—the Tagish people call it *Témil Shó*, the "big fishnet."

A short distance north of the bridge is the junction with the South Klondike Highway, which leads south to Carcross and Skagway. You have arrived in Whitehorse, though it will be a few kilometres before you reach the access road to the downtown area. At MacRae, the first gas station you encounter, you simultaneously cross the abandoned White Pass & Yukon Route Railroad and the 135th meridian. You may appreciate how far north you are, but you may not realize just how much you've travelled west—you are now about 12 degrees of longitude west of Vancouver, which translates to almost 650 kilometres at this northern latitude.

To the east is a striking, rounded mountain that is capped with bare, grey rock—appropriately referred to as Grey Mountain by locals. However, the stampeders of '98 called it Canyon Mountain because its presence on the skyline warned them the perils of Miles Canyon and the Whitehorse Rapids. Grey Mountain is a massive block of limestone—a reef laid down in the early days of the Whitehorse Trough, over 200 million years ago.

At about kilometre 1416, a modest sign points east to the Miles Canyon Road. Even if you don't plan to visit Whitehorse, Miles Canyon is worth the short (1.3 kilometres) side trip. If you are planning to stop in Whitehorse, this road is by far the most scenic way of entering the city.

Tucked in behind the Coast and St. Elias Mountains, Whitehorse has the driest climate of any city its size in Canada, with a paltry 267 millimetres annual precipitation. However, it is cool—more than half of that modest precipitation falls as snow, the average daily minimum in January is -22°C and freezing temperatures are recorded on

REST STOP

Miles Canyon

MILES CANYON IS a narrow gorge of the Yukon River, where the jade-green water has been forced to cut through vertical walls of columnar basalt. The river originally flowed farther to the east, but that route was filled by glacial sediments during the last ice advance of the Pleistocene, and the river has taken this recent detour. The basaltic lava erupted 8.3 million years ago from a vent about 8 kilometres to the south, near the base of Golden Horn Mountain. The lava is about 120 metres deep here, even though only the top 10 metres are visible to you. Before the hydroelectric dam was built a few kilometres downstream in 1959, the water ran much more swiftly through the canyon, and the resistant rock of the canyon also created a steeper river bed at the canyon mouth—the White Horse Rapids. Now the water in the canyon is 10 metres deeper and flows more smoothly, and the Whitehorse rapids are largely submerged under the Schwatka Lake reservoir.

The suspension footbridge leads to a network of trails on the other side. The walk along the canyon rim upstream takes you along some dry, relict grasslands with early summer wildflowers and creeping juniper. Violet-green swallows and cliff swallows nest in the canyon's rock walls, and Townsend's solitaires sing from the forest edge.

Above: Miles Canyon. CAMERON ECKERT

220 days per year. Average July daily highs are 20.5°C, and it is usually hard to find a lake that is warm enough to have a comfortable swim in.

The silt bluffs that flank Whitehorse are the sediments of Glacial Lake Laberge, a proglacial lake that formed here at the end of the last ice age. The runway of the city's airport runs along the flat, tabletop surface of the lake bottom above the town.

In Whitehorse, the Yukon River is the focal point for a naturalist. In the summer, Arctic terns wheel and cry over your head—they breed here after spending the northern winter in Antarctic waters. Mew gulls, herring gulls, bank swallows and bald eagles also nest along the river. Beavers are very active along here, too—you probably won't see one, but you will certainly see freshly cut trees, stripped of branches for the beavers' food stores. In the late summer, you can watch chinook salmon negotiating the fish ladder on the east side of the river, below the dam.

➤ Whitehorse to Haines Junction:
The Takhini and Dezadeash Valleys

On this section of your journey, the highway leaves the valley of the Yukon River and heads west to Haines Junction and the St. Elias Mountains through a wide gap in the mountains. You first follow the Takhini River upstream, and then cross a low divide and follow the Dezadeash River into the Shakwak Trench and the abrupt face of the Kluane Ranges.

At kilometre 1437, you reach the junction of the North Klondike Highway, which is not treated in this guide. The North Klondike is the route to Dawson City and the Klondike, crossing the great Pelly and Stewart Rivers along the way. From the Klondike, the Dempster Highway can take you all the way to the Mackenzie Delta, through some of the most stunning subarctic tundra anywhere. Many travellers make a circle route, taking the Top of the World Highway from Dawson back to the Alaska Highway.

At this point, the Alaska Highway curves west to follow the Takhini River, which enters the Yukon River a short distance north of the Klondike Highway junction. Takhini is from the Tagish *tahk heena*, meaning, unfortunately, "mosquito river." This stately stream has its origins high in the Coast Mountains to the southwest, between the Chilkoot and Chilkat Passes; its mostly gentle waters make it a favourite family canoe route for Whitehorse residents. It flows through long, sinuous Kusawa Lake and then, entering this valley, winds its way through the sands and silts laid down in Glacial Lake Champagne. At an early stage of deglaciation, when a glacier still occupied the Yukon River valley and blocked this eastern end of the Takhini drainage, Lake Champagne occupied this entire valley and drained north through the Taye Lake valley into the Nordenskiold drainage south of Carmacks. Later on, when the Yukon valley glacier had retreated as far south as Whitehorse, Lake Champagne could drain out through Glacial Lake Laberge, so its water level dropped significantly, and the two lakes merged into one. After the glaciers had vanished, the lake drained away completely, leaving the entire valley bottom covered in glacial lake silts, and deep sand deltas laid down where rivers had entered the lake from side valleys.

At first, the highway follows the south edge of the east-west valley, which means the roadside forest doesn't get a lot of sun in the winter. The soils are very cold, and permafrost is widespread, especially in the north-facing draws. In addition to seeing drunken forests on frozen ground, you will feel the effects of permafrost as the highway crosses these gullies, breaking up in waves where the frozen ground thaws below.

Two kilometres west of the Takhini River bridge, the older spruce trees in the forest vanish and a young fire forest appears. In many places in this valley, it is hardly a forest and could better be called a savanna. This is the product of an extensive fire that tore through the valley in the summer of 1958. Now, more than fifty years later, the trees are still small and sparse in this dry, cold environment. At this eastern edge of the burn, lodgepole pine is a common pioneer tree, along with trembling aspen and white spruce. But 3 kilometres farther to the west, that tree drops out of the scene, except for a few

REST STOP
Takhini Salt Flats

AT KILOMETRE 1467.9, the Takhini salt flats lie to the north of the road. This complex of salt lakes, ponds and dry basins is one of the rarest and most interesting ecosystems in the territory. If you are so inclined, park your car safely here and walk in for a closer look—this is public land. Among the fascinating plants that grow here is a bright-red succulent that carpets the salty white ground—this is a type of glasswort or sea asparagus. Exactly what species it is, though, is debatable. It is not the maritime glasswort that lives over the hill in the salt marshes of Alaska and may be a species unique to this valley. Whatever the taxonomists decide, it is a long way from its other interior cousins on the prairies and on the southern grasslands of British Columbia. Two species of small ground beetles that prowl the lake edges are also a long way from their nearest brethren on the prairies. The whole community is a relict of a postglacial period when the climate was warmer and drier than it is today, when dry grasslands linked the southern Yukon with the prairie grasslands.

Salt flats occur where evaporation is greater than precipitation, so any salts in the underlying glacial sediments are continually drawn upwards and concentrated in shallow basins. The geological origin of the sediments varies from place to place in the valley, and so some areas contain more salts than others.

Above: Glasswort on the Takhini salt flats. JOHN MEIKLE

rare individuals. Why would a common fire pioneer like lodgepole pine not spread across the whole valley? If you've come up the Alaska Highway through the fire forests of the Liard, this absence is hard to comprehend. The answer seems to be simply because this is the edge of the lodgepole pine's interior range—it just hasn't moved into the far western Yukon since the glaciers left.

The open woodland and savanna of the Takhini Valley are great habitat for Elk. Elk are deer that would rather not browse; they eat grass. At the end of the Pleistocene, Elk were an abundant member of the steppe megafauna in Beringia. Then they shared the grasslands with bison and mammoths but, like both of those species, they vanished from the Yukon's interior a long time ago. They were first reintroduced into the region in 1951 and moved into this area after

Spruce Bark Beetle

About 1990, a spruce bark beetle outbreak began in the forests of Kluane National Park. This is a native species of beetle—a boreal relative of the mountain pine beetle familiar to many British Columbians—that normally remains at low numbers in the spruce forest, but occasionally undergoes population explosions and kills most of the mature trees over a large area. Younger trees are spared, so the insect acts as a forest renewal agent. By 2007, the beetles of this outbreak had killed over half the mature spruce in an area of 380,000 hectares, from the Kluane icefields to the Mendenhall River, and from the north end of Kluane Lake to the Haines Highway in British Columbia. Apparently the beetles have been aided in this outbreak by a series of warmer autumns and winters—early autumn frosts, or extended winter periods of -40°c weather will kill larvae. Some birds, especially three-toed woodpeckers, benefit greatly from beetle outbreaks.

Spruce bark beetle

the 1958 fire opened the forest up. Spring and fall are the best times to see them along the road—if you don't see them close to the highway, check out the grassy, south-facing slopes to the north for their cream-coloured rumps.

At kilometre 1487, a viewing area to the south offers panels that discuss the 1958 fire and the wildlife that inhabit the valley today. The big gap in the mountains to the south is the valley of Kusawa Lake and the headwaters of the Takhini River. Each small valley coming out of the Coast Mountains to the south is a classic U-shaped hanging valley that has been deeply sculpted by glaciers.

Past the Kusawa Lake road junction, you leave the fire forest behind, but the forest you drive through from here to Haines Junction is still a very simple one. The cold, arid climate in the rain shadow of the massive St. Elias Mountains doesn't foster diversity. There is one conifer—white spruce—and one broad-leaved tree—trembling aspen. That's all: this is a very easy place to be an expert on trees!

Soon you pass the Mendenhall River, which now is only a large creek, but at the end of the ice ages, its valley held the headwaters of the early Yukon River draining Glacial Lake Champagne. Past the Mendenhall, the highway climbs up a low rise, and the side road to Champagne enters from the south. The whole area around Champagne is awash in dunes, some home to rare plants such as the Baikal sedge. Straight down the highway to the west, the Kluane Ranges of the St. Elias Mountains form a distant wall drawing closer by the kilometre.

Between kilometre 1538 and kilometre 1540, look up onto the alpine ridges to the north—the smooth backbones of the mountains are ridged with spines. These are unglaciated tors, an indication that the glaciers pouring north out of the Coast Range were thinning here, leaving these ridge tops exposed as ice-free nunataks.

Soon, the Aishihik River flows in from the north, and you can stop at a pull-off along its banks across from the small community of Canyon. The Aishihik drains two large lakes in a semiarid basin surrounded by alpine plateaus. Because it drains into the Alsek, it is one of the two Yukon rivers with a native population of rainbow trout. Those of you old enough will have seen the Aishihik's Otter Falls on the back of the 1954 series five dollar bill.

After the highway dips in and out of the valley of Marshall Creek, it swings slightly southwest and looks directly down the Dezadeash (Alsek) River's gap in the Kluane Ranges. Look beyond the stunning mountains in the foreground—on a good day, you can see over a hundred kilometres through the gap to the snow-white summits of Mt. Hubbard (4557 metres) and Mt. Kennedy (4300 metres) in the heart of the Icefield Ranges of the St. Elias Mountains. Although the great distance diminishes their apparent size, they are almost twice the elevation of the peaks in front of you. The glaciers that flow from them and their sister peaks form the world's largest nonpolar ice field; Mt. Logan (5959 metres), the highest peak in Canada, is out of sight to the north.

The highway passes Pine Lake and descends into the Shakwak Trench, the great geological lineament that defines the eastern wall of the St. Elias Mountains. Shakwak is a Tlingit name meaning "between the mountains." From Kluane Lake north, the trench follows the line of the Denali Fault, but here in its southern reaches its geological *raison d'être* is obscure, hidden beneath hundreds of metres of sediments washed off the Kluane Ranges. Whatever feature has created the Shakwak, it bounds most of the tectonic forces that are raising the mountains to the west. At Haines Junction, the trench is occupied by the meandering, braided Dezadeash River, but that river soon turns south and, apparently defying gravity, cuts through the mountains to find the Alsek.

The Kluane Ranges form a glorious backdrop to Haines Junction with a rock glacier flowing out of every cirque. What are rock glaciers and how do they form? As the steep cirque walls erode, deep rock rubble fills their basins. Water then flows into the rock pile, and the lower depths become permanently frozen. When the rock-ice mass becomes deep enough, the entire mass can flow slowly downhill in the same manner as a glacier.

Surging Glaciers and Temporary Lakes

At kilometre 1588, if you look to the southwest down the Dezadeash valley, you can see a series of horizontal stripes crossing the big talus slopes—the old beach lines of Glacial Lake Lowell. They aren't "ancient" beaches, just "old," because the lake covered this valley as late as 1852 and perhaps even later. The lake was created when the Lowell Glacier surged across the Alsek River and dammed it 60 kilometres downstream from here, and it was created a number of times over the past 10,000 years. The Little Ice Age of the nineteenth century seems to have been a particularly active time for the Lowell. At its deepest, the lake flooded the lower reaches of what would become Haines Junction—in fact, as you turned at the junction, you were driving along its uppermost beach line. When the lake became deep enough to float the toe of the glacier, water began to flow under it. Relatively quickly, the water eroded a large tunnel through the glacier, and the huge lake drained catastrophically in one or two days, causing a massive flood downstream. In the 1852 flood, at least two Tlingit villages along the lower Alsek were wiped out, with considerable loss of life—all of this is recorded in the oral history of the local First Nations. The Champagne and Aishihik people call the Lowell Glacier *Nàlùdi*—"fish stop"—because it blocked the salmon migrations.

Above: Ancient beach lines cross talus slopes in the Dezadeash Valley, west of Haines Junction. SYDNEY CANNINGS

Here the Haines Highway meets the Alaska Highway. The Haines Highway follows the Shakwak Trench south, and the Alaska Highway makes a right angle turn and follows it north.

➤ Haines Junction to Burwash Landing:
Kluane and the Shakwak Trench

This portion of the highway follows the Shakwak Trench north to the far end of Kluane Lake, with the Kluane Ranges rising up steeply to the west and the broad valley and lake providing expansive views of the Ruby Range to the east. Cold air often descends from the nearby mountains and pools in the Shakwak Trench, depressing the temperatures. In Haines Junction, the average daily minimum temperature in January is −27°c and the average daily July maximum is 20°c. The climate is dry in the mountains' rainshadow; the average annual precipitation is 290 millimetres, less than that of the southern Okanagan Valley in British Columbia.

Haines Junction is the administrative centre for Kluane National Park, and one of the key stops for anyone interested in natural history is the park's Visitor Centre, now housed within the Dä Kų Cultural Centre. But the real world is outside, and the open road beckons.

The highway leaves Haines Junction through aspen parkland, with the extensive wetlands and willow thickets of the Dezadeash River to the southwest. The ice-capped peak in front of you is Mt. Archibald (2588 metres), and the smaller, pyramidal peak to the north is Mt. Decoeli (2332 metres). Mt. Decoeli isn't that massive, but it is one of the big landmarks of Kluane because it projects into the curve of the Shakwak Trench and can be seen up and down the valley for a great distance.

As it leaves the Dezadeash drainage, the highway begins to climb up the huge alluvial fan of Bear Creek and its neighbouring streams. A few kilometres up the hill, there is a pull-off to the west for the Spruce Beetle Interpretive Trail. This is a beautiful little loop trail through spruce forest with a series of signs interpreting the forest and the effects of the spruce bark beetle outbreak that killed most of the mature trees in this valley from 1994–2010.

REST STOP

Alsek River Valley Trail

AT KILOMETRE 1589, the road to Nygren subdivision comes in from the south. This inconspicuously marked junction leads to the spectacular valley of the Dezadeash (although this portion is often referred to as the Alsek), and trail access to its junction with the glacial Kaskawulsh River. You can drive 700 metres south to a parking lot and explore farther on foot or by mountain bike or, if you have a vehicle with high clearance, you can drive 15 kilometres to a second trailhead. On a short walk, you cross open meadows that cover the old sandy, gravelly shores of Lake Lowell. Arctic ground squirrels abound and are hunted by the local Harlan's hawks. Harlan's hawks are either a Beringian subspecies of the red-tailed hawk, or a full species that diverged from a red-tailed hawk ancestor during the Pleistocene. Upland sandpipers, uncommon shorebirds that breed in northern grasslands, scold you from the treetops. In late spring and early summer, these meadows are covered in flowers—prairie crocus, few-seeded draba and three-toothed saxifrage, among others. But the most interesting plant is the Yukon draba, a small mustard species with white flowers that blooms at the end of May and in early June. Until 2011, despite extensive searching in the region, this species was known in the world only from this meadow. In that year, it was discovered in the Aishihik valley to the east. A unique subspecies of the Pacific fritillary is also known in the world only from this valley. Kluane is more than just glaciers: it is home to a whole host of species that were isolated in Beringia and on mountain nunataks during the Pleistocene.

If you drive, hike, or bike farther down the trail, you will cross old beach ridges of Lake Lowell, two impressive alluvial fans and their very active creeks, and extensive meadows. Dall's sheep and mountain goats are common on the precipitous ridges above you, and grizzly bears are abundant throughout—take appropriate measures! Trumpeter swans nest in the rich wetlands of the wandering Dezadeash. At the junction of the two rivers (3 kilometres past the final gate), large dunes covered in Yukon lupine and the threatened Baikal sedge create a strange landscape in the mountains.

Yukon draba

The highway continues to climb and eventually crosses Bear Creek at the summit—at 1004 metres, this is the highest point of the Alaska Highway north of the Rocky Mountains. Like the grasslands below, the alpine zone of the Kluane Ranges is home to animals and plants that are found nowhere else in the world or are far removed from their close relatives—among them, a disjunct, showy variety of Arctic locoweed and Vahl's alkali grass. A large species of tiger moth with bright pink hindwings was first discovered on the barren tundra of Mt. Archibald in 1991—and subsequently was found in the unglaciated Mackenzie Mountains of the Northwest Territories in

The Cycles of the Snowshoe Hare

Central to the ecological web of this simple forest is the snowshoe hare, which consumes the willows in the open woodlands and is preyed upon by Canada lynx, great horned owls and northern goshawks. Snowshoe hare populations cycle dramatically, going from almost absent to exceedingly abundant over a period of ten or eleven years, and their predators' populations shadow these cycles. The peak period of the hare population usually lasts two years, but in the winter of the third year, 95 per cent of the hares die and the population cycle begins again. It seems that predators play a key role in reducing the hare numbers, and this role is probably enhanced by the reduction in food supply. Intriguingly, the hare population cycles seem to be linked to decadal cycles in rainfall, which are also linked to similar cycles in sunspots.

Snowshoe hare. RICHARD CANNINGS

2010. Presumably, it is scattered more widely through unglaciated Beringia, but we have a lot to learn.

The region of the trench from Sulphur Lake to Kluane Lake is one of the most intensively studied areas of boreal forest anywhere. For almost forty years, teams of researchers from a variety of universities have investigated the complex web of ecological relationships that binds this relatively simple, northern forest.

One of the animals that has been studied extensively here is the red squirrel, which depends on the seeds of the white spruce for the bulk of its food. Squirrels are efficient harvesters of cones and store them in large middens, which not only makes them easy to get at in the winter, but also hides them from the squirrels' main competition, white-winged crossbills. Every few years, the white spruces in the region overwhelm the seed predators by producing massive bumper crops of cones. White-winged crossbills deal with this by wandering across the continent looking for these bumper crops, but the squirrels don't have that luxury. Amazingly, the squirrels somehow anticipate the bumper crops and have larger-than-usual litters even before the cones are available. How do they do this? Researchers aren't sure, but they theorize that the squirrels may be able to count the cone buds, or perhaps they can detect changes in the trees' hormones by sampling the cone buds.

The highway continues over the low rise between Sulphur Lake and Christmas Creek, and you leave the Alsek's Pacific watershed and return to the Yukon River watershed. The striking, glacier-topped peak to the south is Mt. Cairnes. This portion of the Kluane Ranges is sliced by the Duke River Fault and more than a dozen other strike-slip faults—the geological map of Mt. Cairnes looks like a stripy, multicoloured dessert topped with whipped cream. The Denali Fault, an older, longer sibling of the Duke River Fault, has emerged from behind Mt. Archibald and Mt. Decoeli and parallels the highway to the west—from here north, it defines the Shakwak Trench. The lower part of the Mt. Cairnes range is a sliver of Wrangellia; the upper part—west of the Duke River Fault—is part of the Alexander Terrane.

The young delta of the Slims River spreads into the southwestern corner of Kluane Lake, with the south-facing slope of Sheep Mountain forming the backdrop.
SYDNEY CANNINGS

Over the rise past Christmas Creek, the view of Kluane Lake set in the broad trench is breathtaking. Its waters are tinted azure by the pale glacial silts brought in by the Slims River, which is born at the toe of the great Kaskawulsh Glacier. The Kaskawulsh actually gives birth to two rivers, the other being its namesake, the Kaskawulsh River, which flows south into the Alsek. But it wasn't always this way, and Kluane Lake wasn't always this colour—before about 350 years ago, Kluane Lake was a non-glacial lake that drained westward, *out* the Slims River valley into the Alsek watershed. What happened to change that? During the Little Ice Age, between 300 and 400 years ago, the Kaskawulsh Glacier advanced and dammed the valley, just as the Lowell Glacier blocked the Alsek. Kluane Lake rose 13 metres but, before it could find a way under or around the Kaskawulsh, it found a new drainage at its north end, where one of its now-flooded inlet streams spilled over a low pass into the watershed of the Donjek and Yukon Rivers. By the time the glacier had receded, the northern drainage had been carved deep enough that it was a smidgeon lower than the Kaskawulsh—and thus Kluane Lake was captured by the Yukon River system. If you look carefully along the far shore of the lake, you can see some of the former beach lines, up to 13 metres above the lake.

Kluane Lake is deep, cold, and relatively unproductive, but a perfect place for lake trout to thrive and dominate. Other fish that live here are chum salmon, Arctic grayling, lake whitefish, burbot and, in shallow bays, northern pike. The name Kluane is a transliteration of Tlingit *Lùxh-àní*, meaning "whitefish country."

As you drive down the long, gradual hill toward Kluane Lake, you are crossing the immense alluvial fans of Silver and Topham Creeks, which still move tons of debris from the mountains into the trench each summer. The highways department, however, has entrained the creeks between dikes to reduce washouts. The dry forest surrounding the creeks doesn't look that productive, but one of the primary understory shrubs here is soopolallie, a favourite food of grizzly bears, and bears are often seen along this stretch of road.

Past Silver Creek, the access road to the Kluane Lake Research Station of the Arctic Institute of North America leads to the right. This station has been and still is the hub of hundreds of scientific research projects studying geology, glaciology, high-altitude physiology and ecology in the region. Tourist flights into the remarkable otherworld of the Icefield Ranges are offered from its airstrip.

Just west of the Arctic Institute road, the hidden, northwest-southeast trace of the Denali Fault crosses the highway—the land to the west has been displaced at least 350 kilometres north relative to the land to the east. The tectonic forces that are causing uplift in the St. Elias Mountains also cause the movement along the Denali, and the transfer of force along the fault prevents the region to the east from being affected by those tectonic forces.

The boreal forest is, as a rule, shaped by fire, and the Shakwak Trench is a typical boreal patchwork of different-aged forests, each defined by the last major fire. As you approach the shore of Kluane Lake, the forest on the south side of the road hasn't experienced fire for more than four hundred years, though most of its older trees have been killed by the recent spruce bark beetle outbreak.

After following the shoreline of Kluane Lake for a short distance, the highway crosses the remarkable delta of the Slims River. As mentioned earlier, this is a young delta, less than four hundred years old. Immense quantities of silt and mud ground off the St. Elias Mountains by the Kaskawulsh Glacier are deposited here, gradually filling this corner of the lake. In the middle distance, the Duke River Fault cuts across the valley just past the knife-edged limestone ridge; the mountains of the Donjek Range in the distance are all part of the Alexander Terrane, those in the foreground are underlain by Wrangellia and by younger rocks.

Soon after you leave the visitor centre, there are pull-offs on both sides of the road—the one on the north side leads you to the old highway and the Soldier's Summit monument, which commemorates the opening of the Alaska Highway here on a snowy November 20, 1942. If you walk up that trail and turn right instead of left, you walk through a major rock slide made up of large basalt blocks from the Nikolai formation above you. These basalts are the hallmark of Wrangellia, and characterize the terrane from southern Vancouver Island to Alaska. Across the lake, the Ruby Ranges are underlain by younger rocks of the Coastal Plutonic Complex— the Kluane Schist and the Ruby Range Batholith.

As you continue north, the theme is erosion. The highway crosses one dryas-covered alluvial fan after another, some small and others gigantic, but each containing a gravel- and cobble-choked creek, and each a testament to the active mountain building and active mountain erosion to the west.

Katabatic winds are winds caused by heavy, cold air over the ice caps to the west descending and accelerating as it falls. The winds pour out of the Slims River valley and turn north, guided by the topography of the Shakwak Trench—such a wind gave Destruction Bay its name by blowing away the highway construction camp there. The same type of wind fanned the flames of a fire that began in the community landfill 8 kilometres south of Burwash Landing on June 12, 1999. In just over 24 hours, the fire had raced almost 15 kilometres north to the Duke River and had burned over 3200 hectares.

REST STOP

Tachäl Dhäl (Sheep Mountain)

AS YOU CROSS the Slims delta, a steep, south-facing slope of grass, rock bluffs and talus rises directly in front of you. This is Tachäl Dhäl or, as it is more widely known, Sheep Mountain. The Tachäl Dhäl Visitor Centre of Parks Canada (open May to early September) provides interpretive programs and panels and viewing telescopes. Strong, katabatic winds that descend from the high glacial plateau of the Icefield Ranges keep the ridge almost snow free, and the mountain's steep south aspect ensures that any remaining snow melts quickly in the spring. The winds also bring down quantities of glacial loess from the Slims Valley and lay it down on the slopes, creating fertile soil for grasses and forbs. Consequently, this is ideal winter range for Dall's sheep. Unfortunately, most visitors are here during the summer when the sheep are more widely dispersed in the alpine meadows beyond the ridge top. If you are here from September to May, though, you are almost guaranteed a view.

But there is more than sheep on Tachäl Dhäl. The sagebrush steppe on its slopes may be reminiscent of the mammoth steppe of the Beringian Pleistocene, and a number of rare plants and insects live on its slope, including rock wormwood, a disjunct Asian sage. The silty, mineral-rich flats around the visitor centre are also a botanical paradise—the Yukon Aster, a rare Kluane endemic, is dominant here.

If you have time and energy, a day hike to the summit offers unparalleled views of Kluane Lake and the terminus of the Kaskawulsh Glacier, not to mention the chance of seeing Dall's sheep close up. Singing voles chirp and squeak from their tundra tunnels, and Brewer's (timberline) sparrows sing in the shrub subalpine on the west slope. Use the Sheep Creek trail on the mountain's west slope for access—hiking up the south face is discouraged, especially during spring lambing season.

Rock wormwood

At Burwash Landing, you can visit the Kluane Museum of Natural History for an introduction to local geology, wildlife and culture. If you are visiting in April and May, trumpeter swans and other waterfowl gather here near the outlet of Kluane Lake, where the ice opens up early.

➤ Burwash Landing to Alaska:
The Northern Shakwak Trench and Beringia

Along the northernmost stretch of the Alaska Highway in Canada, the highway follows the Shakwak Trench as far as the White River, where the trench fades out and the Denali Fault curves to the northwest. On its way north, it follows the Kluane River for a short distance, then crosses the Donjek River before reaching the White River. The landscape becomes distinctly more subarctic the farther north you go, with permafrost and peatland formations increasing as the highway approaches the extreme continental climate zone of central Alaska.

About 8 kilometres north of Burwash Landing and 500 metres south of the Duke River bridge, a small road leads northeast into the Duke Meadows. These grasslands, formed on the alluvial fan of the river and kept open by past fires, are home to plant species of the southern prairies such as spike-oat and are the breeding grounds for upland sandpipers and sharp-tailed grouse. Some upland sandpipers in the Yukon nest in lowland grasslands like these but, to the surprise of most southern birders, the majority of them nest in wet tussock tundra at or just above timberline. The dikes along the river near the highway have allowed balsam poplar and white spruce trees to colonize the floodplain in the last fifty years.

The bridge over the Duke River was replaced in 2009 with a new structure built to withstand serious earthquakes—a nod to the fact that the Denali Fault transects the gravel cliff 300 metres upstream. Three serious, surface-rupturing earthquakes have occurred within two kilometres of this point in the past 3000 years, about 1000 years apart. The latest one has been dated to 1050 AD, so it may be time for the next one—and it thus makes good sense to make the bridge as secure as possible.

North of the Duke River, permafrost becomes more widespread, the road becomes more unruly as it copes—or doesn't—with the melting and slumping ground, and sloping fens on top of the permafrost become a common sight in the spruce woodlands.

At kilometre 1726, a viewpoint on the northeast side of the highway overlooks the Kluane River as it exits the Shakwak Trench on its way to the Donjek, White and Yukon Rivers. As mentioned before, this is a relatively new river, only carving out this northern exit for Kluane Lake in the last 300 to 400 years. Chum salmon have discovered the new route, though—each year in mid-September, they reach here after swimming upstream 2500 kilometres from the Bering Sea. The warm upwellings in the sloughs of the Kluane River make ideal rearing pools for the salmon eggs and fry.

On the way north to the Donjek River crossing, the highway crosses the shallow slopes of the trench, covered here in extensive muskeg woodlands of black spruce and broad fen meadows. These meadows are home to sharp-tailed grouse that, at least formerly, met for their fascinating mating displays on the shoulder of the highway along this stretch.

At kilometre 1755.5, the Donjek River breaks through the Kluane and Donjek Ranges, and a large pull-off to the west offers the most expansive views you will get from the highway of the big peaks of the Icefield Ranges, including Mt. Steele (5081 metres) and Mt. Lucania (5261 metres). The Donjek drains three of the great glaciers that flow out of the icefields—the Kluane, Donjek and Steele.

The highway continues up the narrow, northern Shakwak Trench, entering a zone thick with shallow lakes that are important for both

Chum salmon. MARK CONNOR

Glimpses of the big peaks of the Icefield Ranges can be seen up the broad valley of the Donjek River. SYDNEY CANNINGS

migrating and breeding waterfowl. Most of the lakes are thermokarst in origin; that is, they form when a patch of permafrost melts and collapses, exposing more permafrost that is susceptible to summer melting. As the basin gets larger and larger, a lake forms.

Look for bands of light-coloured ash in the slumping banks of the lake at kilometre 1776, and in the banks of Lake Creek, 3 kilometres farther north. This is the White River ash, the product of two tremendous eruptions from Mt. Churchill, an Alaskan stratovolcano 95 kilometres to the southwest of the highway. One explosion in about 110 AD and another in about 860 AD blew an astounding total of 50 cubic kilometres of ash into the atmosphere, and strong westerly winds carried these ash plumes over 340,000 square kilometres of the Yukon and Northwest Territories. The Mt. St. Helen's eruption of 1980 was puny in comparison—it produced only 1 cubic kilometre of ash. The two eruptions must have had a tremendous impact on the biota of the Yukon, including the humans living in the ash zone. Genetic evidence from caribou remains frozen in ice in the southern Yukon indicates that the resident caribou vanished and were subsequently replaced by unrelated immigrants.

At kilometre 1798, as Pickhandle Peak looms straight ahead, you can look north, up the valley of Long's and Wolf Creeks and see the tor-spined ridges south of Koidern Mountain. These crests are just over 1500 metres and were ice-free nunataks during the last glaciation. A kilometre farther on, you drive by a high road cut that provides a rare and easily accessible view of the contact between Yukon-Tanana Terrane and oceanic rocks of the Slide Mountain Terrane. The two formations are folded together, so it's a bit complicated, but the light-coloured rock at the south end of the road cut is a pale gabbro of the Slide Mountain ocean floor, whereas the high, cliff-forming, layered rock in the middle of the cut is made up of quartzite and amphibolite of the Yukon-Tanana Terrane.

At Pickhandle Lake, the wetland complex is much more extensive than the view from the highway indicates. Hidden behind the low ridge of trees across the lakes is a crescent-shaped basin filled with dozens of lakes and ponds on the floodplain of the Koidern River. This network of wetlands is vitally important to the migrant waterfowl that fly north and south along the trench every spring and fall. The many fens and marshes in this part of the trench are also ideal moose habitat.

The White River emerges from a narrow gap in the Kluane Ranges at the Alaska Highway bridge, and immediately spreads out in broad gravel braids over the large valley to the northeast. The White was named for its thick mixture of glacial silt and volcanic ash that it carries. At the White River crossing, the highway meets the Denali Fault for the last time—from here, the fault curves to the northwest and the road heads north to Beaver Creek. High on the ridge to the northwest of the bridge is a large, active landslide that begins near the ridgeline and fills the canyon just upstream. Will it let go totally and block the White River? If you stop at the bridge, watch and listen for the harsh cries of peregrine falcons—they nest in the canyon and hunt for shorebirds and ducks over the wetlands to the south.

Spiked saxifrage. SYDNEY CANNINGS

The highway winds up the hill out of the White River valley and onto the Klondike Plateau. Two of the small stream courses that cross the highway from east to west—Dry Creek and a northern headwater feeder of Sanpete Creek—are home to the spiked saxifrage, a tall wildflower that is found only in Alaska and the Yukon and is extremely rare in Canada. For a short distance, you drive through the headwater plateau of Dry Creek to Snag Junction. The road leading to the northeast at kilometre 1849.3 goes to Snag, an abandoned airstrip with the claim to fame of being Canada's official coldest weather station, with a reading of –63°c on February 3, 1947 (but see p. 261).

About 5 kilometres north of the Snag Junction campground, the road cuts through a large moraine that marks the northern limit (along the highway) of the McConnell glaciation, the final glaciation of the Pleistocene. North of here you travel through land shaped by the Reid glaciation, about 200,000 years ago. Beyond this moraine, the highway traverses a muskeg plain of fens, bogs and shallow lakes—sharp-tailed grouse country—on its way to Beaver Creek.

Just after passing the community of Beaver Creek, you pass by the Canada Customs station, but the Canada–U.S. border is still 29 kilometres to the northwest. At the highway crossing of Snag Creek, you are driving through a flat basin clothed in willows, scrub birch, sedge fens and scattered, stunted black spruce. Snag Creek flows into the White River drainage, but somewhere in the next 2 kilometres, you cross an invisible, movable and very wet line into the Mirror Creek and Tanana River drainage. All this water, though, ends up in the Yukon River.

Watch for nesting trumpeter swans in this area, especially at the small lake on the east side of the road just north of the Mirror Creek crossing. This shallow lake is an exceptionally good place to look for spring waterfowl and shorebird migrants, and peregrine falcons and foxes sometimes pay a visit.

At kilometre 1891.8, an unobtrusive pull-off to the west leads to the Little John archaeological site, where people have camped and looked over the Mirror Creek valley for 14,000 years. This dig has been a joint project of the White River First Nation and Yukon College. At this point, the 141st meridian—the Alaska border—is only one kilometre to the west, but the road swings north and enters the drainage of Scottie Creek.

Along the peaty lakeshores in this valley, look for the purple flowers of the beach-head iris—this is the only area of Canada where this beautiful flower makes its home. In among the irises and the sedges, you may see a tiny, metallic-green

Beach-head iris. BRUCE BENNETT

damselfly with a blue tail—the sedge sprite, a southern boreal species whose nearest cousins live in the far southeast of the territory. At least as far as wetland ecosystems go, you have entered a different world from that of most of the Yukon. This is a zone of intensely cold winters but warm, sometimes even hot summers—at least when compared to the rest of the Yukon. For species that don't care about cold winters but love warm, short summers, this part of the world is ideal.

You are entering Beringia—the Scottie Creek valley has not been covered by ice since early in the Pleistocene, about 2.6 million years ago, and the hills ahead of you and to the east have never been glaciated. During cold periods in the Pleistocene, when ice covered the rest of Canada, this land was covered in steppe or tundra and was home to wandering herds of mammoths, horses, bison and prides of lions.

At kilometre 1902.5, you reach the U.S. border—you are over 1500 kilometres north of Vancouver and, at this latitude, over 900 kilometres to the west.

THIRTEEN

The Sea to Sky Highway

HIGHWAY 99

IGHWAY 99 is British Columbia's newest route through the Coast Mountains. It starts as a wide commuter freeway racing across the Fraser Delta, makes its way through downtown Vancouver on congested streets, then crosses Burrard Inlet on the Lions Gate Bridge. Once the highway reaches the North Shore, it is at home in the mountains, winding along steep bluffs above Howe Sound and climbing up the granitic canyons of the Cheakamus Valley to Whistler; then it descends again to the Pemberton Valley. From Pemberton it takes its newest track through the eastern ranges of the Coast Mountains, following Cayoosh Creek to the semidesert grasslands of Lillooet. Crossing the Fraser, it makes one more pass through the mountains at Marble Canyon before meeting Highway 97 at Hat Creek.

➤ **White Rock to West Vancouver:** The Fraser Delta
Just before the first exit north of the border, Campbell River (not to be confused with a larger river on Vancouver Island) flows under the freeway to empty into Semiahmoo Bay. Although less than 15 kilometres long and more of a glorified creek than a river, this stream

has spawning populations of chinook, coho and chum salmon, as well as steelhead and cutthroat trout.

Beyond the Campbell the highway climbs over a low ridge to the lowlands east of Mud Bay, the shallow northeastern arm of Boundary Bay. Two more small streams enter the ocean here. The southernmost is the Nicomekl River, which rises in Langley and meanders westward to Mud Bay. It has a colony of great blue herons in the high trees along its banks just east of the highway. More than six hundred herons feed in the productive shallows of Boundary Bay, but most nest on Point Roberts, just south of the border on the west edge of the bay. The Nicomekl colony consists of about twenty-five pairs. North of the Nicomekl, you cross the Serpentine River. As its name suggests, this stream winds tortuously south from the Tynehead region of eastern Surrey. Ducks Unlimited has developed a waterfowl sanctuary on the south side of its delta at Serpentine Fen.

North of the Serpentine, the highway turns due west along the shores of Mud Bay. Mud Bay is so shallow that it is almost completely exposed at low tides, creating a vast expanse of mud flats. Although mud flats may look unappealing to the human eye, they are one of the richest of all habitats. This richness is often best appreciated by looking for the bird life that comes to feed on it. Loons and grebes dive to catch fish at high tide, huge flocks of dabbling ducks graze on algae and other plants, and thousands of sandpipers and plovers probe for tiny invertebrates and slurp the slimy biofilm off the surface of the mud.

North of Mud Bay is the forested ridge of Panorama Park, one of the newest protected areas in the Lower Mainland. This 176-hectare park preserves mixed forests and lowland fields that support a variety of wildlife. Around ten thousand years ago, when the Surrey upland was a peninsula surrounded by the sea, waves broke along the foot of these steep slopes.

As the highway swings northwest around the shore of Mud Bay, it continues to travel through farm fields and pastures. These fields are one of the best wintering grounds for hawks and owls in Canada, since their high vole (meadow mouse) populations are rarely protected by snow cover. Northern harriers are almost always in view over the fields, and you can usually see several Red-tailed and rough-legged hawks along this section as well. The rough fields on the sea side of the Boundary Bay dykes are favourite feeding and roosting grounds for short-eared and snowy owls. The short-eared owls are looking for voles, while the snowy owls are there for the ducks.

The most conspicuous birds along this stretch of the highway are the gulls. They gather in the fields by the thousands, usually resting and preening after visiting the area's real attraction for them, the Delta landfill, just north of the highway on the southern edge of Burns Bog. Most of these gulls are glaucous-winged gulls, the common gull of the B.C. coast. These birds nest on various islands around Vancouver, mostly on Mandarte Island, 50 kilometres to the southwest near Sidney. The colony there is littered with chicken bones and other fast-food remains gleaned from the dump on the birds' daily foraging flight.

Unlike most of its nocturnal relatives, the short-eared owl typically hunts during daylight hours. SYDNEY CANNINGS

The dark forest edge of Burns Bog is visible beyond the farms north of the highway. This is a roughly circular bog about 5 to 7 kilometres across, an island of natural life in an urban and agricultural sea. Burns Bog is unique for its size and composition this far south along the Pacific coast. Its peat moss ponds and fields of cottongrass attract bird and insect species more often associated with habitats of the Far North. Sandhill Cranes nest in the bog, and several species of dragonflies found there are not known to occur anywhere in Washington State, only 10 kilometres away.

Highway 99 swings north around the east side of Burns Bog, passes an interchange with Highway 17, then dives under the south arm of the Fraser River through the George Massey Tunnel. Just before it goes under water, it passes Deas Slough and Deas Island, a natural oasis of tall cottonwoods and other riverside vegetation. Deas Island marks the upper limit of tidal flow in the Fraser River; that is, the river flows backward as far as this point at high tide. The influence of the tides is felt as far upstream as the Pitt River, since the river basically stops flowing at high tide, causing waters to back up the valley.

Once out of the tunnel, you are on Lulu Island, the largest of the islands in the Fraser delta. Lulu Island once consisted almost entirely of salt marshes and bogs, but a foreshore dyke built early in the 1900s allowed most of the land to be converted to agriculture; now much of the island is covered with the sprawling residential developments of the city of Richmond. The land is still below sea level on average, and there is some concern that if an earthquake liquefies the muddy soils of Richmond, buildings will topple and dykes will be breached.

> **Vancouver to Squamish:** Forests and Fiords

The next section of Highway 99 is radically different from the first, passing from a flat, deltaic plain into rolling hills, then precipitous mountain slopes above a deep fiord. Once through Vancouver, the highway travels up Howe Sound, a fiord carved into the Coast Mountains by a succession of huge glaciers during the Pleistocene Epoch. Howe Sound is also a transition point from drier forests of Douglas-fir and arbutus to the true coastal rain forests of western hemlock and western redcedar.

At the north end of Lulu Island, you cross the north arm of the Fraser on the Oak Street Bridge, leaving the Fraser Delta behind and entering the city of Vancouver. The rolling landscape of Vancouver is underlain mostly by thick glacial deposits, but here and there bedrock protrudes to form the higher hills. Little Mountain, east of Oak Street around 33rd Avenue, consists of volcanic rock.

Despite the complete urbanization of its shores, English Bay remains a vital wintering ground for thousands of western grebes, surf scoters and other waterfowl.
RICHARD CANNINGS

You can enter downtown Vancouver on either Cambie or Granville Street; either way you cross over False Creek, a former muddy inlet turned industrial area now lined with expensive condos and trendy shops. As you drive amid the skyscrapers of the urban centre, it is humbling to remember that many of the trees felled to clear the land for this city rivalled these buildings in height—some were giant Douglas-firs more than 90 metres high.

From downtown Vancouver you enter Stanley Park on a causeway that separates Lost Lagoon from Coal Harbour. The lagoon, now a freshwater lake but formerly a brackish lagoon joined at high tide to the sea, is literally covered with ducks from October to April. Those clustered at the east end of the lagoon near the highway are mostly goldeneyes and scaup. Coal Harbour, on the east side of the road, is named after low-grade coal deposits found around its shores. This coal comes from organic material laid down in sand, silt and mud deposited at the mouth of a westward-flowing river (like today's Fraser) 35 to 50 million years ago. Much of Vancouver is built on these sedimentary rocks.

Stanley Park is famous for its large trees, and two-thirds of its forest is more than 100 years old. The peninsula was selectively logged in the 1800s, however, and windstorms in 1962 and 2006 blew down substantial areas of forest, so the areas of true old growth (more than 250 years old) are small and not located along the highway. These are typical coastal forests, dominated by western hemlock and western redcedar, though the largest trees are generally Douglas-firs. The highway leaves the park near Prospect Point, a headland of volcanic rock where magma cooled at the Earth's surface about 35 million years ago. The cliffs of Prospect Point provide nesting sites for Pelagic Cormorants and Pigeon Guillemots.

The Lions Gate Bridge provides a stunning view of Burrard Inlet on either side and the mouth of the Capilano River just north of the east end of the bridge. Burrard Inlet is an important wintering area for several species of waterfowl, especially western grebes, Barrow's goldeneyes and surf scoters. The Capilano River has a fish hatchery and significant salmon runs, so it attracts sports fishermen to its mouth as well as large numbers of gulls and ducks. About ten thousand to forty thousand coho salmon return to the river each year, with lesser numbers of chinook and steelhead.

The route winds its way up through West Vancouver to Highway 1 (this section is known locally as the Upper Levels Highway). The freeway to Horseshoe Bay is cut through granitic rocks of the Coast Mountains. Young Douglas-firs cloak the hillsides, while under the power lines above the road, young arbutus trees have grown in profusion. Butterfly bushes are the common shrub along the median, their lilac-like flower clusters attracting butterflies and hummingbirds alike in midsummer.

North of Horseshoe Bay, the mountainsides are even steeper as you begin to follow Howe Sound. The sound is a deep fiord with a few large islands—Bowen, Gambier and Anvil—in its broad mouth. North of Porteau Cove, the sound is a more typical fiord—a U-shaped trough scoured out by glaciers and now partly filled by the sea. Glaciers that are flowing into the sea do not float until the water is almost as deep as the ice is thick. The Howe Sound glacier was more than 1000 metres thick, whereas the sea was much less than even 900 metres deep. As a result, the glacier was grounded and eroded the valley bottom, deepening it well below sea level. As the ice melted around twelve thousand years ago, it was replaced by the sea. At first, sea level was about 200 metres higher than it is today because the weight of the ice sheet had depressed the land. Streams flowing into the fiord formed deltas along this high shoreline—you can see these delta deposits today as a series of gravel pits adjacent to most streams along the highway.

Along the eastern shore of Howe Sound, slopes underlain by granitic and metamorphosed volcanic rocks plunge steeply into the water, leaving few options for easy highway construction. The highway winds across rocky slopes forested with broadleaf maples and young Douglas-firs.

A few kilometres on, you cross Disbrow Creek, the first of many mountain streams along this route. This section has become infamous for the disastrous debris torrents down these creeks. During periods of heavy rain, minor landslides in the upper reaches of these creeks trigger torrential flows of mud, trees, rocks and other debris that roar down the gullies, taking out bridges and occasionally homes. These torrents began to occur with disturbing frequency in the 1970s and 1980s, perhaps exacerbated by clear-cut logging practices on the slopes far above the highway. Between 1981 and 1984, fourteen of these torrents caused widespread damage and killed twelve motorists. Nine of these people lost their lives on the night of October 28, 1981, driving into the chasm of M Creek, unaware in the blackness that the bridge had been swept away. Since those disasters, considerable work has been done to construct catch basins, grille openings and concrete sills to slow down or stop debris torrents before they wreak havoc on the highway and settlements below.

You leave the serious torrent hazard area as the highway descends to Porteau Cove Provincial Park. Porteau Cove marks the site of an underwater ridge, or sill, that stretches across Howe Sound. This is the terminal moraine of one of the glaciers that carved the sound.

Fiord sills are areas of vibrant underwater life, since sunlight can reach the shallow seafloor to allow a rich growth of undersea plants, and four times a day tidal currents surge across the sill, bringing oxygen and nutrients. Not surprisingly, Porteau Cove is a popular location for local divers wishing to explore this undersea life.

At Furry Creek the highway crosses one of the few somewhat level modern creek deltas on Howe Sound, now part of a golf course development. The forest changes around this point to the true coastal rain forest of western hemlock, with a thick growth of red alder on recently disturbed gravel soils along the road. Alders are especially dominant as the highway descends to Daisy Creek, a little farther on.

From Daisy Creek you can look across the sound to Woodfibre, a large pulp mill accessible only by ferry, and you soon reach another major industrial site at Britannia Beach. This was the site of a major underground copper mine that opened in 1904 and by 1929 was the largest copper producer in the British Commonwealth. The mineshafts of Britannia extend below sea level in a 150-kilometre-long network. The rich mineral veins at Britannia were formed in a deep undersea vent much like those still present off the B.C. coast. The scalding water that pours out of these vents is rich in minerals, which precipitate out as black sulfides on the sea floor.

Although it closed in 1974, the mine is still the source of serious metal pollution, and a complex water treatment system—costing $100 million over 20 years—was opened in 2005 to deal with this problem. On October 28, 1921, Britannia Creek was also the site of one of the most devastating floods in B.C. history. During heavy rainfall, an upstream logjam burst, releasing a deluge of water carrying boulders and uprooted trees that destroyed half the town and swept some houses out to sea; thirty-seven people lost their lives. This was not the worst tragedy to befall Britannia Beach; on March 22, 1915, an avalanche, perhaps triggered by tunnelling activities, brought 100,000 cubic metres of rock down onto a mining camp, killing fifty-six people.

After crossing Britannia Creek, the highway climbs once again to avoid sea cliffs, passing Browning Lake in Murrin Provincial

Park. As you begin to descend, you can see the massive granitic half-dome of the Stawamus Chief, one of the most popular rock-climbing sites in Canada. Just beyond the Chief lies Squamish, a port at the head of Howe Sound at the mouth of the Squamish River.

➤ **Squamish to Pemberton:** Fire and Ice
At Squamish the highway crosses its last stretch of tidewater at Mamquam Blind Channel and begins to travel along the relatively flat floodplain of the Squamish River. The Squamish delta provides a patch of rich habitat in the generally unproductive waters of Howe Sound. Its salt marshes are the winter home of many ducks and a small population of trumpeter swans.

Valley of Eagles

The big birding event in the Squamish area—indeed one of the biggest wildlife spectacles on the continent—is the midwinter gathering of bald eagles on the lower Squamish River and its tributaries. Starting in December, the eagles come from all over western North America, from Arizona to Alaska, to feast on spawning chum salmon. At the peak of the gathering, in mid-January, there may be more than three thousand eagles in the valley, roosting on large cottonwoods and conifers along the rivers, sometime more than fifty birds per tree. The big concentrations are just out of sight of the highway, along the Squamish River and lower Cheakamus River in the town of Brackendale, but eagles can often be seen from the highway bridge over the Mamquam River just north of Squamish.

Bald eagle

The broken summit of Mt. Garibaldi towers over the Squamish Valley.
RICHARD CANNINGS

From Squamish you can see Mt. Garibaldi (2678 metres) on the skyline 25 kilometres to the northeast. It is the centrepiece of Garibaldi Provincial Park, an area of high volcanic activity in the Pleistocene, when fiery lava met a world of ice. Mt. Garibaldi was formed by an eruption about thirteen thousand years ago, at a time when the great ice sheets were gradually melting but were still 1350 metres thick in this valley. The eruption built up an impressive cone-shaped summit of ash and cinders, but the western half of the cone rested on the glacial ice. As the ice sheet melted, half of the volcano collapsed into the valley below, leaving the broken west wall of the peak now visible.

Beyond Brackendale the highway climbs gradually past Alice Lake Provincial Park to the Cheekye River crossing. The Cheekye River drains the western face of Mt. Garibaldi, the face that collapsed when the valley glacier melted. This face of the mountain is still unstable, and periodic landslides trigger debris flows in the lower rock gorge of the Cheekye. All the land traversed by the highway since Brackendale has been on the Cheekye fan, which was formed by the many debris flows over the last few thousand years. The most recent big flow, after a rainstorm in August 1958, sent a 3-metre-high wall of logs and volcanic rock debris down the Cheekye to dam the Cheakamus River, about 2 kilometres downstream from the highway crossing.

Around Cheekye the forests are dominated by second-growth Douglas-firs, with many western hemlock seedlings growing beneath, a typical situation in local rain forests. Old, veteran Douglas-firs can be seen on the ridge ahead of you north of Cheekye Creek. Interpretive trails at Brohm Lake provide information about these forests. Just beyond Brohm Lake, lodgepole pine becomes a common component of the young forests, suggesting a cooler, drier climate, or at least drier, well-drained soils.

A viewpoint 3 kilometres north of Brohm Lake provides excellent views of the glacier-covered peaks of the Tantalus Range on the western wall of the Squamish Valley. About 10 kilometres farther on, you enter the Cheakamus Canyon, the highway winding along granitic walls above the tumultuous river. Beyond the canyon the valley opens again, the river lined with large western hemlock, Douglas-fir and western redcedar. As you approach Rubble Creek, the highway climbs a gently rising fan. The source of this fan material is the Barrier, a 500-metre-high cliff at the head of the Rubble Creek. The Barrier was built by a large lava flow that erupted out of a vent on Clinker Peak (1940 metres), 11 kilometres southeast of the highway, around the same time that Mt. Garibaldi was active—ten to thirteen thousand years ago. The lava dammed Rubble Creek to form Garibaldi Lake, then flowed toward the Cheakamus Valley. There it was stopped cold by an immense valley glacier, forming the cliff wall you see today. It is a rather unstable cliff and has generated many rockslides, some of which have travelled as far as the Cheakamus River.

Lichen, moss and kinnikinick at Daisy Lake. RICHARD CANNINGS

As you cross the Cheakamus River, you can see the Cheakamus Dam, which forms the reservoir of Daisy Lake. Immediately beyond the bridge over the Cheakamus, the highway begins to pass through basaltic lava flows along the west side of Daisy Lake. Some rocky road cuts and a quarry display the splendid columnar jointing that is typical of basalt flows. The long island in the middle of the lake and the peninsula just south of the island are thought to be a volcanic esker, formed by lava flowing through a tunnel beneath glacial ice before solidifying. A similar steep-sided ridge can be seen at the railway crossing just south of Brandywine Falls Provincial Park. A toothlike peak on the southeastern horizon—the Black Tusk—is another volcanic remnant formed when lava melted its way up through a glacier.

About 10 kilometres north of Brandywine Falls, you leave the Cheakamus River; it flows out of Cheakamus Lake 8 kilometres to the southeast. Following the course of Millar Creek, you come to the ski resort of Whistler, built around a series of small lakes—Alpha, Nita, Alta and Green—at the headwaters of the Green River, a tributary of the Lillooet River. At Whistler Village you can see Whistler Mountain (2194 metres) to the southwest, Blackcomb (2438 metres) to the southeast and the pyramidal peak of Wedge Mountain (2891 metres) to the east. A pull-off 6 kilometres north of Whistler will help you sort out the names of local peaks. As you approach the eastern side of the pass at the Emerald Estates subdivision, the forests become more diverse as the climate takes on Interior characteristics.

The highway then begins the 25-kilometre descent to Pemberton, down the Green River valley. It first follows the river fairly closely, then swings northwest around a ridge at the outlet of the Soo River valley. On the north side of this ridge, the highway crosses the toe of the prehistoric Mystery Creek rock avalanche. This huge rockslide originated at a jagged black wall on the west face of Mt. Currie (2590 metres), across the Green River valley to the east. About 35 million cubic metres of diorite (granitic rock) fell about 1 kilometre to the foot of Mt. Currie, crossed the Green River, climbed a rocky ridge in the centre of the valley, then descended again to where the highway is now located. Judging from the large trees now growing in the Green River floodplain, this slide occurred more than four hundred years ago and possibly several thousand years ago. The highway continues to follow the Soo River, then crosses its glacial blue waters just above its confluence with the Green River. The Green River pours over granitic bedrock at Nairn Falls, visible only from a trail in the provincial park.

At Pemberton the highway reaches the Lillooet River floodplain, with glacier-spangled Mt. Currie towering over the valley to the south. The Pemberton Valley has a Shangri-La reputation in British Columbia history—a warm, fertile valley that was only connected by a good road to Vancouver in 1975. Because of this isolation, local farmers specialized in growing disease-free seed potatoes for many years. The valley has a mix of coastal and Interior plants and animals; the open forests on its eastern slopes are dotted with large Douglas-firs, while Interior birds such as veeries, American redstarts and Nashville warblers nest in riparian shrubbery along the river.

➤ **Pemberton to Lillooet:** The Eastern Ranges
The road follows the Lillooet River floodplain for about 15 kilometres south to the village of Mount Currie. Past the village the highway travels along the south side of the Birkenhead River as it meanders along the northeast side of the Lillooet River delta before emptying into Lillooet Lake itself. This stretch of the Birkenhead is an important spawning ground for sockeye salmon in August and September, attracting flocks of crows and gulls to the feast. Lesser numbers of coho, chinook and pink salmon spawn here as well.

At Lillooet Lake, the highway swings northeast and begins to climb the steep valley walls in a series of switchbacks, eventually straightening out and following Joffre Creek. At the top of the hill about 13 kilometres along you are at the upper limit of a western hemlock forest intermixed with redcedar, western white pine, red alder and Douglas-fir. This forest changes to a coastal subalpine mix of mountain hemlock and amabilis fir over the next few kilometres. These latter species are typical of coastal snow forests, indicating a tremendous winter snow pack. A luxurious growth of creamy witch's hair lichen also indicates long periods of moist, foggy weather.

Beyond Joffre Lakes you cross over a pass into the Cayoosh Creek drainage, its upper valley dominated by steep alpine ridges streaked with avalanche tracks, with Mt. Rohr (2940 metres) in the Cayoosh

REST STOP

Joffre Lakes

A DEEP WINTER snow pack is conducive to the formation of alpine glaciers on the northeast side of higher local peaks. Just before the height of land, you pass the trailhead to Joffre Lakes, a series of three exquisite tarns set in the northern slopes of Joffre Peak and its glaciers. Lower Joffre Lake is very close to the highway, and the other two are reached by trail; these lakes fill the depressions left by more extensive glaciers in the past.

Above: Joffre Glacier. KEN WRIGHT

Range on the north and Mt. Chief Pascall (2200 metres) to the south. In several places earth berms have been constructed to deflect avalanches from the highway. Duffey Lake fills the narrow valley for 7 kilometres. At its east end, the forests change once again, this time to a diverse Interior subalpine mix of Engelmann spruce, lodgepole pine, western redcedar and Douglas-fir.

The Cayoosh Creek valley becomes deeper and steeper as you travel eastward, and within 15 kilometres of Duffey Lake, there are rock faces towering above you, many dramatically striped with pale dykes of rock that was intruded into the highly deformed sedimentary beds as they were melted and folded. The road crosses Cayoosh Creek three times in this narrow valley; just beyond the third bridge, there is a viewpoint before it begins the steep descent to Lillooet. As you descend to warmer altitudes, the forests open up, and ponderosa pine quickly becomes the dominant tree.

Only 5 kilometres from the viewpoint, you come to the lower treeline at Seton Lake and enter sagebrush grasslands. The east end of Seton Lake has a small dam that diverts water into a canal that feeds a small hydroelectric plant beside the Fraser River south of Lillooet. Seton Lake contributes to the turbines not only water from its own drainage, but also water from the Bridge River drainage to the north. The Bridge River is dammed at the east end of Carpenter Lake, and water from that lake is piped through Mission Ridge to another set of powerhouses near the west end of Seton Lake at Shalalth. To mitigate the effects of the dams on spawning salmon, two sections of spawning channels have been built beside the Seton River. These primarily benefit pink salmon; the channels can produce up to 27 million young pink salmon, of which 750,000 reach the sea and 250,000 return to the Fraser.

The highway enters the Fraser Valley at Lillooet. This large valley has been dug by rivers and glaciers along lines of weakness associated with a series of major faults—the Fraser River Fault Zone—over the past several million years. Land movement along these faults has been both lateral and vertical; rocks on the west side of the valley have moved hundreds of kilometres to the north relative to rocks on the east side, and the land west of the fault zone has been pushed up about 600 metres more than land to the east. Consequently the fault zone and the Fraser Valley separate two major regions: the rugged Coast Mountains to the west and the uplands of the Interior Plateau to the east.

The highway crosses the mighty Fraser on the Bridge of the 23 Camels, named to honour the animals brought to British Columbia in 1862 to pack supplies into the Cariboo goldfields. They were turned loose after they were deemed impractical for the terrain and climate, and the last one died in 1905.

Lillooet is built on three different levels. The highest undulating bench that you can see south of the bridge was formed by glacial meltwater streams, which deposited vast quantities of gravel in a depression surrounded by ice. The highest of the flat terraces is the remnant of an old glacial outwash plain, but the three lower terraces—for example, the terrace immediately east of the bridge—were formed after the valley glacier melted as the river eroded down and sideways simultaneously, cutting into old glacial deposits. Silty sediments deposited in a glacial lake are visible under the terrace gravels in the eastern riverbank south of the bridge. All of the terraces are capped by about a metre of fine soil deposited by the wind—this stone-free veneer produces agricultural soil that is far superior to that derived directly from river gravels.

Once across the Fraser, the road meets Highway 12 coming north from Lytton. You turn north here to follow the Fraser for about 30 kilometres to Pavilion. About a kilometre north of the junction, the road cuts reveal gravel with large round boulders—this was the bed of the Fraser River when it was cutting through old glacial sediments about six thousand years ago. Most of this section is along terraces that are naturally vegetated with bunchgrasses and sagebrush, but many have been cultivated and planted to alfalfa or ginseng.

About 8 kilometres north of Lillooet, you can see the Bridge River entering the Fraser from the west. Bridge River drains extensive snow fields and glaciers of the central Coast Mountains close to the headwaters of the Lillooet River. But unlike the sediment-laden Lillooet, the Bridge River is relatively clear because most of its sediment is trapped in two large reservoirs—Downton Lake and Carpenter Lake.

At Pavilion the highway turns east into a valley separating the Clear Range on the south and Marble Range on the north. Both of

White calcium carbonate deposits on its bottom give Pavilion Lake a beautiful blue-green colour. DOUGLAS LEIGHTON

these ranges are dissected remnants of the high rim of the Interior Plateau, where steep-sided valleys have been cut into a gently undulating upland. The Clear Range consists primarily of old volcanic and sedimentary rocks, which weather into a claylike material that moves downslope, forming many slow-moving earth flows. The highway crosses the toe of one of these earth flows immediately after the railway crossing at Pavilion; watch for reddish road cuts. This slow landslide descends gently for about 10 kilometres from the slopes of Mt. Cole (1710 metres) at the northern end of the Clear Range. The toe of the earth flow is now stationary, but slow movement—a few centimetres per year—is still continuing farther upslope.

The bulk of the Marble Range, north of the highway, consists not of marble but of pale grey limestones laid down as coral reefs in tropical seas, probably on the western side of the Pacific Ocean. About 7 kilometres east of Pavilion, you reach Pavilion Lake, a beautiful blue-green colour from the white calcium carbonate marl that lines its bottom. Nestled in a mountain range formed from coral, the lake is famous for its own coral-like underwater structures. Under its surface are strange calcite formations called microbialites, formations found nowhere else on Earth. Some are shaped like delicate cauliflowers, others like artichokes; some of them are up to 4 metres high. The structures are covered with green and purple microbes called cyanobacteria (formerly known as blue-green algae), but scientists are still not sure whether the cyanobacteria make the structures or whether they simply grow on their surface. What is clear is that these microbialites closely resemble marine fossils described from the Cambrian Period 530 million years ago. Scientists from NASA are studying the microbialites to better understand how primitive life forms can produce uniquely shaped rock material, perhaps providing a key to discovering evidence of life on other planets. Dating techniques show that the Pavilion Lake structures are about eleven thousand years old and so began growing in the lake shortly after the glaciers melted in this area.

By Pavilion Lake the sagebrush so prevalent along the Fraser has given way to ponderosa pines and Douglas-firs, with many Rocky Mountain junipers on the steep slopes north of the highway. These junipers attract Townsend's Solitaires, slim grey thrushes that feed on the gin-flavoured berries all fall.

The highway continues past Crown Lake and soon the valley forests open up to grassy meadows and dry bunchgrass hillsides with rabbit-brush at Hat Creek. Spruce line the creek at first, then alder and willow at lower elevations. As you come out of the mountains into the broader Bonaparte Valley, you can see the flat green skyline of the Arrowstone Hills, a remnant of the relatively level ground that comprises the upland surface of the Interior Plateau. The road crosses the Bonaparte River and almost immediately meets Highway 97; you are back in the sagebrush again.

Appendix

HIGH-SPEED BOTANY

SITKA SPRUCE
Habitat and function: In coastal valleys and along marine shorelines; fast-growing pioneer species

Distinguishing characteristics: Scaly bark; long, horizontal branches

WHITE/ENGELMANN SPRUCE
Habitat and function: Engelmann is dominant in mature subalpine forests in the Interior; white spruce is common in Interior valley bottoms and throughout the north

Distinguishing characteristics: Sweeping branches; scaly, "corn flakes" bark; small cones

BLACK SPRUCE
Habitat and function: Found in bogs and on poor river gravel soils; common north of Quesnel

Distinguishing characteristics: Narrow form; knobbly top

Facing page: Western larches. STEVE CANNINGS

WESTERN HEMLOCK

Habitat and function: Characteristic tree of coastal rain forests and Interior wet belt; climax species—can germinate in shady understorey

Distinguishing characteristics: Drooping tip; dark green needles; finely furrowed bark; tiny cones; mountain hemlock similar, but needles are greyer and it grows at higher elevations

DOUGLAS-FIR

Habitat and function: Climax species of moderately dry forests in the southern Interior and on southern Vancouver Island; pioneer species in some coastal rain forests; thick bark of mature trees can withstand fire

Distinguishing characteristics: Deeply furrowed bark; old trees usually flat-topped; younger trees with straight top (not drooping) and smooth grey bark; small brown cones hanging down

SUBALPINE FIR

Habitat and function: Climax species in many Interior subalpine forests; often grows with Engelmann spruce

Distinguishing characteristics: Spirelike form; purplish cones standing up straight from branch like fat candles; smooth grey bark; short grey-green needles curling up on branch like brush-cut

LODGEPOLE PINE

Habitat and function: Abundant in the Interior; pioneer species after fires and logging; prefers sandy and gravelly soils; found in bogs and on rocky soils on the coast

Distinguishing characteristics: Ramrod-straight trunk on most trees; finely scaled bark; needles about 4 centimetres long; short branches; small round cones

PONDEROSA PINE
Habitat and function: Typical species of dry Interior valleys; grows in open, parklike stands; thick bark of mature trees can withstand fire

Distinguishing characteristics: Reddish bark; furrowed and scaled bark; very long needles; rounded form in mature tree; large round cones

WESTERN WHITE PINE
Habitat and function: Pioneer species in wet forests at low to moderate elevations

Distinguishing characteristics: Long, horizontal branches; long, bananalike cones; grey bark; greyish-green needles

WESTERN REDCEDAR
Habitat and function: Very tolerant of wet soils; often restricted to river bottom habitats

Distinguishing characteristics: Massive trunk; stringy bark; scalelike needles; tiny cones

BLACK COTTONWOOD
Habitat and function: Found mostly along creeks, rivers and lakeshores

Distinguishing characteristics: Furrowed bark; massive trunk

TREMBLING ASPEN
Habitat and function: Common in burned-over areas in the Interior; grows in clonal clumps

Distinguishing characteristics: Smooth white bark; small, round grey-green leaves; white birch is similar but has papery bark and greener leaves

➤ Other species

MOUNTAIN HEMLOCK
Has droopy tip, as in western hemlock, but with greyer needles and larger cones. Grows at high elevations in coastal mountain snow forests (Coquihalla Summit on Highway 5 and upper Cayoosh Creek on Highway 99). Indicator species for Mountain Hemlock Zone.

GRAND FIR
Similar to subalpine fir, but needles are medium green, arranged horizontally on the twig; grows at lower elevations in moderately wet coastal and Kootenay forests.

AMABILIS FIR
Similar to grand fir, but needles are dark green above and silver below; grows at higher elevations in coastal mountain snow forests.

WESTERN LARCH
Has soft, light green needles that turn gold in October and fall off in early winter. Mature trees have orange bark and massive trunks. Common in southern Interior mountains, where it is a pioneer species after fire or other disturbance.

ALPINE LARCH
Similar to western larch but smaller; grows near treeline in southern Interior mountains. Although not close to highways, it can be seen from a distance in fall when needles turn gold.

TAMARACK
Similar to western larch but smaller; grows in boggy habitats in the northern half of British Columbia (patchy on Highway 16 west of Prince George).

YELLOW CEDAR
Similar to western redcedar, but branch tips hang down rather than spreading out; has round, juniper-like berries instead of small cones. Grows at high elevations in coastal mountain snow forests (Coquihalla Summit on Highway 5).

WHITE BIRCH

Has a white trunk similar to that of aspen, but bark is papery and often has brownish patches; leaves are bright green. Grows throughout the province except in dry valleys of the southern Interior.

RED ALDER

Has a smooth grey trunk, sometimes whitened by lichens in wet situations or greenish from algal growth. Has long reddish catkins in March. Abundant pioneer species in coastal forests after logging or other disturbance. Indicator species for Coastal Western Hemlock Zone.

BROADLEAVED MAPLE

Large deciduous tree with furrowed bark, often moss-covered; leaves very large. Grows in rich, moist soils in coastal forests.

ARBUTUS

Distinctive broad-leaved but evergreen tree with smooth, coppery-coloured bark. Indicator species for Coastal Douglas-fir Zone.

Index

Maps, photos and illustrations
indicated in *italics*

draba: few-seeded, 293; Yukon, *293*

dragonflies, 310; boreal snaketail, 138, *140*, 185; Canada whiteface, *186*; Hudsonian whiteface, *270*; variable darner, *137*

ducks: American wigeon, 155, 225; Barrow's goldeneye, 71, 114, *223*, 256, 312, 313; bufflehead, 71, 155, 225; harlequin, *68*; lesser scaup, 178, 225; mallards, 155; mergansers, 32, 71, 156, 214, 216; pintail, 225; ruddy, 219, 226; scaup, 256, 312; scoters, 256; surf scoter, 178, 312, 313; teal, 225; wood, 114, 216

eagles: bald, 17, 34, 50–64 *passim*, 127, 153, 210–11, 216, 244, 282, 285, *316*; golden, 83, 213, 247–48

elderberry: blue, *92*; red, 233

elk, 46, 56, 101, 189, *190*, 258, 261, 288–89

eulachon, *126*, 127, 173

false box, 71

false Solomon's seal, 233

ferns: bracken, 19, 37; Mexican mosquito, 114; ostrich, 265; southern maidenhair, 192; swordfern, 62

fir: amabilis, 62, 106, 320; grand, 97, 330; subalpine, 40, 62, 72, 90–94 *passim*, 106–8 *passim*, 143, 167, 176, 183, 234, 235, 246, 252, 275, 320–30 *passim*

fireweed, 56; narrow-leaved, 259

fisher, 140

flycatchers, 74; alder, 273; northern alder, 121, *228*; southern willow, 121, *228*

foamflower, 247

fritillary, Pacific, 293

frogs: bullfrog, 155, *156*; northern leopard, *97*; Oregon spotted, *16*, 156

Garry oak, 15–16, 19, 50, 53, 55, 154

geese: Brant, 56, 150; Canada, 137, 155, 206

geological history, 2, 4–5, 7–8

ginseng, 29, 222, 323

glasswort, *287*

goats, mountain, 41, 71, 77, *78*, 129, 135, 168, *196*, 213, 293

goatsbeard, 37, 115, *142*, 176

gooseberry, 36

grasses: beargrass, *94*; bluebunch wheatgrass, 25, 77, 164, 192; bunchgrass, 109, 323, 325; canary reedgrass, 34; cottongrass, 125, 167, 234; crested wheatgrass, 27, 30; fescues, 84, 233; foxtail barley, 46, 165, *166*; junegrass, 25; moss-grass, 34; needle-and-thread, 25; rough fescue, 25; salt grass, 99; Vahl's alkali, 294

grasslands, 162

grayling, Arctic, 180, 263, 274, 297

grebes, 216, 309; eared, 96; red-necked, 96, 220, 242, 271; western, 34, *36*, 96, 228, 312, 313

grosbeaks: black-headed, 209; rose-breasted, 248, 266

ground squirrels: Arctic, 178, 280, 293; Columbian, 227

grouse, sharp-tailed, 164, 300, 301, 305

guillemot, pigeon, 313

gulls, 65, 214; Bonaparte's, *153*, 225–26; Franklin's, 256;

moles, 15
moose, 134, 135, 142, 171, 176, 194,
    196, 232, 258-77 *passim*, 303
mosses, 20; campion, 262; peat
    (Sphagnum), 125, 258, 260
moths: satin, 144; tiger, 294
mountain-avens, yellow, 45-46, 259
Mt. Edziza, 178
muskrats, 164, 226, 243
mussels, 55, 56

nettle, Lyall's, 265

oceanspray, 52, 89
olives, Russian, 31
opossums, 15
orcas, *see* killer whales
orchids, 179, 262, 265; giant
    helleborine, 192; rein, 115, 262;
    round-leaved bog, 273; white
    adder's-mouth, 265; white bog, *180*
orioles: Baltimore, 248, 256, *257*,
    266; Bullock's, 209, 228
osprey, 13, 31, 96, 108, 138, 156, 184,
    214, 244
otters, 156; river, 243
ovenbirds, 248, 256
owls: barn, 203, *204*; barred, 140;
    breal, 198; flammulated, 160; great
    gray, 160; long-eared, 27; northern
    hawk, *198*; short-eared, *310*; snowy,
    310; spotted, 69
oysters, 56

paintbrush: Raup's Indian, 262;
    red, 115, 232
penstemon, 75; Davidson's, *52*
peregrine falcons, 13, 303, 305
phacelia, Franklin, 280

pike, northern, 180, 254, 283, 297
pine: lodgepole, 42-46 *passim*, 63,
    72-98 *passim*, 107-19 *passim*,
    125-41 *passim*, 160-68 *passim*,
    174, 191, 195, 225-36 *passim*,
    239, 243, 250, 254-86 *passim*,
    318-28 *passim*; ponderosa, 21-33
    passim, 62, 75-100 *passim*, 108-14
    passim, 189-95 *passim*, 213-36
    passim, 322-29 *passim*; western
    white, 63, 89-98 *passim*, 115, 320,
    329; white, 34-38 *passim*
plovers, 164, 309; American golden-,
    166
poorwill, common, 160
poplars, 17; balsam, 245, 264, 266,
    267, 300
potatoes, 320
purple martins, 13, 54

rabbit-brush, 28, 88, 111, 192, 194, 214,
    223, 229, 233, 325
rabbits: mountain cottontails, 83;
    snowshoe hare, *294*; white-tailed
    jackrabbits, 80-81
redstart, American, 320
rest stops: 100 Mile Marsh, 226;
    Albert Creek Migration Monitor-
    ing Station, 273; Alsek River Valley
    Trail, 293; Bear Lake, 242; Beatton
    Provincial Park, 256; Bijoux Falls
    Provincial Park, 247; Boya Lake,
    184; Buckinghorse Provincial Park,
    259; Chilanko Marsh, 164; Cran-
    berry Marsh, 117; Creston Valley
    Wildlife Management Area Inter-
    pretation Centre, 95; Dalrymple
    Creek, 61; Hardy Falls, 214; Joffre
    Lakes, 321; Liard River Hot Springs,